THE STRUGGLE FOR SURVIVAL

THE
STRUGGLE
FOR
SURVIVAL

Indian Cultures and
the Protestant Ethic
in British Columbia

Forrest E. LaViolette

**UNIVERSITY OF
TORONTO PRESS**

University of Toronto Press

Diamond Anniversary 1961

FOR

PETER R. KELLY AND WILLIAM SCOW

Foreword

MANY ARE the parts of the world where a number of tribes, separate in organization and more or less different in culture, have been brought under a single authority by invaders. The invaders take over sovereignty almost completely; they reorganize the economy, the social institutions, and the style of life in varying degree. They may be content to let the native gods live; they may, on the contrary, feel called to rout them out. Generally, although not always, the people of greater economic and military power have taken the land from the native tribal peoples. Where the native population has used the land fairly intensively, as in parts of what is now Latin America, the invaders have sometimes left them on the land but have changed the mode of ownership, the organization of labour, and the marketing of the produce. In much of black Africa, Australia, and New Zealand the European invaders took what land they wanted for agriculture, forest produce, or mining, leaving what they did not especially need to the natives for subsistence agriculture, and employing the excess labour in plantations, mines, and other enterprises.

Of all the modern "discovered" lands, North America was most congenial to the Europeans. They conquered and occupied it, adapting their style of agriculture and industry to the soil, the climate, and the raw materials. Only in the region now comprising the southern United States did they depart from the northern and western European system of agriculture; there they found it profitable to adopt a system of large-scale agriculture. Since they could not get a labour force from among the natives, as the Spanish had done in certain colonies, they imported one from Africa; the effects on American history are still deep and sometimes violent.

British Columbia belongs to that part of the continent where the Europeans took, in effect, whatever land they wanted. The province has more of what C. A. Dawson called the "chronic frontier" than many parts of North America; there was more territory in which the native Indians might, after a fashion, survive. This book is devoted to their struggle to do so in the face of attacks by white men upon their land and their institutions. The book's importance lies precisely in the fact that it does report one case of a kind not only numerous, but fateful, in our epoch. For we are in a time when there is a general resurgence among peoples whose ancestors were thus dispossessed. Some of these people are more resentful than the Indians of British Columbia seem to be. Some are more numerous; some more oppressed. The case of British Columbia is not one of those that may spark a world controversy. Nevertheless it is of interest and of importance.

The story deals not only with the problem of land but also with a native institution which furnished the basic principle of organization in pre-conquest life. The potlatch of British Columbia has become one of the best known, in name at least, of "native" institutions. The *kula* in the South Seas, *lobolo* in parts of Africa, and head-hunting in Melanesia are all institutions which were the rallying points of enterprise—centres about which economic effort, the struggle for power and prestige, and festivities were mobilized. All of them have been attacked by European conquerors, settlers, missionaries, and entrepreneurs as incompatible with western civilization and as bad for the natives. The latter have, in all cases but with varying degrees of stubbornness and success, resisted. The attack and the defence appear always to have some part in drawing the hitherto separate tribes into some sort of unity.

And again we find this book related to a recurrent theme of modern history. For it is a story of collective self-consciousness, of the halting progress of collective action. The struggle for land and the resistance to the attack upon a basic institution (albeit one most certainly damned by the progress of a new economy even without attack) are the themes of the story; but it must not be overlooked that, as in many such cases, the new self-consciousness stems also in large measure from the desire, not to restore a dead world, but to find a better place in the new.

Many historians are now studying situations of this general kind. In a sense, one can say that the historical method is supplementing the field-work of the ethnologist in the study of native peoples. Perhaps this is because historians have to find new fields to till; perhaps it is because the documents have accumulated to such point that the historian can now profitably work where only missionaries and anthropologists worked before. Perhaps it is because political movements—a favourite of historians—are now found among what were not long ago tribes with only lore and no documents. At any rate, this is a document of a kind that is becoming common and will form an ever more important part of the historical and sociological record of this, the period of "decolonizing."

EVERETT C. HUGHES

Preface

DURING WORLD WAR II numerous Canadians travelled in and became acquainted with the Canadian North. Trends of national development were such that even before hostilities had ceased the Canadian Social Science Research Council was directing its attention to northern Canada as an area for new settlement, with resources for exploitation but with difficult conditions for its peoples—Eskimo, Indian, and European-derived groups. The Council provided grants for a number of investigators, and under the editorship of Professor Carl Dawson, who himself went to the Northwest in the summer of 1944, the observations and studies of some of the scholars were published in *The New North-West*.

A less general line of activity emerged from this period of Council work. Professor Harold Innis, President of the Council, appointed a committee on Indian Research, with Professor Dawson as its first chairman, consisting of Professors Bailey of the University of New Brunswick, Jean-Charles Falardeau of Laval University, Brown and McIlwraith of the University of Toronto, Hawthorn of the University of British Columbia, and Hall, Keyfitz, and myself of McGill University. It was the intention of Professor Innis that this committee prepare a programme of research on contemporary Indian life in Canada and that the Council would secure, if possible, fairly large funds for supporting the work. So that the committee could initiate its work, funds for travel and small grants for research were made available immediately. It developed, however, that funds on a large scale could not be secured as several of the foundations already had commitments to assist European universities and libraries in their plans of reconstruction. The Council did, none the less, continue to make available smaller grants to individual scholars. Since I had succeeded Professor Dawson as chairman of the committee, the Council provided me with a grant for the summer of 1946, thus creating an ideal opportunity for the writer, after spending some time at Indian Lorette and on the Caughnawaga Iroquois Reserve in the Montreal area, to return to the west, in particular to British Columbia.

It had become clear to me during the years spent in gathering and preparing materials for *Americans of Japanese Ancestry* and for *Canadian Japanese and World War II* that British Columbia had been, and apparently would continue to be for some decades, a region in which the creative processes of social organization had some historical depth but still not so much but that they could be observed easily in contemporary actions. Hence, while just "looking around," I was impressed with the amount of talk among the coastal Indians about the land title question and about "getting back those potlatch goods," as Guy Williams expressed it while we were chatting one day at the Indian Village. These were the items, I learned later, which were shipped to Edward Sapir as part of the settlement of the Alert Bay trials in 1922. In 1950 Douglas Leechman showed to me some of them retained in the National Museum at Ottawa.

However, when I went to Ottawa in the summer of 1950, on a grant from the University Research Council of Tulane University, it was with the intention of making a study of the roles of the several churches in the formation of policy with respect to Indian affairs and church influence in the administration of that policy. It was around this interest that my work on the Indian Committee had finally centred. But it is a difficult project and a longer than expected convalescence from surgery dictated the necessity of something less difficult, at least for that summer. Circumstances did, however, permit me to work on the Potlatch File in the Ottawa office of Indian Affairs, and so it is from this, the field work of 1946 among the Indians, and my own files of Japanese materials, as well as discussions with Director McKay and Secretary T. R. L. MacInnes that a major theme was formulated.

To the two Councils concerned with research, Directors Hoey and McKay, and a very learned civil servant from British Columbia—the late Loftus MacInnes—and to the deeply respected Rev. Dr. Peter R. Kelly and Chief William Scow, I extend my greetings and appreciation for their assistance. And to anthropologists Jenness and Barbeau I am indebted for various kinds of assistance, the latter making his personal "potlatch file" available. In that file were some materials of Mr. E. K. DeBeck who in 1953, while serving as Clerk of the Provincial Assembly of British Columbia, gave me permission to use any of his letters or memoranda which I could locate. Finally to William Poweles, M.D., I owe recognition for the perspective I gained on an Indian-white community, Alert Bay, as a result of his and Mrs. Poweles' insistence that I stay long enough to learn something about what a medical practitioner observes in his daily care of whites and Indians.

To Professor Kalman Silvert, a political scientist at Tulane, and to several colleagues on the Committee on Indian Research, Carl Dawson, T. F. McIlwraith, Oswald Hall, Nathan Keyfitz, and Jean-Charles Falardeau, I want to acknowledge that it was they who assisted me in gaining a perspective on Canadian life—through committee work and through various academic enterprises undertaken while I was on the staff of McGill University—for until that perspective was achieved, British Columbia was only a place where my uncles and cousins from Scotland lived and were visited by kinfolk and where there had been much agitation about Orientals.

FORREST E. LAVIOLETTE

New Orleans
May, 1959

Contents

THE STRUGGLE FOR SURVIVAL

THE PROTESTANT ETHIC

"Industry was the outstanding character trait required of all those who aspired to success. Idleness was condemned by Franklin and by generations after him as injurious to the person as well as a detriment to the well-being of society. Perseverance was another prized quality required for success and was outstandingly evident, it was said, among those who carefully and diligently saved their money until they amassed great wealth. Sobriety was on the list, as was also the stricture against 'the pleasures of bad company' that not only caused one to waste money foolishly but also would lead one astray. Additional virtues that were stressed included punctuality and a ready willingness to perform extra services without extra pay or special recognition."

LEONARD REISSMAN
Class in American Society, p. 17

1. British Columbia,
An Area of New Settlement

THE NORTHWEST COAST

THE PACIFIC COAST of Canada, stretching between Juan de Fuca Strait on the south and Dixon Entrance on the north, encompasses the major portion of what has become known as the Northwest Coast culture area. As a geographic area it is widely recognized as a region of unusual grandeur and exceptional interest, but its beauty is mixed with some difficult physical features. The waters of the Inside Passage to Alaska move in dangerously swift tidal currents. Frequent fogs, occasional great storms from the Bering Sea and Gulf of Alaska or from the reaches of the Pacific as far distant as the Philippine Islands, sudden local storms with high winds blowing down off the mountains which line the seemingly innumerable waterways of the Passage, create conditions of weather hazardous to work and travel. In spite of their dangers, the Pacific Ocean and the Inside Passage were, for centuries, reliable sources of many foods for the natives; and the forests provided fabricating materials for numerous other needs—clothing, shelter, canoes, tools, and works of art. These natural resources were so extensive and so easily exploited that even a technology of the primitive fishing and hunting type made possible, until recent times, one of the few major concentrations of natives on North or South America.

For some centuries prior to the arrival of the Europeans, the natives of the region had been developing an elaborate cultural system which for a variety of reasons has become one of the better known non-literate cultures of the world. This system, as anthropologists have demonstrated, developed within well-defined geographic limits. The "Note on the Accompanying Paper," which precedes Boas' *Ethnology of the Kwakiutl*, states that:

Many Indian tribes, distinct in physical characteristics and distinct also in languages, but who are one in culture, occupy the Pacific coast of America between Juan de Fuca Strait and Yakutat Bay. This they are because, in large measure, their industries and arts, their beliefs and customs, differ so markedly from those of all other Indian peoples. Notwithstanding this great uniformity of culture, however, a closer study of the elements discloses many things that are peculiar to single tribes, which show that this culture is the natural result of a gradual and convergent development from several distinct sources or centers, every one of these tribes having added something peculiar to itself to the sum of this development.[1]

Although this general cultural system reaches northward into southeastern Alaska and southward into the northern part of the coastal area of the State of Washington (as far south as northern California according to Drucker), it was the almost exclusively Canadian tribes[2] —the Nootka, Haida, Kwakiutl, and Tsimshian—who developed its characteristic features, and because of public and scholarly interests, they are the tribes which have become best known of all tribes in the Northwest Coast area.

In discussing the development of anthropology in Canada, McIlwraith reports that it was not until the 1860's that scientists in Canada became interested in the Indians. He states that about that time Dr. George Dawson, one of Canada's most distinguished geologists, began collecting cultural artifacts and linguistic data from the tribes which he contacted during his field trips.[3] However others may have contributed, the major recordings of this cultural system were made in the 1880's and 1890's by Franz Boas. The significance of the work of Boas was, of course, increased markedly by the use of it— particularly the materials dealing with the Kwakiutl, and most specifically that of the tribal customs associated with potlatching—by Ruth Benedict in *Patterns of Culture*, published in 1934. A paperback edition later sold, so it is understood, to the extent of hundreds of thousands of copies.

For the purpose of appraising somewhat more effectively the importance of these cultural data and the interpretations or use made of them outside the field of anthropology, the author, with the assistance of Dr. Fred Adams, made a cursory survey in 1955. Forty-five books well known to sociologists and social psychologists were found to use Northwest Coast materials. Of all the major tribes of the area, the Kwakiutl group and its potlatch were the most generally known.

[1]American Bureau of Ethnology, *Annual Report*. 1913–14, part I, pp. 39–40.
[2]The distribution of these tribes, including others, is best portrayed in *British Columbia: Atlas of Resources*, Map No. 12, "Native Indians: Distribution of Ethnic Groups—1850." Other maps in this publication provide a compendium of geographic facts with respect to the major features of the Northwest Coast.
[3]See Marius Barbeau, *Totem Poles: A By-product of the Fur Trade*. An historical survey with data most pertinent to this point and chapter is found in chapter one of *The Tlingit Indians*, a translation by Erna Gunther of Aurel Krause, *Die Tlingit Indianer*.

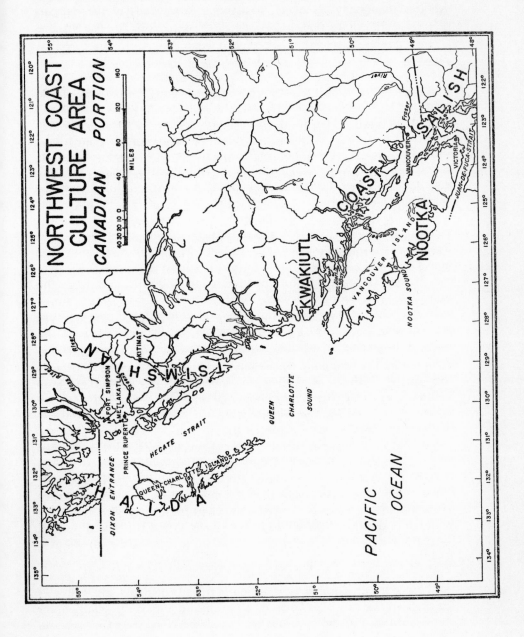

NORTHWEST COAST
CULTURE AREA
CANADIAN PORTION

MILES
40 30 20 10 0   40   80   120   160

HAIDA

QUEEN CHARLOTTE ISLANDS

HECATE STRAIT

DIXON ENTRANCE

PRINCE RUPERT

FORT SIMPSON

METLAKATLA

KITIMAT

RIVER

TSIMSHIAN

QUEEN

CHARLOTTE

SOUND

KWAKIUTL

COAST SALISH

NOOTKA

NOOTKA SOUND

VANCOUVER ISLAND

Campbell

Fraser River

Vancouver

VICTORIA

JUAN-DE-FUCA-STRAIT

PACIFIC

OCEAN

Five authors made comparative use of Kwakiutl materials; seven authors described their social organization, all using the potlatch data and several limiting their selections to it; eight authors cited data or interpretations from Ruth Benedict. Twenty-five authors referred to *Patterns of Culture* or presented the idea of "themes" or "patterns" as developed by Benedict. The work of Boas, through Benedict, led social scientists to an interest in those materials. In the forty-five books analysed, the authors used the basic ideas for: (1) the formulation of a hypothesis of cultural themes-patterns in social organization; (2) the development of a typology of competition-co-operation; (3) evidence of culturally based abnormalities, such as found in megalomania, acquisitiveness, competitiveness, and egotism; and (4) description of unique aspects of a cultural system. The diffusion of Northwest Coast interpretations of social scientists and psychiatrists throughout Canada and the United States has become extensive; the Boas-Benedict work has become classic in character. The other Canadian Northwest Coast tribes—the Tsimshian, Haida, Nootka, and Coast Salish—are well known to anthropologists, but among the other social sciences, they can be said to be unknown by comparison with the Kwakiutls.

Anthropologists and historians have shown that after their first contacts with Europeans in the 1770's and with the beginning of the fur trade in 1785, the tribal cultures of the Northwest Coast started to change rapidly, becoming transitional in character. They have been so ever since.[4] With the beginning of colonization after 1849, the rate of cultural change increased even more markedly. As much as the Indians may have wished for the departure of the gold miners, missionaries, and settlers, they became actors in the processes inevitable in the development of a regional social system. They became involved in that social development because of the organization and dynamics of their remarkable cultural system based upon fishing and wood, especially cedar. Unlike the Tasmanians they did not disappear as a consequence of foreign immigration as shown on the chart with its graphs comparing population trends of the whites in the province and the coastal Indian.

Peaceful Penetration

The history of European expansion is full of incidents and struggles among national states, or between a power and a native population, for the control of a given area. In the case of the Northwest Coast, Spain

[4]See C. E. Denny, *The Law Marches West.*

and Britain made rival claims to the region. These claims were settled by diplomacy after the Nootka Sound Incident in 1789. In keeping with British colonial philosophy and thus the policies of that period, Pitt's willingness to go to war over the claim was a sign that colonization of the region would be undertaken.

After general claims were established, each colonizing power has had necessarily to formulate a policy with respect to the ownership and use of the land. In West Africa, now the state of Ghana, the British refused to permit any European to possess land; it is said today that this principle of land control facilitated the evolution of the tribal people and the emergence of Ghana as an independent state. In the Belgian Congo, immigrants are permitted to own land, but the Belgian government, before the disturbances of 1959, regulated migration to the area so that immigrants would not compete with the natives in any kind of economic activity. In Canada, the acquisition of land for settlement was secured in most instances by the Crown through title negotiation with the several Indian tribes. It was assumed that their tribal organization made them sovereign nations. This was, of course, a continuation of the historic British policy.

In the settlement of Canada west of the Ontario border, official action regarding land preceded the arrival of any important number of settlers. The treaty system, developed as the result of experience in Ontario, was applied to Manitoba, Saskatchewan, and Alberta, when those areas were being opened for settlement. Although the documents signed were not treaties in the strict sense of the word, since they were not negotiated, none the less the British, by using this so-called treaty system, recognized native rights on the principle of prior occupancy of the land. By extinguishing the native title to the land, by transferring the title to the Crown, and by creating reserves, the government gained absolute control of the disposition of vast tracts of land.[5] This control of land, furthermore, was managed with the utmost care through the introduction of legal institutions and police support. Law and order were not permitted to emerge haphazardly through the fights of rival settlers; they were established by the government, which had formulated a plan of action for acquiring land and opening it for settlement.

From the point of view of the settlers of British Columbia, land

[5]The historical discussion as to whom the land belonged is very involved, including court cases. This issue has been sketched briefly by Chester Martin in "The Colonial Policy of the Dominion," *Transactions of the Royal Society of Canada*, Series III, XVI (1922), s. II, pp. 35–47. Professor Martin mentions the fact that none of this discussion was going on in Canada before nor was it involved at the time the colony of British Columbia joined the Dominion.

acquisition through settlement and without negotiation generally worked smoothly. But for the natives, land presented a problem from the beginning of settlement. Although there had been conflict between several groups of Indians and the maritime fur traders,[6] that type of commercial contact did not involve questions of land. Resentment and hostility among British Columbia Indians against the white man began to emerge in an important way during the gold rush of 1858: the inflow of miners, the development of capital, and the opportunities for trade were the first stage in the emergence of acute problems for the native inhabitants.[7] As settlement proceeded and governments were established, reserves were set aside for individual bands and groups, and to the white settlers all seemed well. None the less, the Indians became increasingly preoccupied with questions of land ownership and use as they became Canadianized. For the majority of them the central question came to be: "Who owns British Columbia?" The increasing agitation over land ownership became a movement, and from it emerged an Indian conception of how the land title had been acquired by the British and Canadians—a conception quite different from that of the British Columbians. In 1926, for example, when the Allied Indian Tribes of British Columbia presented their land title claims to the Canadian Parliament, the Reverend Peter Kelly, chairman of the Allied Indian Tribes and a member of the Haida tribe, stated flatly and emphatically, in reply to a remark by the Hon. Mr. McLennan, "We have not been conquered." Mr. McLennan replied: "Well, call it peaceful penetration in British Columbia, fortunately."[8] His conception of the mode of settlement represents what the people of British Columbia have come to accept about their province. British Columbia was settled and title to the land acquired through peaceful penetration: that is, occupation without the Indian wars and extensive violence that characterized settlement in other areas, especially the United States. In contrast the Indians came to look upon the British claim to

[6]A careful appraisal of all known data on the subject of the earliest Indian-European conflict has been made by F. W. Howay, "Indian Attacks upon Maritime Traders of the Northwest," *Canadian Historical Review*, VI, pp. 287–309.

[7]There was, of course, some violence during this period. See, for example, the account of Father Morice with respect to the Humalhkhoh massacre, in *History of the Northern Interior of British Columbia*, pp. 314–17; see also George Edgar Shankel, "The Development of Indian Policy in British Columbia," unpublished doctoral dissertation, University of Washington, and *The Year Book of British Columbia, 1911*.

[8]Special Joint Committee of the Senate and House of Commons appointed to inquire into the *Claims of the Allied Indian Tribes of British Columbia, as Set Forth in their Petition Submitted to Parliament in June, 1926: Report and Evidence*, p. 156. Henceforth cited as *Claims*.

title to the province as unjust because only a small northeast portion of it was ceded to the Canadians through negotiation. Thus the Indians, by prior occupancy, owned the land. This definition is a consequence of part of the struggle for survival and a more detailed analysis follows later.

The settlement of British Columbia began in earnest in 1849 when the Hudson's Bay Company was given a grant for colonizing the area. At that time only 450 white people, it is estimated, were living on Vancouver Island. When it became clear that the Hudson's Bay Company could not work successfully as a colonizing agent for Vancouver Island and when difficult conditions were being created on the mainland by the gold rushes, arrangements were made to cancel the grant "as soon as convenient," establish colonial governments for Vancouver Island and British Columbia, and promote settlement. British interest in emigration and colonization during this period was very high, and the cancellation was part of the effort to retain British North America. Riddell states the essential feature of Canadian concern about the West prior to Confederation:

For Canada . . . expansion was born of an inner necessity within the life of the country. . . . The St. Lawrence Valley had provided Canadians with a great highway of communication leading naturally into the interior of the continent. Across the upper reaches of this valley had been drawn an international boundary which turned what the Canadian had hoped would be a corridor into a cul-de-sac. In the hopes of sharing the fruits of American expansion, Canadian governments for half a century had pushed forward the construction of a system of communications—first canals and later railroads—from Montreal to the international boundary on the St. Clair River. For a variety of reasons the promised flow of trade had never come. The Province of Canada found itself, in the 1860's, with a system of transport and all accompanying economic structures, much too much for its needs, much to costly for its resources. At this point the Canadian west appeared as the possible frontier of settlement in the development of which this capital equipment could be put to use.[9]

As early as 1850, eight years before the miners started arriving, Sir James Douglas, simultaneously governor and head officer for Hudson's Bay, had undertaken the responsibility for managing the problems of land title. In 1850, 1851, and 1852, he made agreements with the Coast Salish natives in the immediate vicinity of Victoria in which cash payments were made for small portions of Vancouver Island, with reservation to the natives of their village sites and enclosed fields. According to the Report of the Royal Commission on Indian Affairs for the Province

[9]Alexander Begg, The History of British Columbia, p. 201.

of British Columbia, the Indian question was given considerable prominence, because of threats of fighting,[10] at the first meeting of the Legislative Assembly of the Colony of Vancouver Island in the summer of 1856, two years before the gold rush. The *Report* stated that in his inaugural address "Governor Douglas, after referring to the feeling of insecurity engendered 'by the presence of large bodies of armed savages' who visited the Colony from the North, said: 'I shall nevertheless, continue to conciliate the good will of the native Indian tribes by treating them with justice and forbearance and by rigidly protecting their civil and agrarian rights.'" (I, 15) Thus was declared a portion of official policy, supported by the cabinet in England.[11]

In 1859, the Secretary of State for the Colonies, Lord Carnarvon, wrote to Sir James Douglas on the Indian question, apparently in response to some of the Governor's reports. The Secretary felt that the subject of relations with the Indians was extremely important, and concurred with Sir James in his concern for their welfare:

Proofs are unhappily still too frequent of the neglect which Indians experience when the white man obtains possession of their country, and their claims to consideration are forgotten at the moment when equity most demands that the hand of the protector should be extended to help them. In the case of the Indians of Vancouver Island and British Columbia, Her Majesty's Government earnestly wish that when the advancing requirements of colonization press upon lands occupied by members of that race, measures of liberality and justice may be adopted for compensating them for the surrender of the territory which they have been taught to regard as their own.[12]

Lord Carnarvon nevertheless did not want any checks or obstacles placed in the way of settlement, and just a few weeks after the above dispatch was forwarded, another was sent, according to the *Report,* in which the Secretary advised the Governor that "whilst making ample provision under the arrangement proposed for the future sustenance

[10]W. H. Collison, in *In the Wake of the War Canoe,* p. 89, describes the raiding and war-making activities of the Haida tribesmen who lived on the Queen Charlotte Islands, and speaks of "the courage and ambition of these adventurers." On one occasion (date not given) "they threatened to attack Victoria, and Sir James Douglas, who was then Governor of the Colony, had to order the marines around from the vessel of war lying at Esquimault, in order to drive them back to their camp outside the city limits and thus preserve the peace."

[11]The complete inaugural address of Sir James Douglas is reported in Begg, pp. 207–9. For Governor Douglas' first-hand experiences with Indian violence in the interior of British Columbia, see Morice, chap. IX, "An Episode and Its Consequences."

[12]*Report of the Royal Commission on Indian Affairs for the Province of British Columbia,* I, pp. 14–15.

and improvement of the native tribes, you will, I am persuaded, bear in mind the importance of exercising due care in laying out and defining the several Reserves, so as to avoid checking at a future day the progress of white colonists."

On March 5, 1861, Governor Douglas directed the Chief Commissoner of Lands and Works to take steps for marking out "distinctly the Indian Reserves throughout the Colony." By the time British Columbia had been organized into a single royal colony through the union of Vancouver Island and British Columbia in 1866, just five years before joining Confederation, a schedule of Indian reserves had been made.

According to the laws effective when the colony became a province, a non-Indian settler could pre-empt unsurveyed lands, or homestead or purchase surveyed lands. Legally recognized Indians were attached to reserves without the right of pre-emption and although it was legally possible, they were unable for numerous reasons to purchase land. Since 1871 any readjustment of reserves to meet changing conditions has had to be negotiated through the Superintendent-General of Indian Affairs in Ottawa or petitioned from the Parliament of Canada. Canadians had acquired complete control over the land in a manner consistent with British colonial policy—by some negotiation but chiefly by occupation, by settlement, and by reserving lands for the Indians. In their conception the title to the province of British Columbia was acquired in a moral manner, legally, and in accordance with their ideas of justice even though a treaty was never negotiated, as in the other provinces. Thus when British Columbia joined the Dominion, there existed a basis for the distribution of the land and its ownership. By then the coastal and interior Indians were possibly, but if so barely, outnumbered; they were in any case outgunned. The Indians had become a displaced population without war or much informal violence. Peaceful penetration had so far been successful.

WARDSHIP

Peaceful penetration in the Canadian West went through several phases as Indian-white relationships developed. The creation of reserves designated exclusively for the benefit of specified tribes of Indians was the first major step taken in establishing a segregated social system based upon legal sanctions. The reserves provided an ecological base for the system; they fitted neatly into schemes for civilizing the Indians and at the outset gave explicit expression to a British social philosophy which later became Canadian. This segregated system maintained the identity of Indian groups and tribes so that later when they did become knowledgeable regarding the techniques of modern economic life and political action, the natives existed as groups with potential power rather than as individuals who might have dropped or drifted to the lowest social stratum of the Canadian community.

Until 1845 the policy of administering Indian affairs in British North America was essentially military in character; nevertheless, here and there one finds humanitarian motives expressed. The introduction to the *Annual Report, 1927*, of the Department of Indian Affairs, Ottawa, has a short history of Indian administration entitled, "The Canadian Indians after Sixty Years of Confederation," which gives evidence of such motives:

> The military police had looked upon the Indians as potential allies or foes, and, during the pioneer days, the feeling was balanced between hope and apprehension. They were kept quiet by presents of scarlet cloth, silver gorgets, brass kettles, and ammunition, with an occasional ration of rum. The fur-traders used the latter fluid as the most precious means of exchange and barter, and the restless, dejected people that were handed over to the province were indeed a problem. One Governor of Upper Canada, seeing them so wretched, resolved to send them back to nature for healing, and to remove them to hunting grounds where they might recuperate or die away unseen. But better counsels prevailed. The missionaries claimed them as materials for evangelization, and protested that they were capable of lasting improvement. Upper and Lower Canada, not long after that, began a systematic endeavour to educate the Indians, supported by zealous missionary effort. This informal union between church and state still exists, and all Canadian Indian schools are conducted upon a joint agreement between the Government and the denominations as to finance and system. The method has proved successful, and the Indians of Ontario and Quebec, in the older regions of the provinces are every day entering more and more into the general life of the country . . .
>
> On the whole it may be said that the Indians have reason to be grateful to the Canadian Government for the benefits and consideration that they have received, while Canada may well be proud of what has been accomplished by the members of the aboriginal race. (p. 7 *et seq.*)

In spite of these claims of good care and good intentions, Indians have for decades carried on protest activities, including visits to the King or Queen in London, against the settlers and the government. As early as 1830, Indians from Lorette, a reserve located about eight miles northwest of Quebec City, sent a deputation to London to see about their land claims. After references to conferences and a legal decision, a dispatch from a Downing Street official to Lt. General Sir James

Kempt, commander of the imperial forces from September of 1828 until October of 1840, concludes with these charitable instructions:

I apprehend that after the legal decision which this claim of the Indians has undergone, it is impossible now to extend their limits in the way they desire. . . . I am, therefore, desirous that immediate steps should be taken for placing such of the families of the Hurons of Lorette as may be inclined to emigrate, upon the nearest Crown Lands which can be granted to them, leaving it to your discretion to assign the quantity which should be granted to each family willing to accept this boon from the Crown; and that such arrangements be made for the repair of their Church (which is represented to be in ruins) as the immediate circumstances of the case may appear to require.[13]

The same humane concern was evidenced by Lord Carnarvon in his dispatches to Sir James Douglas when he stated that the "Government wishes . . . [that] measures of liberality and justice may be adopted." It is in such statements that one can observe the influence of the philanthropic movement and Christian humanitarianism in the formation and administration of policy. It was most effectively expressed when the Canadian legislation of 1869 was entitled "An Act for the Gradual Enfranchisement of Indians, the Better Management of Indian Affairs, and to Extend the Provisions of the Act 31st Victoria, Chapter 42."[14] It is no longer good form to express in the titles of Canadian statutes philosophic hopes or social objectives, but in 1869 there was considerable zeal in the young Dominion of Canada. In addition to zeal, however, there was held the general assumption that the Indians would disappear either by extermination through diseases and inability to control alcohol or by amalgamation and assimilation. And there is, in fact, a residue of that assumption still current in contemporary Canada. As a statement in point the brief of the Church Missionary Society to a Special Joint Committee in 1947 states that "it has been common to think and to speak of Indians as a 'dying race' and perhaps the idea that they were doomed to become extinct has had something to do with producing the indifference to their state which has been so common. As recently as twenty-six years ago it was possible for competent authorities to accept the extinction of Western tribes as a practical certainty. . . ."[15] There is no necessity of government officials

[13]Public Archives of Canada, Series G 1, vol. XX, p. 201, duplicate no. 84.
[14]*Statutes of Canada*, 32–3 Vic., c. 6.
[15]See Special Joint Committee of the Senate and the House of Commons, *Minutes of Proceedings and Evidence* (henceforth cited as *Minutes*), 1947, no. 9, p. 403. See also H. B. Hawthorn, C. S. Belshaw, and S. M. Jamieson, *The Indians of British Columbia*, pp. 58–9, regarding attitudes to the Indians.

to take liberal, humane, or philanthropic attitudes towards the natives who are being or have been displaced by invading settlers. The variations in policy and attitudes in Africa and other areas under British domination are well known.[16] Therefore, from what is known about the policy of wardship during the past century, one cannot state that the national goals and public policy which emerged in Canada are an integral part of any social philosophy requiring peaceful penetration. One feels that it ought to be, but one can have the same feelings about the policy of "indirect rule," a principle of colonial administration which apparently originated with the Treaty States in India and then was applied in 1918 to Northern Nigeria and in 1925 to the different conditions in Tanganyika. As stated by MacMillan:

British tradition has always been shy of anything resembling a set programme or formula. Though it has in fact been more uniform than is usually admitted we have taken pride rather in its elasticity. The older policy was thoroughly national, and perhaps a subconscious effort to carry men of all parties over this break with tradition inclined some exponents of Indirect Rule to allow the new experiment to harden into a doctrine, almost as text of orthodoxy.[17]

Prior to the completion of the first phase of peaceful penetration of the area now represented by the Prairie Provinces and British Columbia, the policy of wardship had been fully formulated and applications made of it in Quebec and Ontario. Influenced by national trends and contrasting actions regarding Indians in the United States, by the philanthropic movement in England, as well as by imperial diplomacy and the development of a free trade economy, the Canadian policy of wardship emerged from colonial experience with these major components:

First, a system of land reserves in which each reserve is for the exclusive use of the band to whom it was assigned. Buttressed by administrative rules of the Dominion Government and the authority of the band, the system gives protection from trespassers, from non-Indian squatters, and from wasting of natural resources.

Second, the concept of wardship envisages Indian self-support and self-sufficiency. Gradually over the years this has become increasingly influenced by the more recent ideas of governmental responsibility for

[16]See the various relevant sections in Ralph Linton, ed., *Most of the World: The Peoples of Africa, Latin America, and the East Today;* also, A. Grenfell, *White Settlers and Native Peoples: An Historical Study of Racial Contacts between English-Speaking Whites and Aboriginal Peoples in the United States, Australia, and New Zealand,* especially with respect to Australia and New Zealand.

[17]W. H. MacMillan, *Africa Emergent,* p. 214.

individual welfare as represented in relief allowances, old age pensions, and health programs.

Finally, wardship involves the gradual preparation for Canadian citizenship. Hence, Christianization is necessary; education is necessary. When the individual or the band is prepared, then individual or band enfranchisement can take place. Thus the legislation of 1951 makes provision for the conversion of reserves to local municipalities.[18] These major principles of wardship have been modified by a careful administrative scrutiny and supported by a relatively small annual appropriation until after World War II. Within that framework of administrative action, the idea of progress towards the Canadian ideals of citizenship has persisted.

Canadian officials hesitate to use the term "wardship," although occasionally they have. Harper, Price, and MacInnes have claimed that the policies which have been formulated are in fact the policies of guardianship. The Indian has a specialized status in the Canadian system, but it is not one of dependence.[19] Although some claim that it is not a system which involves the perpetual legal status of childhood, many Indians do feel that way about it, and white judges in British Columbia courts continue to refuse to accept the testimony of an Indian witness. Many actions appear to be those based upon the idea of wardship; but stated public policy and public ideals are those of guardianship.

There are several aspects of this system, as it has worked in British Columbia, which are pertinent to the discussions to follow. At the time that the colony joined the Dominion, a schedule of reserves was at hand. Important as that has been administratively, it has also been important historically in organizing provincial attitudes towards the federal government and the Indians. The thirteenth article of the Terms of Union has three provisions: that (1) "the charge of the Indians, and

[18]The most detailed statements on the Canadian system of administration and the assumptions on which it rests are to be found in an article by Dr. Allan Harper entitled "Canada's Indian Administration: The Treaty System" in *America Indigena*, V (2), VI (4), and VII (2); also T. R. L. MacInnes, "The History and Policies of Indian Administration in Canada," in C. T. Loram and T. F. McIlwraith, eds., *The North American Indian Today*, especially p. 158, and "History of Indian Administration in Canada," *Canadian Journal of Economics and Political Science*, XII pp. 387–94.

[19]In August, 1946, Mr. Andrew Paull, president of the North American Indian Brotherhood, circulated "Contravention of Certain Rights." On page ten evidence in the form of federal legislation and three court decisions is adduced to support the assertion that "the Indian is a ward of the Crown, under the guardianship and protection of the Dominion Government and, as such, is not a British subject in the accepted sense of the term."

the trusteeship and management of the lands, reserved for their use and benefit, shall be assumed by the Dominion Government"; that (2) "a policy as liberal as that hitherto pursued by the British Columbia Government shall be continued by the Dominion Government after the Union"; and that (3) "to carry out such policy, tracts of land of such extent as it has hitherto been the practice of the British Columbia Government to appropriate for that purpose shall from time to time be conveyed by the local Government to the Dominion Government, in trust for the use and benefit of the Indians."[20]

The province has from time to time manifested a keen sensitivity, when federal legislative action was involved, to the provisions of the Terms of Union, especially the second one. This item, as interpreted by members of the House of Commons and others, assumes that the early settlers and the founders of government formulated and applied a liberal policy. It is well known that between 1849 and 1871 officials did set out reserves for the Indians, following the example set during the colonial period when Sir James Douglas arranged for the Salish near Victoria to retain land for their own use. Outside of this, it might be established upon further inquiry that the colonial government pursued the policy of peaceful penetration with little regard for Indian rights. Upon joining confederation in 1871, British Columbia was relieved of any responsibility, since the federal government's policy of wardship was extended to the Indians of the province. It was not until decades later, however, that the wardship policy was made particularly effective, except upon assumption of this responsibility Ottawa did encourage the activities of the mission stations. The resulting contradiction with regard to this aspect of the complicated relationship between the two governments can be stated in this form: today British Columbians believe that the colonial government did a great deal for the Indians; Ottawa believes that it has since 1871 kept the agreement of the Terms of the Union. Meanwhile the British Columbia Indians feel that Ottawa has failed to live up to its agreement.

In some localities the reserve system is highly influential in Indian-white relationships, while in others it appears to have little influence on them. There is still pressure here and there for whites to take over Indian areas good for farming lands or those needed by cities for expansion, especially where industrial sites are possible.[21] Moreover,

[20]Quoted in the *Report of the Royal Commission on Indian Affairs for the Province of British Columbia*, I, pp. 15–16.

[21]A Squamish Indian informant explained to the writer that an incorporated city had advertised part of his reserve as excellent water front property for industrial development. See also Hawthorn, Belshaw, and Jamieson, pp. 469–70.

wardship, even though benevolent guardianship, involves contradictions for the wards, in band politics for example and in their view of themselves in relation to the past, the present, and the future. Their orientation in the coastal area of the province is based on efforts made by missionaries, Indian agents, and Sir John A. Macdonald to legislate social change; on a movement of protest against the procedures associated with peaceful penetration; and on a struggle for identity which appears to have emerged out of the first two and to have prepared the way for the creation of the Native Brotherhood of British Columbia.

2. Native Conduct:
"The Thraldom of Heathenism and Sin"

MISSIONARIES

STUDIES OF THE modern history of the Northwest Coast describe how explorers and traders initiated for the Indians a period of rapid social change. In the case of other peoples, the acquisition of metals, firearms, alcohol, and new diseases from Europeans have precipitated either their disappearance or major, persistent crises requiring radical changes in native social organization. The tribes of British Columbia were no exception. It may be noted that the first significant social changes, those induced by the fur trade, were based upon casual and informal contacts.

The changes inaugurated during the period of the first contact had not been completed when new inducements to change were encountered. Even though this aboriginal population was remote from Great Britain, the world was shrinking rapidly and descriptions of their extreme heathenism spread quickly. Hence it was not long before they were discovered again, this time by missionaries in Great Britain and eastern Canada. A small leaflet published, about 1934 in Alert Bay, by the Church Missionary Society reports that the "Anglican missionary enterprise on the Pacific Coast dates back to the year 1819 when the attention of the C.M.S. in the Old Land was drawn to the dire needs of the Indians, whose members at that time were estimated to total almost one hundred thousand." It was not, none the less, until the earlier days of colonization that a need for formal action to bring about radical transformations in native conduct had somehow become defined. The casualness of the fur trading type of contacts could no longer be tolerated. Hence, with the arrival of the missionaries and their Christian ethic the task of converting the natives began, and peaceful penetration entered a new phase, based upon an institutionalized mode of cultural dismemberment and reconstruction.[1]

[1]See Wilson Duff and Michael Kew, "Anthony Island, a Home of the Haidas," *Annual Report*, Provincial Museum of Natural History and Anthropology, 1957, p. 37.

Central to the theory of the origins of and changes in institutions is the element of social unrest. Individual unrest is unimportant until it becomes social, that is, characteristic of a group; often the first indication of social unrest is the development of epidemic-like behaviour sweeping through groups and at times over vast areas. There is evidence that before the missionaries arrived in coastal British Columbia, the Indians of the Northwest were manifesting social unrest as a consequence of the fur trade and of settlements in the Oregon country to the south and even in eastern Canada.[2] The missionaries themselves were products of the social unrest in Great Britain which had become effective long before 1800. There the forces of unrest generated by radical social change had become channelled toward colonization, large-scale emigration, industrialization, and urbanization. Several social movements resulted, some dominated by ideas of reform and several by notions of Christian humanitarianism. Out of the religiously-oriented movements grew the Society for Promoting Christian Knowledge (1698) and the Society for Propagating the Gospel (1701). Their purpose was brilliantly clear and their intent continued strong until the early 1900's.

Among these movements born of social unrest, the Wesleyan and Evangelical revivals are of particular interest; they were under way when Captain Cook located a good rendezvous at Nootka Sound in 1778, and enthusiasm and support for the revivals persisted long after the death of John Wesley in 1788. The discovery of British Columbia as a land of opportunity for missionaries as well as traders and settlers came in the later stages of these great movements. According to the theory of revivals, reforms, and social revolutions, the earlier stages are dominated by excitement and the phenomena of social contagion. Under those conditions it is imposible to achieve the goals which they define, and unless a relatively permanent organization directed towards goal achievement can be created, the efforts and interests of participants will be re-channelled or frittered away. These two revival movements evolved permanent organizations in the form of the Methodist Church and the Church Missionary Society of the Church of England. They thus became equipped for continuing the unfinished business of their earlier years of development, namely the extension of Chris-

---

[2]In his *History of the Northern Interior of British Columbia*, p. 225, Morice speaks of a movement agitating the southern Carriers around 1834: "This can be traced to two natives of Oregon, who boasted a semblance of education received at Red River. According to J. McLean, it spread with amazing rapidity over the country, and its ceremonial was . . . restricted to singing and dancing." See also pp. 238–40 for his statements regarding the Indian prophet Peni.

tianity to the whole world.[3] It was possible, then, to direct interest, energy, and capital toward Japan, China, India, Africa, and North America. All of those vast areas and nations were affected profoundly by this organization of great resources for missionary purposes. The final institutionalization of some of that social unrest is typified by the Church of England's Church Missionary Society which, founded in 1799, had by 1920 expended some $4,000,000 for its Indian-Eskimo programmes in Canada. Through that Society the Church of England took the lead among Protestants in the conversion of natives. Cultural change which heretofore had been the result of casual and informal contacts with the fur traders was now accelerated by the pressure of an organized and purposeful group—the missionaries.

It is not clear whether the experiences of the earliest explorers and fur traders by giving rise to certain opinions or beliefs about the natives of the Northwest Coast were influential in formulating this need for changing native conduct. By 1825 more than 230 vessels were trading yearly along the coast,[4] and their experiences are significant insofar as they communicated news to Europe and eastern North America and insofar as they were confirmed by the somewhat parallel experiences of the early missionaries. At least three passages from John Meares' *Voyage from China to the Northwest Coast of America* (1791) contributed, we may suppose, to the widely held belief that the natives of the Northwest Coast were cannibals:

On the 8th, a strange canoe with several people in it entered the cove, and, coming alongside the ship, sold us a number of small sea otter skins:— they also offered for sale an human hand, dried and shrivelled up; the fingers of which were compleat, and the nails long; but our horror may be better conceived than expressed, when we saw a seal hanging from the ear of one of the men in the canoe, which was known to have belonged to the unfortunate Mr. Millar, of the Imperial Eagle, whose melancholy history was perfectly well known to every one on board . . . ; and from his manifest confusion in conversing on this subject, and various other concurring circumstances . . . , we were very much disposed to believe that Maquilla himself was a cannibal. There is, indeed, too much reason to apprehend that the horrible traffic for human flesh extends, more or less, along this part of the continent of America. Even our friend Callicum reposed his head, at

---

[3]Archibald G. Baker gives important attention to "characteristic missionary organization." Each of our denominations has succeeded "in building up a closely articulated missionary machine." And in referring to the oriental peoples, he states that "they see behind him [the missionary] and his labors a vast array of men, institutions and resources." He indicates that abroad this organization has resulted in the notion that "The secret of power lies in organization." *Christian Missions and a New World Culture*, pp. 49–50.

[4]Duff and Kew, p. 54, from Howay's study.

night, upon a large bag, filled with human skulls, which he showed as the
trophies of his superior courage; and it is more than probable, that the
bodies of the victims to which they belonged, had furnished a banquet of
victory for him, and the warrior who shared his savage glory. (pp. 124–5)

With reference to the houses which the natives occupied:

. . . Festoons of human skulls, arranged with some attention to uniformity,
were disposed in almost every part where they could be placed, and were
considered as a very spendid decoration of the royal apartment. (p. 139)

And finally an experience of members of his crew:

The boat had advanced a considerable way up the Straits of de Fuca, and
had entered a bay or harbour; . . .
As they returned down the straits, they were met by a small canoe
paddled by two men, who were the subjects of Wicananish, and from whom
they purchased some fish. But words cannot express the surprise and
abhorrence of our people, when the natives held up two human heads, but
just cut off, and still streaming with blood, by way of offering them for sale.
They held these detestable objects by the hair with an air of triumph and
exultation; and, when the crew of the boat discovered signs of disgust and
detestation at such an horrid spectacle, the savages, in a tone, and with
looks of extreme satisfaction, informed them, that they were the heads of
two people belonging to Tatooche, whom they had murdered, as that chief
had lately declared war against Wicananish. This circumstance threw a damp
upon the spirits of the crew, which continued, more or less, through the
whole of the voyage. (p. 178)

There is no evidence that the natives were ever cannibals, but such
accounts, coupled with the missionaries' own observations of some of
the ceremonials, strongly supported the belief.[5]

In his *History of British Columbia*, Begg reported that in 1859 there
were eleven missionaries at work in Vancouver Island and on the
mainland in the colony of British Columbia: four of them were from
the Methodist Church; three of them had been sent by the Society for
the Propagation of the Gospel; the Rev. E. Cridge who had first gone
as a chaplain of the Hudson's Bay Company; and Mr. Duncan who had
started work with the support of Miss (later Baroness) Burdett-Coutts.
Although Catholic missionaries had arrived a decade earlier,[6] it was
with the arrival of Mr. Duncan in 1857 that the formal and direct

[5]Philip Drucker, in *Indians of the Northwest Coast*, p. 151, is of the opinion
that in the great dramatic productions which incorporated the *tamanawas* (medicine dance) and the potlatching activity, the "corpse" was a simulation of a
cadaver; in any case, according to Drucker, "it was prepared."

[6]Morice, chap. xv. Begg, *History of British Columbia*, p. 477, says that the
first Catholic missionary, Father, later Bishop, Demers, arrived in 1842. It was
not until later, however, that a permanent Catholic mission was established.

attack upon the native social organization was initiated, inspired, and given direction by the Church Missionary Society, for which he was a lay missionary.[7] Commander R. C. Mayne published in 1862 his well-known *Four Years in British Columbia and Vancouver Island*; portions of the book were based upon the file materials of Mr. Duncan:

Upon H.M.S. "Satellite" being commissioned in 1856, Captain Prevost offered to give a free passage to a missionary if the Church Missionary Society would send one.[8] This Society, which had been endowed by an anonymous benefactor with the sum of 500 pounds to be devoted to such a purpose, offered the work to Mr. Duncan, who had been trained at High-bury College, and who readily accepted it. The "Satellite" sailed in December, 1856, and reached Vancouver Island in June, 1857 . . .

After some question with the colonial authorities as to where he should begin his work, considerable desire being expressed on the Hudson Bay Company's part to place him at Nanaimo, it was determined that he should go to Fort Simpson on our northern boundary. This post has been previously fixed upon by the Society at home for the scene of Mr. Duncan's labors. The Indians were known to be more free from the contagion of the white man, and were assembled in larger numbers than at any other place on the coast. Another advantage possessed by this locality was that at Simpson the trade of the fort brought a great number of different tribes together. (p. 307)

No other missionary in this region became so famous nor so great a *cause célèbre* as did Mr. Duncan; he not only opened the assault on native institutions but he and his programmes became the model which others aspired to follow.[9]

It was Mr. Duncan who was the first to describe selected aspects of native conduct, to understand its motivation, and thus confirm and enlarge upon the earlier, brief reports of Meares and others who had visited the Coast. Commander Mayne reported that before Mr. Dun-

[7]On the Northwest Coast residents who know about Mr. Duncan have informally bestowed the title of "Father" upon him as an indication of the esteem in which he is still held. Philip Drucker, *The Native Brotherhoods*, refers to him as "Father Duncan" without calling attention to the fact that Mr. Duncan was not an ordained clergyman.

[8]Collison, *In the Wake of the War Canoe*, reports several instances where he had found bibles in the possession of natives, left by Captain, later Admiral, Prevost. Apparently Admiral Prevost was keenly interested in Christianizing the natives.

[9]Much of the story of the activities, tactics, strategies, and successes of Mr. Duncan are described in John W. Arctander, *The Apostle of Alaska: The Story of William Duncan of Metlakahtla*, and in Henry S. Wellcome, *The Story of Metlakahtla*, Arctic Bibliography item 19275. Important as missionaries have been in the history of modern Europe and the extension of its civilization, little attention has been given to them by anthropologists and sociologists. For a review of the literature see the unpublished doctoral dissertation of Virgil Annakin, "The Missionary, an Agent of Cultural Diffusion."

can moved out of Fort Simpson to the site where he established a village for his converts, he had observed conduct of the Tsimshians as follows:

Sometimes slaves have to be sacrificed to satiate the vanity of their owners, or take away reproach. Only the other day we were called upon to witness a terrible scene of this kind. An old chief, in cold blood, ordered a slave to be dragged to the beach, murdered, and thrown into the water. His orders were quickly obeyed. The victim was a poor woman. Two or three reasons are assigned for this foul act; one is, that it is to take away the disgrace attached to his daughter, who has been suffering for some time from a ball wound in the arm. Another report is, that he does not expect his daughter to recover, so he has killed his slave in order that she may prepare for the coming of his daughter into the unseen world. . . .

I did not see the murder, but immediately after, I saw crowds of people running out of those houses near to where the corpse was thrown, and forming themselves into groups at a good distance away. This I learned was from fear of what was to follow. Presently two bands of furious wretches appeared, each headed by a man in a state of nudity. They gave vent to the most unearthly sounds, and the two naked men made themselves look as unearthly as possible, proceeding in a creeping sort of stoop, and stepping like two proud horses, at the same time shooting forward each arm alternately, which they held out at full length for a little time in the most defiant manner. Besides this, the continual jerking their heads back, causing their long black hair to twist about, added much to their savage appearance.

For some time they pretended to be seeking the body, and the instant they came where it lay they commenced screaming and rushing around it like so many angry wolves. Finally they seized it, dragged it out of the water, and laid it on the beach, where I was told the naked men would commence tearing it to pieces with their teeth. The two bands of men immediately surrounded them, and so hid their horrid work. In a few minutes the crowd broke again into two, when each of the naked cannibals appeared with half of the body in his hands. Separating a few yards, they commenced, amid horrid yells, their still more horrid feast. The sight was too terrible to behold. I left the gallery with a depressed heart. I may mention that the two bands of savages just alluded to belong to that class which the whites term "medicine men." The superstitions connected with this fearful system are deeply rooted here; and it is the admitting and initiating of fresh pupils into these arts that employ numbers, and excite and interest all, during the winter months. This year I think there must have been eight or ten parties of them, but each party seldom has more than one pupil at once. (pp. 284-6)

Further paragraphs from Mr. Duncan's file materials described in more detail the initiation ceremonies for the admission to secret societies. Of the several societies, the most dreaded were the members of the Cannibals.

. . . I was called to witness a stir in the camp which had been caused by this set. When I reached the gallery I saw hundred of Tsimsheans sitting in their canoes. I was told that the cannibal party were in search of a body to devour, and if they failed to find a dead one, it was probable they would seize the first living one that came their way; so that all the people living near the cannibal's house had taken to their canoes to escape being torn to pieces. It is the custom among these Indians to burn their dead; but I suppose for these occasions they take care to deposit a corpse somewhere, in order to satisfy these inhuman wretches.

These, then, are some of the things and scenes which occur in the day during the winter months, while the nights are taken up with amusements— singing and dancing. Occasionally the medicine parties invite people to their several houses, and exhibit tricks before them of various kinds. Some of the actors appear as bears, while others wear masks, the parts of which are moved by string. The great feature in their proceedings is to pretend to murder, and then to restore to life, and so forth. The cannibal, on such occasions, is generally supplied with two, three, or four human bodies, which he tears to pieces before his audience. Several persons, either from bravado or as a charm, present their arms for him to bite. I have seen several whom he has thus bitten, and I hear two have died from the effects. (p. 287)

Other modes of behaviour which caused apprehension for physical safety as well as moral indignation were those of the blood-feud, the techniques of securing revenge, and those which were motivated by a sensitivity to shame so extreme that it must have seemed pathological to European Christians. An instance of the blood feud was witnessed by Mr. J. A. McCullagh, who, with Mr. Tomlinson and Rev. Alfred E. A. Green, began to work in the Nass River country a few years after Mr. Duncan founded his village near Fort Simpson. In the Nass River area, of course, the Tsimshian had not been converted; hence the native conduct which those three missionaries described was undoubtedly much as it had been upon the arrival of Mr. Duncan at Fort Simpson in 1857. In the instance of the blood feud experienced by Mr. McCullagh, a medicine-man prohibited a father from giving his adolescent a certain name. The youth died shortly thereafter, and the father revenged his son's death by killing the medicine-man.

Almost a week after this event the relatives of the murdered medicine-man came to me to report the circumstances of the crime and saying that they would not perpetuate the feud if the Queen's law could be set in motion. I wrote informing the Indian Agent of the murder, and in a short time fourteen specials were despatched to arrest poor Shegit. In attempting to carry out their instructions they shot him and nearly brought a hornet's nest about, not only their own ears, but the ears of every white man in the district. The Indians, however, held a council at which they fixed the blame of Shegit's death on me, because I had given information to the authorities . . .

The Indians apparently went to avenge Shegit's death, but Mr. McCullagh was away from home. They waited for three weeks, and since he was delayed even further in returning, "they concluded that I had got wind of them, and would, therefore, not come up at all, so they left."[10]

From Mr. Duncan's materials, Mayne provided an analysis of other characteristics, among them one that quickly became recognized as a major motive of the Indians of the Northwest Coast:

. . . pride or conceit is the passion they most strikingly exhibit. It is astonishing what they will do or suffer in order to establish or maintain dignity. Yesterday a young man fell down, and cut himself a little with an axe. On arriving home his father immediately announced his intention to destroy some property which was to save his son from any disgrace attached to the accident. When a few people or friends were collected to witness the brave act, the father would carry out his vow, with no small show of vanity. I hear that instances are numerous where persons who have been hoarding up property for ten, fifteen or twenty years (at the same time almost starving themselves for want of clothing), have given it all away to make a show for a few hours, and to be thought of consequence. (p. 295)

As part of that same context, Mr. Duncan further described their motives when he reported that:

Sometimes, when calamities are prolonged or thicken, they get enraged against God, and vent their anger against Him, raising their eyes and hands in savage anger to Heaven, and stomping their feet on the ground. . . . Revenge with them . . . is so dire . . . that many years and change of circumstances cannot extinguish it. Several instances have been known where it has burst forth in terrible vengeance more than twenty years after its birth, and simply because an opportunity to satisfy it never occurred before. But, as I said before, pride or conceit is the passion they most strikingly exhibit . . .

The numerous occasions for extreme ego-involvement in minor accidents and the tendency towards interpersonal conflict created for the Christian missionaries many dangerous situations. In his chapter on feuds and bloodshed, Rev. Thomas Crosby described what he called an "awful night." Two chiefs had been holding a grudge against a third chief, and upon being informed of the possibilities of "big fights," Mr. Crosby went to the Indian house.

The building was all in darkness, except for a few embers of a fire. In the dim darkness I could see two wild, savage-looking men, mercilessly assaulting the old man, Qual-la-kup, whom they had dragged out of bed. A number of others were standing around with clubs, looking wild enough and ready to knock a man down at any moment.

I rushed towards the group, and with what seemed to me supernatural strength I flung myself upon them, sending one one way and another

---

[10]J. W. W. Moeran, McCullagh of Aiyansh, p. 60.

another. With that the old man seized his advantage, and getting up, all
bruised and bleeding, he hid himself behind me, spreading my overcoat
tails to hide him from his pursuers.

At the same time the old chief stood dancing in front of me with
fiendish yells, his knife in his hand, ready to strike the old man when the
opportunity came.

. . . Now the friends of both parties rushed in from all sides of the village,
and in a few moments the great Indian house, some seventy feet long by
thirty broad, was filled with a quarrelling multitude. Fortunately some
torches were lighted, which enabled us to take in the scene, and for hours
and hours Amos Cushan and I were rushing between quarrelling parties
to stop their fighting. . . .

Suddenly Quin-num, the son of old Qual-la-kup, dashed in. He had just
heard of the trouble, away at the other end of the village, and jumping out
of bed . . . he seized the first weapon to hand, a claw-hammer, and hurried
to the rescue of his father.

I saw him rush in, trembling with anger, and I said, "Quin-num, be good!
Don't fight!"

"Oh," he said, and his voice was wild with rage, "I could listen to what
you say, but look at the blood of my father."

And with that he let out an awful yell, and wheeling around, struck
with the hammer the old chief who had clubbed his father, cutting his
eye nearly out.

Then the fighting commenced with renewed vigor and continued until
four in the morning . . .

Early the next day Tsil-ka-mut and others came to the mission house to
thank me for being there that night, for they said, "O missionary, if you
hadn't been there perhaps six or twelve men dead this morning. Then there
would be such a savage angry feeling in all our hearts, which would not
leave us for many moons."[11]

The preceding descriptions show that the natives of the region did
not behave according to European and Christian ideals of conduct.
With little provocation, the Indians would commit murder and what
was thought to be cannibalism; they had no conception of the Christian
principle of brotherly love; for almost any small passion, they would
destroy or apparently give away property as a means of supporting
personal dignity. These personal motives were, we may suppose,
sufficient to demonstrate for the Europeans of those decades that
native personal conduct was the very essence of heathenism. The more
highly elaborated expression of these motives found in great ceremonial feasting, dancing, dramatic productions, and gift giving was
to become known as the potlatch and defined by Europeans as an
even greater demonstration of heathenism. The efforts of Mr. Crosby

[11]Thomas Crosby, *Among the An-ko-me-nums or Flathead Tribes of the Pacific
Coast,* pp. 74–7.

to stop the fighting were admirable but certainly inadequate to bring about the magnitude of change required to transform these pagans into Christians. In an analysis of the techniques of missionaries, Annakin has classified their methods in two categories: direct evangelism, which includes preaching, personal work, and the use of literature; and indirect evangelism, which includes medical missions and education.[12] Mr. Duncan made plans to use all these methods and to go so far as to attempt to change the natives' mode of living and working completely. Extreme steps had to be taken and circumstances permitted their contemplation.

Upon his arrival at Fort Simpson Mr. Duncan was allotted a small house in the Fort of the Hudson's Bay Company. This he used for a school as well as a dwelling. Mayne further reports that Mr. Duncan found in the Fort:

. . . eighteen men assembled—one Scotch, one English, three Sandwich Islanders, and thirteen French Canadians, each having an Indian woman living with him. There were also seven children and he was told there were some half-breed children scattered about the camp, who, if he pleased, might be received in the Fort for instruction.

On Sunday, the 11th October, he first performed Divine Service in this scene of his new and arduous labors, and on the 13th he opened school with but five half-breed boys belonging to the Fort as pupils, the eldest not five years old.[13]

For five years Mr. Duncan continued his school, conducted religious services, and studied the Tsimshian language. During this time he thought intensely about Christian ideas, ceremonies, and rituals in relation to the cultural heritage of the Tsimshian. He had observed them closely, at least from the gallery where he could see what was going on along the beach and on his trips outside the Fort. He concluded that certain Christian ideas and rituals could not be accepted by the Indians without too much conflict or too many questions, and should therefore be modified. When he felt that he understood the culture and language, he gathered together a group of converted Tsimshian so as to found a new village, a Christian one. In this manner Canadian Metlakatla was established in 1862.

The *Annual Report*, 1879, of the Department of Indian Affairs considered the undertaking of Mr. Duncan to be very hazardous. This

[12]Annakin, pp. 65–86.

[13]Mayne, p. 308. Collison reports that about 3,000 Tsimshian Indians were living around Fort Simpson, where they had moved so as to be able to trade more easily. Other tribal groups, such as the Haida, went to Fort Simpson on trading expeditions. Apparently the Tsimshian were the only ones who took up residence at the Fort.

appraisal was based in part, we suppose, upon the extreme steps which he had taken, almost any one of which could arouse general hostility and persistent enmity and could lead, it was assumed, to organized reaction from the Indians. Mr. Duncan assumed unusual responsibilities and risks in establishing his own village: a new, radical economic system was being developed for a people who were traditionally salmon fishermen—now they were to operate sawmills, stores, and manage a co-operative; and a new polity for the village had to be devised. Again, and from the other side, Mr. Duncan risked losing the support of the Church Missionary Society because he modified church services and disputed with his superiors over the form and proper use of Christian ritual and ceremony for those considered to be former cannibals. In addition, of course, there were the undermining influences of the unconverted Indians and the traders, and the larger changes developing over the whole of the Northwest Coast. All these had to be contended with continually.

With respect to church services and symbolism, Mr. Duncan had decided, according to Wellcome, that "the distinctive dress of the ministers and Bishops, as well as the order of the Service of the Church—especially in the administration of the Lord's Supper—were calculated to bewilder, rather than to edify the Indians with whom he had to do, in their present state of progress." (p. 172) The Tsimshian faced further confusions in attempting to distinguish between sacramental wine and hard liquor, Church law and law of the Queen, the elements of communion and cannibalism. With respect to the latter, Wellcome commented:

To those who formerly regaled themselves at banquets of human flesh, how fine would be the point of distinction, and moral consideration, between the *emblem* which was assumed to *represent* the substance; and the *real* substance, to partake of which, they were now taught, was a most atrocious sin. They who had tasted flesh in their days of heathenism, benighted as they then were, would have recoiled with horror, at the bare thought of consuming, even by emblem, a part of one of their gods.[14]

Mr. Duncan worked out a modified form of the Lord's Supper. He felt the Indians should be kept in a probationary stage for a long period: "Baptism might be compared to a label on a can of salmon, to signify, and vouch for the quality of the contents."

[14]This quotation is part of the context in which Wellcome is dealing with the issues of evangelism *versus* ecclesiasticism. He devotes chapters VI, VII, and VIII to this conflict as it became an issue between Mr. Duncan and his superior officers of the Church Missionary Society. The conflict became a *cause célèbre*, leading eventually to Mr. Duncan moving his entire group to New Metlakahtla, on Annette Island in Alaska, just over the Canadian boundary from Fort Simpson.

The Department of Indian Affairs, Ottawa, in its *Annual Report*, 1879, devoted considerable space to the results of Mr. Duncan and the means by which he was achieving them. For such success, it was necessary for him to exercise supreme control. Contacts and association with white men were deterimental to the converts' progress; Fort Simpson was too limited in space; and it was desirable to isolate his "protegés from the sights and thraldom of heathenism." Just as important, Mr. Duncan had formulated a set of rules, a "regular programme of what their future conduct at the 'Christian City' was to be," to which the Indians had to assent, prior to joining Mr. Duncan's group. These rules required according to the departmental statement of 1879, that the Indians were:

(1) To give up their "Ah-lied," or Indian deviltry;
(2) To cease calling in conjurors when sick;
(3) To stop gambling;
(4) To cease potlatches or giving away their property for display;
(5) To cease painting their faces;
(6) To cease drinking intoxicating liquors;
(7) To rest on the Sabbath;
(8) To attend religious instructions;
(9) To send their children to school;
(10) To be cleanly;
(11) To be industrious;
(12) To be liberal and honest in trade;
(13) To build neat houses,
(14) To pay the village tax.

It was hazardous, to be certain, and undertaken in the mood of great adventure, but the success of Mr. Duncan can only be termed the more remarkable. William Carey in India had "toiled almost seven years for his first convert." Likewise, Joseph Verbeck had worked in Japan for seven years before he baptized his first followers. Yet, quite astoundingly, William Duncan had had about fifty converts by the end of the first month of work in the fort and when he was ready to move to his own village after only five years of work, some 400 Indians joined him.[15] The same *Annual Report* called attention to what was considered a most amazing feat: "He has built by *means of Indian labor alone*, one of the finest churches in the Province, capable of seating, comfortably, 800 people." In fact, the building of that church

[15]The success of Mr. Duncan can be appraised more effectively if the experiences of missionaries in other fields are compared. See Stephen J. Corey, *Ten Lessons in World Conquest,* Arthur J. Brown, *The Foreign Missionary,* and John McLean, *Indians of Canada.*

edifice symbolized far more than any writer of a report in 1879 could realize, for a perspective greater than seventeen years in depth was required to reveal the profound influence of Mr. Duncan and his first 400 converted Tsimshian; they were among the first natives on the Canadian Northwest Coast who were fully precipitated into a period of extended crises and institutional creativity.

The influence of Mr. Duncan pervaded the whole of the Northwest Coast for at least a half century. Other missionaries also gained important reputations; the localities they represented are rather spotty in geographic distribution, and the materials which are available describe or analyse different aspects of their work. But there is sufficient information to know that what they experienced in the way of problems due to the native cultural system were similar to those of Mr. Duncan. The *Annual Report* of Indian Affairs, 1879, noted that Mr. Green had established a mission station in northern British Columbia on the upper Nass River. Around this station the town of Aiyansh developed, populated by the Nishga and after 1883 served by Mr. McCullagh. Early in *McCullagh of Aiyansh* appears a description of the *Ha-Alaid*, or Indian deviltry, the first item on the list of behaviour proscribed by Mr. Duncan.

There is among the Nishgas [a Tsimshian group] a Society called the *Alaid*, a semi-secret Society, consisting of four degrees of mysteries to be initiated into which is the ambition of every Indian who can afford it. Originally this Society was composed of only chiefs and leading men, but now that articles of property can be acquired by any industrious Indian from European trading-posts and stores, it is open to every one who can give the required feasts and presents to the tribe. Anyone not belonging to this Society is classed as Um-gigiat—unmade, rude, or raw-made; . . . On the other hand those who have taken their degrees are styled "Shim-gigiat" or literally made-men, real men, i.e., chiefs. The "um-gigiat" have no special position at all in the tribe, while the "shim-gigiat" are classed according to the number of degrees they have taken. The first degree is Milthat (plural Gamilthat, sons of being); the second Lulthim (dog eaters); the third, Ulala (cannibals); while the fourth is Hunanlthit (destroyers). The fourth degree is open only to members of the third, the third to those belonging to the second, the second to those in the first, while the first is open to anyone who can afford to give a big feast and who makes a distribution of property. (p. 55)

Some of the initiation ceremonies were described for each of the degrees in the hierarchal organization of the *Ha-Alaid*. The initiations required a gradual building up of frenzy and miracles of behaviour completely repugnant to European Christians: ritualistic dog eating, ritualistic cannibalism, and running amuck through the village, destroying articles of property in each house for which the frenzied person later made restitution. "A greater honour than this no Indian can attain." (pp. 59–60)

Then, too, in addition to nudity, and what Europeans considered sexual promiscuity, superstition, cannibalism, and Indian deviltry, the missionaries found that the natives engaged in warring and raiding parties during which they gathered slaves. The number of slaves present in any one tribal group seems to be unknown, but the missionaries learned that slaves were at times murdered, occasionally by being put in the hole prepared for the erection of a totem pole. Mr. Collison has described how Mr. Duncan helped some slaves to escape, as the missionaries all felt intensely about slavery. The anti-slavery movement in England had reached its climax in 1833 with the freeing of the slaves, and at the time that the several churches were establishing their first mission stations on the Northwest Coast, the American Civil War and the issue of slavery were very much to the forefront of public attention. Slaves became then one more reason why the missionaries felt it necessary to change the social system of the Indians.

If the missionaries had had only the conduct of the natives based on Indian institutions to transform, they would have had a sufficiently difficult and extended task. But that was not to be; the missionaries could only control partially the changing milieu and the response of the natives to it. The exploitation of the forest and the sea by settlers was developing rapidly; land was being prepared for farming and other uses; and traders, some of whom were bootleggers of liquor, were very active. The lure of the emerging urban settlement with its excitement and its possibilities for native purposes was becoming a fact even prior to the arrival of Mr. Duncan in 1857. The European invasion and settlement of the Northwest Coast had brought not only the European conception of sin, but also some specific forms of it, particularly prostitution and drunkenness. In both of these, the Indians became deeply involved. With settlement and sin came the Indian agent whose job, along with the missionary's, was concerned with civilizing the aboriginal salmon fishermen of British Columbia.

Indian Agents and the Potlatch

Marius Barbeau and Diamond Jenness, two of Canada's most eminent anthropologists, have noted in their writings and have emphasized in their public discussions that the whole of native life seems to have come unhinged as a result of new opportunities to earn money, the availability of new trade goods which could be purchased with that money, the discovery of new locations for homes and new means of travel, and thus, new chances to escape tribal responsibilities. In 1871 the federal Indian agent became an additional factor working toward the disintegration of the old mode of native living. British Columbia became a province of Canada that year, and thereafter the federal government assumed responsibility for Indian policy and its administration. Although the history of Indian administration in any one of the Canadian provinces has not yet been written, it is still possible to secure sufficient information to indicate the general policy, to outline how enforced acculturation was begun both formally and informally as the Indian agents exercised guardianship over their Indian wards, and to show how peaceful penetration continued.

T. R. L. MacInnes, the late Secretary of Indian Affairs, wrote that the major function of his department was the "management of Indian reserves and lands." A number of tribes have trust funds, and the Indian administration manages those, too. According to the Secretary, the department is also concerned with "relief, education, medical services, and agricultural and industrial supervision."[16] But these functions of today were only in the process of definition in the 1870's; the Indian agencies of British Columbia had not yet been established when the colony became a province. Although the administration of Indian affairs was in its infancy, the policy of wardship and acculturation had already been formulated. It was thought, for example, that a land economy would have to be developed for the salmon-fishing Indians so as to settle them. At the same time it was recognized that Indians were radically unlike Europeans in their attitudes to property, the rhythm of work, and the saving of surpluses. These attitudes would have to be changed, it seemed obvious, if the Indians were to become self-supporting. It was clear that the Indian agent was in the field to do more than exercise juridical control, minimize conflict, and adjust wrongs or grievances. He was there to be the planner, the director, and the reporter of progress in the programmes of Parliament and the Department of Indian Affairs. In the *Annual Report, 1871*, as an instance, attention was called to the fact that the federal legislation of 1868 and 1869 was designed to "lead the Indian people by degrees to mingle with the white race in the ordinary avocations of life." Legislators and administrators claimed that the native system of political control was an irresponsible one; they intended to substitute a responsible form of government through the development of band

[16]In Loram and McIlwraith, eds., *The North American Indian Today*.

councils. These band councils as conceived in 1871 were to have seven major functions: to see to "the care of public health," to make certain that "order and decorum at assemblies" were observed, to undertake the "repression of intemperance and profligacy," to prevent "the trespass of cattle," to undertake "the maintenance of roads, bridges, ditches, and fences," to undertake the "construction, maintenance and repair of schoolhouses, council houses, and other Indian public buildings," and finally to provide for the "establishment of pounds and the appointment of pound keepers." The Indian agent now had his work outlined for him in general; the details he would meet in the field and there decide upon specific applications.

The *Annual Report* of 1872 presented an official interpretation of the conditions of the natives of British Columbia. It was based on details furnished by the Superintendent, Dr. I. W. Powell, whose office was in Victoria, in his annual report to the Deputy Superintendent-General in Ottawa who in turn reported them to Earl Dufferin, the Governor-General of Canada.

The Hydah and Ahts build superb canoes, perfections in design and workmanship; and Dr. Powell states that the lines of the first clipper ship built in Boston were taken from a Nootka canoe. But, on the other hand, the people are depraved. Virtue is unappreciated, and vice and intemperance prevail. Hence may be accounted for the decreased population which is evidently now taking place.

The necessity for, and the duty of effecting a thorough change, and of vigourously and systematically carrying out plans for improvement, are clearly established by Superintendent Powell's Reports. And strenuous efforts, as he plainly shows, are required with a view to bringing about amelioration in the condition and habits of those coast northern bands. It is evident that the individual responsibilities of each member of society in those Indian communities are not understood, and general degradation is the consequence. Dr. Powell, in his comprehensive and excellent reports, urges that an enlightened and liberal Indian policy should be adopted and pursued towards them. His description of their practices and propensities renders it abundantly manifest that civilization in its best sense, and humanizing agents are absolutely required as a means of elevating their condition, and also for rendering their future intercourse with an inflowing white population what it ought to be.

. . . Under Governor Douglas's administration of British Columbia, it appears that a policy was in the year 1858 inaugurated, which gave to the Indians the status of British subjects, the effect of which seems to have been to diminish the sort of despotic power exercised in former times by individual chiefs, and to render the Indians sensible that they are amenable in the same manner as other subjects of the Crown to the laws of the country. The chiefs still, however, employ practices peculiar to themselves, in order to maintain as large a share of influence as possible with their people.

Some of them donate, under the name of "Patlache" [*sic*], to their people, blankets, food, firearms, etc. etc. . . . The Superintendent considers that these usages have an injurious tendency, and encourages idleness, and expresses a hope that the custom will in time become obsolete. (pp. 9–10)

Apparently Dr. Powell had suggested an industrial school and small hospitals at the centres of Indian population and called attention to the success of Mr. Duncan, although he did not mention his name.

The following year, again dealing with British Columbia, the *Annual Report* referred to the problem of settling Indians on the land and making farmers of them. Undoubtedly the writer had chiefly in mind the Indians of the Victoria and lower Fraser River areas; little experience had been had with other areas simply because agencies had not been established. One of the Indian agents had hoped, according to the *Report*, to have each family settled on eighty acres of land but his plan had been delayed; he commented that:

. . . until the Indians are satisfactorily located on lands, and they are judiciously collected into communities, schools for their instruction and other ameliorative arrangements cannot properly be proceeded with. And further, that by limiting, as heretofore, the land of each family to a minimum, agriculture can be nothing else than a mere farce, and it is in vain to tell those people to support their families by farming, unless land enough be allotted to each, out of which to make a farm. (p. 5)

At this period the buffalo was still available on the prairies in sufficient although rapidly diminishing quantity so that the inevitable problem of settling the hunters had not forced Parliament to provide funds for immediate relief and agricultural equipment, seeds, and stocks in a major effort to make the Plains Indians self-supporting. By 1876 in British Columbia a plan for settling the Coast Indians was already under way. But one notices that it was the potlatch, according to the *Annual Report* for that year, that was said to have created the necessity of providing relief, and not the disappearance of salmon.

The Indians generally have a view peculiar to the country and to the value of money; one Band, numbering about fifteen families, applied to me in the spring for some agricultural implements and seeds. I questioned the chief respecting a "Potlache" which he had held at his place during the previous winter, and ascertained that himself and two of his headsmen had given away in presents to their friends 134 sacks of flour, 150 pairs of blankets, together with a quantity of supplies and provisions, amounting in value to about $700, for all of which they had paid for in cash out of their earnings as labourers, fishermen, and hunters. I remarked to the chief that if he had saved his money he would not now be under the necessity of asking me for assistance. Upon reasoning with him, he promised me that the custom should be discontinued in the future. I gave him about $80 worth of implements and potatoes and other seeds. (p. 38)

By 1879 the *Annual Report* indicated that five schools, conducted by several denominations, were receiving grants from the federal government, and a year later the number had been increased to seven, all located in the coastal area. The agents were also again working on the potlatch. The unpublished annual report of one agent had this comment:

The "Potlaches," once so common, are, I believe, gradually dying out. During the last year none of any importance have been held in this Agency, but as many of the chiefs now owe a considerable amount of blankets and other property to Indians of distant tribes, there will be one or two large potlaches given as a kind of final flash before the custom dies out entirely. Most of the chiefs have already promised me that they will only feed their visitors and return the property they owe, and not, as of old, lend more, thus continuing the custom indefinitely.[17]

It is not possible to identify the date and place of origin of the above statement; the following one, however, is dated July 17, 1882, and was written by the agent stationed at Beaver Harbour, north of Victoria.

The question of "potlaching" has engaged my most serious attention.
A general tone of despondency among the elders of the different tribes on account of their being obliged to give up this old custom.
I have pointed out to them over and over again, the evils attending it, which the younger ones do not fail to recognize, and even appreciate its intended abolishment.
They have had due warning, and those who in the future choose to risk or lend their property to uphold such a pernicious system will experience a difficulty in recovering it.
The "tamanawas" was attempted to be carried out last winter in this camp, but the steps taken to prevent it caused the disgusting part of the performance to be abandoned, under threat of prosecution for assault. I have reason to hope it has seen its last days.

In April, 1883, a church group in Victoria, including Indian chiefs from Fort Simpson, Kincolith, and Greenville, submitted a petition to Superintendent Powell, "praying that the system of Potlatching as practised by many Indian Tribes on the Coast of British Columbia may be put down." The petition was enclosed in a letter addressed by Dr. Powell to Ottawa, stating what was being done and, in addition, what could be done if a law prohibiting the potlatch were passed.

[17]This and the four quotations following are from the Potlatch File, Indian Affairs Branch, Ottawa.

Furthermore, he wrote:

. . . I have no doubt, a large number of even those who are obliged now to give Potlatches in order to foster their influence, as well as the Christianized Indians would, as intimated in the petition, gladly welcome and assist in enforcing such a regulation. Meantime, wherever Agents have been appointed they have been instructed to use their best endeavours to induce Indians to give up habits of the kind, and it is certain that in these localities they do not prevail nearly to the extent as formerly.

I presume it is owing to the latter circumstances that the impression prevails with the petitioners "that an Order in Council has been issued to put down Potlaching gatherings in . . . parts of the country." If such assemblages could, indeed, be made offensive to law there would be no difficulty in completely preventing any repetition of them wherever [there] were any officers to put such . . . in force.

The Indian Superintendent went on to say that since there was no law to make potlatching punishable, "much depends upon the efforts of Missionaries, themselves, in inducing Indians to abandon this and other customs incident to savage life." In order to make the programme successful, the Superintendent said, agents would have to be appointed. And, in addition,

Should the system of Municipal Councils contemplated last year be carried into effect it is probable, from the fact that the potlaches or donation feasts are often associated with Gambling, Medicine dances (Tamanawas) and similar Indian vices, that the act should give Indian Councils the power of framing by-laws for their prohibition.

The Indians are generally loyal, have great respect for "the Queen's law" and would stop the Potlach. . . .

In his planned village, Mr. Duncan intended to exorcise potlatching by setting forth a rule which made the Indians agree "to cease potlatches or giving away their property for display." Since he had isolated some Tsimshian, transforming them into modern villagers as well as beginning Christians, he could enforce the rule by controlling residence in his village and by providing substitute forms of behaviour. An important facet of the entire system of potlatch debts and credits, along with native enforcement of payment, was demolished for Mr. Duncan's newly-converted Christians: they were withdrawn from participation and accessibility. Other missionaries either did not or could not emulate Mr. Duncan; yet all concerned came to realize increasingly over a period of almost a century that what was called potlatching was the heart of the cultural system of the Northwest Coast and was related to numerous parts of the complete social system of the natives. Efforts to eliminate potlatch modes of conduct under any conditions could lead only to frustration for missionary and agent alike. There were backsliders among the converts; there were the staunch traditionalists; there were the traders encouraging the holding of potlatches so as to increase sales of goods used in the ceremonies; there were the bootleggers along the whole of the Coast, and there was the glitter of Victoria. For the Indian agent there were additional factors contributing to frustration: he was engaged in a programme designed in general by Parliament, a political body, to promote through the Department of Indian Affairs, a bureaucratic organization, progress towards civilization. In his official capacity he had civil servant superiors to satisfy as to the operations of his agency and, through annual reports, to inform about conditions of native life and progress.

The first instance of welfare declared necessary because of potlatching was reported in 1876. Again in 1879 an Indian agent reported that he was attempting to minimize potlatching; and in 1882 another agent reported that he was repeatedly talking with the Indians about it, analyzing with them the unfortunate effects of the extravagant ceremonies. In 1883 a petition was made to a federal official by whites and Indians in the name of their religious affiliation; concern about the potlatch had gone beyond the missionary in the field to become a problem for the higher administration of his denomination. These sketchy data suggest that between the arrival of Mr. Duncan in 1857 and the petition in 1883, the focus of attention was turning towards the potlatch. The potlatch was more than immoral; it had come to be defined as the grossest of obstacles to the Christian development of the Indians. Opinions, which were also explanations and conclusions, emerged to the effect that if European ideas of progress were to be imposed upon the aboriginals, then much more forceful action would have to be taken. A profound problem of morality had become defined as significant to Indian administration as well as to the churches. Legislation had come to be considered as the only means for solving the moral problem of the religionists and the administrative difficulties of Indian officials. Preaching against and making admonitions about conduct which could lead only to impoverishment had quite distinct limitations as a technique for succeeding in the task at hand.

In the House of Commons, as reported in *Debates*, May 9, 1883, Sir John A. Macdonald explained the need for federal action. He reported that six agencies had been established in British Columbia; he also outlined the commonly accepted beliefs about the Indians in the coastal areas of the province.

Within a very few years ago they were savage; they are now becoming quite peaceable, except in the outlying stations, such as Queen Charlotte's Island. This Island was a very formidable place for white men to visit, because the natives dealt most summarily with the crews of any vessel that called there. Along the outside coast of Vancouver Island there are a large number of scattered Indians, who are so scattered that they can scarcely be said to live in communities. They are now, I believe, very profitably employed in the canneries and establishments of that kind. Indians are now employed as miners and they work very well. But it must be remembered that they are not white men, and civilized, and must be strictly watched. They are very suspicious and easily aroused; the white population is sparse, and the Indians feel yet that they are lords of the country in British Columbia, and they are much more numerous than the whites; the officers are not too numerous and are not highly paid, but they are the best preventive police we have.

The Prime Minister wished to respond favourably to the appeals of the church groups, which were seconded by the Indian administrators. It was, however, his considered judgment that a proclamation might have sufficient influence to make unnecessary any stricter legislation, or police for enforcing it. Since this proclamation is not readily available and since it was the first attempt to solve the moral and administrative problems created by what had come to be called the potlatch, it is quoted rather fully:

Certified Copy of a Report of a Committee of the Honorable Privy Council approved by His Excellency the Governor General in Council, on the 7th July, 1883.

On a report dated 19th of June, 1883, from the Superintendent General of Indian Affairs representing that strenuous measures should be adopted to put a stop to the heathenish custom known as the "Potlack" [sic] and which his department has endeavored through its Superintendent and Agents to suppress, but which still prevails to a large extent among [some] of the tribes in the Province, although some of the more civilized Indians recognize the desirability in their own interests of its being put an end to, and have petitioned the Government to adopt measures to this end.

The Minister quotes the following extract from a Report on the system as it prevails and the evils attendant thereon from the late Indian Reserve Commissioner Mr. G. W. Sproat.

The Potlach [sic] is the parent of numerous vices which eat out the heart of the people. It produces indigence, thriftlessness, and habits of roaming about which prevent home association and is inconsistent with all progress. A large amount of prostitution common among some of the Coast Tribes is directly caused by the "Potlack."

There followed six paragraphs of explanatory statements about the nature of the potlatch—the desire for distinction, the system of credit, the rivalry involved, the deprivation of families, and of course the fact that it was "directly opposed to the inculcation of industriousness or moral habits." The *Proclamation* then continued:

> The Minister advised that the earliest possible measures should be taken with a view to suppress the heathenish and worse than useless custom; and pending legislation which may be had with this object in view at the next session of Parliament, he, the Minister, recommends that Your Excellency will be pleased to issue a Proclamation discountenancing the custom and requesting in her Majesty's name that Her Indian subjects abandon the same.
>
> The Minister is of opinion that such a Proclamation from the well-known loyalty of the Indians generally and their reverence for Her Majesty the Queen will go far to induce them to abandon the heathenish custom of "Potlack."
>
> The Committee concurs in the foregoing recommendations and they advise that a Dispatch based upon this minute when approved together with copies of the Proclamation be transmitted to the Lieutenant Governor of British Columbia with the request that he will use his best efforts for the suppression of the "Potlack," and for the circulation of His Excellency's Proclamation discountenancing the heathenish custom in question.
>
> (signed) JOHN J. MCGEE

When copies of it were circulated, the agents in British Columbia were instructed to keep reminding the Indians about the Proclamation; if that were done, it was argued, it would have the same influence as a legislative enactment.

The administrators in British Columbia were of a different opinion about the adequacy of a proclamation. They felt that "some legal prohibition is necessary before these habits will cease." Mr. Lomas, an Indian agent stationed at Cowichan, close to Victoria, had formulated most clearly a precise and comprehensive statement about the pot-latch.[18] When this statement was transmitted to officials in Ottawa, letters were enclosed from several missionaries working in the area between Victoria and Nanaimo, a distance of some seventy miles, inhabited by the Coast Salish Indians. After preliminary observations regarding his careful analysis and mature reflection on the subject, and drawing the conclusion that legal prohibition is necessary, Mr. Lomas said:

> A few years ago I thought that these dances were only foolish imitations cf their old savage customs, but now I am convinced that they are,—
> (1) The principal cause of the decrease of Population,
> (2) of the destitution and misery of the aged,
> (3) of a great deal of sickness and deaths among the children,

---

[18]Quoted almost completely in the House of Commons, *Debates*, April 7, 1884, p. 1399.

(4) of the difference of the advantage of education,

(5) of the neglect of their farms, cattle and horses during the winter months.

The customs are intimately connected because without a donation [potlatch] of food a dance is never held—And these dances have been sadly on the increase during the present winter, and many young men have impoverished themselves and their families because they had not the moral courage to oppose the custom. Indeed this want of courage or inability to withstand the sneers of the old people always forms one of the greatest drawbacks to the advancement of the native races on the coast.

But in the event of any law being passed it would be advisable to allow a fixed time for its coming into force, as potlatches are in reality a lending of a certain amount of property which has to be returned at an uncertain date with interest, or rather with an additional amount, which at some future date has also to be returned, either by the recipient or if he is dead, by some of his sons.

Thus young men themselves opposed to the custom are often drawn into it. . . .

Local traders derive a benefit from these gatherings, and often encourage the Indians to keep them up, forgetting that were these Indians working their lands, they would be a constant source of profit, instead of being as now only an occasional one.

A few days ago I called a meeting of all the leading men of Cowichan, Chemainus, and Saanich Bands, on the above subject and the matter was well discussed, but I regret to say only a few had the courage to stand up and say they would give up both customs and do their best to influence their relatives to do so; since that time several others have been in to request that their names may be added to this list, and as several of these have had land allotted to them I would suggest that they be supplied with their Location Tickets at once.

Indeed it might have a good effect if only those Indians who give up the custom of Potlatching receive tickets to their lands.

A statement of Father Donckele, a Roman Catholic missionary, was forwarded to Ottawa by the Indian agent to whom it was addressed—possibly Mr. Lomas. The priest said that a petition was "signed by the best and most civilized Indians of Cowichan."[19] This missionary, apparently the only participant of his denominations in this correspondence with field agents and Ottawa officials, pointed out that the pagan Indians were much more numerous than the civilized ones and claimed that:

. . . several of these that had signed the petition not obtaining assistance from the proper authorities, and being daily harrassed and ridiculed by their antagonists have of late forsaken their aspirations of becoming civilized and returned to a life of vagrancy.

---

[19]The quotation given here is part of the letter used by Sir John A. Macdonald in the debate on April 7, 1884, cited above.

For many years I entertained the hope that these heathenish practices would have disappeared as soon as the young people adopted the habits of the whites, and applied themselves to the pursuits of various industries, but now I am sorry to state that many of the young men who for years had improved their fertile lands, built houses and barns on them and made for themselves and their families an almost independent life, have abandoned their farms and become again the adepts of superstition and barbarism.

The evil reached its climax last winter when some of the most prominent dancers insulted some of their Indian Chiefs, because they insisted on their subjects [assuming] the habits of the whites and [giving] up the savage life of their ancestors.

A paragraph was devoted to the need for legislation so as to "ameliorate conditions," and then it was claimed that stringent measures were necessary so that parents could bring up their children properly.

During the whole winter schools are deserted by all those children whose parents attend the dances; when the winter is over they have squandered all their summer earnings and are compelled to leave their homes and roam about in their canoes in search of food, and thus neglect cultivating their lands and sending their children to school. In the summer they leave again for several months, working abroad to earn a few dollars in order to give a dance in the winter, and spend in one winter's night the earnings of the whole summer.

I have lately visited the Indians residing between Cowichan and Nanaimo and in every tribe where dancing is kept up there was general complaint of sickness; and alas! how could it be otherwise? when for about two months they hardly take a night's rest, and when they indulge whole days in ceaseless vociferations.

The statistics of last year show an astonishing decrease of population; the number of births, for instance, was about twenty less than in 1882.

The attitudes of parents toward the moral training of the children were discussed by Father Donckele, and in a paragraph following he again demanded legislation. In defence of the missionaries he claimed that:

It has been thought that clergymen might succeed in abating the evil as they had succeeded in other places. This might have been easy if in former times before a host of wicked white advisors had settled amongst them who for the sake of scanty emolument persuade the Indians to continue their old customs. The fact that some clergymen who for years labored strenuously to extirpate the evil were powerless to do so here, but were successful in some more Northern Sphere is a sufficient proof that the blame is not to be laid to their change.[20]

Rev. Cornelius Bryant, a Methodist missionary located at Nanaimo, stated in his documents, sent to Ottawa apparently by Mr. Lomas, that

[20]This and the three following quotations are from the Potlatch File.

he had had twenty-six years of personal knowledge of the Indians along the east coast of Vancouver Island and the Fraser River. It was his opinion that the potlatch was increasing in frequency. The Indians who participated in them "reduce themselves to beggary and distress." He stressed especially the degradation from intoxication and fighting during which firearms and knives were used freely.

. . . The impoverishment and dissipation already referred to have a most deplorable effect upon hapless children and aged people, who in their dependent condition ought to enjoy comforts of convenient homes and wholesome foods, which are denied them owing to the reckless spendthrift customs which are maintained at these potlatches.

. . . For instance, how many times have I appealed in vain to those who have been hoarding up their wealth in order to give it away at the next "Potlatch," to assist in some sanitary improvement such as the repair or renovation of their own dwelling-house or the grading or laying out of some street or road, or the fencing of or supply of conveniences for their local cemetery. What is true in this respect is no less so in any attempt to elevate the natives intellectually and religiously for,

. . . The Church and school cannot flourish where the "Potlatching" holds sway. . . . Thus all the objects or advantages to be secured by good government are frustrated by this very demoralizing custom; and as the wards of the Government the native tribes should be prevented by judicious counsel and governmental interference, that is by some kind of paternal restraint from indulging in their Potlatching feasts. Of course my knowledge of the Indian character suggests the danger of attempting coercive measures. Added to this the situation of the Government in seeking to suppress the "Potlatch" is rendered the more critical by the ill advice and malignant designs of the dissipated class of whites who commonly hover around the Indian camps, and from whom the natives are only too ready to take counsel. But I have discovered that the Indians have been advised to rebel against the idea of discontinuing the "Potlatch" by respectable traders whose business interests have been temporarily benefitted by the Potlatches being held in their neighborhoods. . . .

But to Mr. Bryant, quoted above, it was not clear that legislative restriction was the best means of trying to down the potlatch system, a suggestion contrary to the dominant notion of the day.

The foregoing observations, claims, and interpretations were sent to Ottawa in January and February, 1884. Their points were apparently the basis for the plans of Sir John A. Macdonald, for Bill 87, among several things, was introduced in its first reading by his short explanation that the several clauses were "a series of amendments which experience has shown to be required." When Bill 87 was given its second reading, Mr. Blake asked for an explanation; Sir John then made a lengthy statement. The first clause of the bill made whisky dealers and smugglers liable to punishment if they sold to the Indians; the second clause dealt with the sale of ammunition, new difficulties having been encountered since the building of the Canadian Pacific Railway. In Sir John's words,

The third clause provides that celebrating the "Potlatch" is a misdemeanour. This Indian festival is a debauchery of the worst kind, and the departmental officers and all clergymen unite in affirming that it is absolutely necessary to put this practice down. Last year the Governor General issued a proclamation on the advise of his Ministers warning the Indians against celebrating this festival. At these gatherings they give away their guns and all their property in a species of rivalry, and go so far as to give away their wives; in fact, as I have said, it is a great debauch. Under this Act to celebrate the Potlach is to be guilty of a misdemeanour.

On April 19, 1884, assent was given to amend the Indian Act, 1880; included in the revision was the first legislation in the *Statutes of Canada* to prohibit potlatching. Section 3, later revised, read as follows in its original statement:

3. Every Indian or other person who engages in or assists in celebrating the Indian festival known as the "Potlach" or in the Indian dance known as the "Tamanawas" is guilty of a misdemeanour, and shall be liable to imprisonment for a term of not more than six nor less than two months in any gaol or other place of confinement; and any Indian or other person who encourages, either directly or indirectly, an Indian or Indians to get up such a festival or dance, or to celebrate the same, or who shall assist in the celebration of same is guilty of a like offense, and shall be liable to the same punishment.

The Potlatch Law as it came to be called, and shall be so designated in the analysis following, remained on the statutes of Canada until the Indian Act was revised completely in 1951, *Statutes of Canada*, Chapter 29, proclaimed on September 4 of that year.

3. The Potlatch Law:
Wardship and Enforcement

INTRODUCTION

MAJOR WRITINGS on the basic tenets of Indian wardship have explained two principles of the system which are of central importance in understanding the application of the Potlatch Law: wardship envisages self-support and self-sufficiency, and is conceived and rationalized as a programme of gradual preparation for Canadian citizenship. When the Potlatch Law was passed in 1884, it was intended to provide a means for solving the moral and administrative problems related to these two principles. It was not a law which had emerged out of a compromise or out of a political debate, for all the field agents and all the missionaries in direct contact with the Indians demanded such a law, and all members of the 1884 session of Parliament saw no reason why Sir John A. Macdonald should not write such a prohibitory act into the *Statutes of Canada*. It appeared eminently sensible, although there was some risk in creating legal sanctions for the use of police and court action. None the less such a law would help, it was felt, in achieving a Canadian standard of self-support and of citizenship for the Northwest Coast Indians. For these reasons, the questions raised in the House of Commons at the time that the legislation was under consideration were only those minor ones conventionally expected of the Opposition.

Thus, it was a surprise when the application of the law became a political question almost immediately. From the available data, at least four distinctly different views on the morality of potlatching can be discerned. Hence there were also differing views on the desirability of the law. The perspective of the missionary-agent group in 1880 has been sketched briefly; it was the only effective perspective when the Proclamation of 1883 was issued and the law of 1884 passed. The perspective of the emerging social sciences, especially that of cultural anthropology, had been worked out before 1900, but several decades were required to pass before it became noticeably influential. The perspective of the journalists was also defined early, but its effect or role has not been more than casually studied. Finally, the perspective of the Indian traditionalists emerged as they faced the problems generated by the new conditions of living in their ancient homeland. The Indians were being swept into a cash economy; the new economy was based on their traditional but now industrialized occupation of fishing and the new occupations of lumbering and mining. Bureaucratic efforts to enforce cultural change involved a negation of the Indian past so that the natives could be fitted, for one thing, into the occupational structure of the new economic system. Efforts to negate the Indian past worked in part through the Potlatch Law. The attempt to legislate morality went on, although spasmodically to be certain, for about seventy years, from 1883 to 1951.

Dr. Powell, the Superintendent of Indian Affairs in Victoria, and his field staff had insisted upon the passage of the Potlatch Law. The existence of the law and the fact that they were the functionaries responsible for its application changed their relationships with the missionaries and the other churchmen, with the Indians, with their superiors in Ottawa, with provincial officials, and with the public in general. The law gave them additional tasks, onerous ones, for in the early attempts to enforce the law the agents were confronted with the difficult role of interpreting the law to the Indians while still administering the other aspects of wardship. They were supposed to secure evidence of the law's infraction, plan court actions, and also be concerned about the consequences of the penalties imposed. All this was very new to the Indian and to the agent, but it was part of peaceful penetration, a policy which, according to Dr. Powell in 1887, was designed to work "for the improvement and control of the Indians." And it is partially through those efforts made for improvement and control that the Northwest Coast Indians gained new conceptions of their individual and tribal position in the Canadian social system, particularly the regional one.

Morality and the Confusion of Change

Shortly after the law had been assented to, Mr. Lomas wrote to Superintendent Powell, from Maple Bay on December 27, 1884, to the effect that as he had travelled among the different bands, he had found a great deal of discontent about doing away with the potlatch.

This, he reported to his superior, was especially true of the older Indians in the West Coast and New Westminster agencies. He explained that the Indians were all in debt to each other and that they were fearful that these debts would not be paid. "Several of the Chiefs share this feeling who are actually anxious to see the 'Potlach' done away with, if only they could get their tribe's 'Potlach' over first. Several of these have promised for some time that they will only return what they or their band owe and lend no more."[1] Mr. Lomas was of the opinion that the enforcement of the new Indian Act should be delayed so that each band could be allowed a special licence to hold just one "returning 'Potlach'" with the distinct understanding that no additional property shall be lent." He also felt that an annual industrial exhibition should be arranged to "stimulate the Indians to increased industry, and at the same time afford each Band an opportunity of paying off their debts in public." Dr. Powell sent the above statement to Ottawa in January, 1885, with the comment that he did not foresee any "bad results" from putting the law in force; possibly in Mr. Lomas' district one or two potlatches might "pass without notice on the understanding that they would be the last." The law had been assented to in the spring of 1884, but no provision had been made for any plan other than it becoming effective January 1, 1885. From the records it seems today that the intent of Parliament was clear and unambiguous; still in the field there was either confusion or intent upon compromise when the realities of enforcement came to be considered. In any case the problem of whether the law should be instituted gradually or suddenly was the first indication of the confusion that was to surround the whole history of the Potlatch Law.

In April, 1885, Mr. Lomas approached some of the Indians in his district and reported almost immediately to his superintendent that it was impossible to make any "amicable arrangement, or, under existing circumstances, to enforce the Act." Therefore Dr. Powell went to Cowichan on April 13 where he found a large assemblage of Indians

[1]Potlatch File, Indian Affairs Branch, Ottawa. Unless otherwise indicated all quotations in this chapter are from this file. In the files of the Kwawkewlth Agency, Alert Bay, all correspondence and reports and any other kinds of pertinent materials are segregated in a "Potlatch File." This is also true at departmental headquarters in Ottawa. In 1946 the author was permitted by Director R. A. Hoey to read the agency file. In the summer of 1950 the author worked intensively on the file in Ottawa, with the permission and consultation of Director McKay and Secretary MacInnis. The Ottawa file contained many documents related to the administrative management of the Potlatch Law which were not in the agency file. Only those of the Ottawa File have been used. Wherever possible public documents or other records have been used. The Potlatch File is not a complete source of data.

"in a very angry mood—who had made up their minds to hold a large Potlach" regardless of the law. He described his visit:

. . . Hearing the speeches made by them both before and after my arrival, I informed the head Chiefs that as I understood they were only anxious to return the property they owed and as they did not intend to continue the practice of potlatching, *i.e.*, lending with the object of having it returned with interest, the Government did not wish to act unjustly towards them, neither did they desire the Indians to act with injustice towards each other, etc. So long as any meeting therefore was intended to witness a return of gifts made on some former occasion, the Indians would not be interfered with. I explained that a Potlatch meant the donation of property in order to get back the original and interest, and that an assemblage such as they now desired did not constitute a Potlach as referred to in the Act.

Shortly after, on April 20, Superintendent Powell sent a long report to his superior in Ottawa describing the various problems he had already encountered with regard to enforcement of the law. On a previous occasion he had called the Deputy Superintendent-General's attention to the fact that the provincial government would not allow his officials to lock up Indians who had broken the liquor clause of the Indian Act. Now he considered it equally impossible to depend upon the provincial Department of Justice for enforcing any of the other clauses. Also, the Superintendent pointed out that, although the law had been enacted a year earlier, "no copies were sent to me until December," and thus "the year of grace permitted in the Act . . . has had no practical application here." In any case, he claimed, the year of grace was insufficient time as it would take an Indian from two to five years to accumulate enough property for paying back his obligations.

The Superintendent's report contained other significant points. He called attention to the fact that the white traders objected vigorously to the law. In addition, only a few Indian agents were on duty, and the whole sum appropriated for Indian affairs in British Columbia was "so small and the Indian population so large" that rapid reform was impossible. In fact it might be well to give up Indian administration in British Columbia entirely.

Were it not that there is abundant reason to believe that the best reserves would soon suffer from the constant encroachments which are even now frequently attempted and that the natives would have no sympathy from those in authority there would be little objection to do away with the Act so far as British Columbia is concerned and allow the Indians to shift for themselves. I say this because the sum now voted is entirely inadequate to permit of any system of improvement such as is afforded in other countries where large sums are devoted by the people for Indian purposes. Were it not that the Indians of British Columbia are industrious, self-sustaining and divided into innumerable small bands among which there is little chance for mischievous combination, a very large expenditure would be necessary to pacify them and make the country habitable for whites. Under present circumstances therefore and especially in view of the large contributions of Indians (being large consumers) to the Dominion revenue, it seems only just that any humane policy should be supplemented with sufficient appropriations to make it effective, and owing to the apparent conflict of authority with the local Department of Justice, there are no means of properly enforcing the Indian Act.

There are no farming instructors, no schools of Industry nor is there even a requisite sum to permit of an Agent travelling more than a stated portion of the year. I trust that I may be pardoned for bringing these insufficiencies to your notice, but I am led to take such a liberty from the helplessness one experiences in attempting with the means at command, to enforce any law such as that prohibiting the Potlach or other evils incident to savage life.

It is gratifying under such adverse circumstances, to state that by my visit to Cowichan and Fraser River, the Indians have so far shown themselves amenable to moral suasion, that the excitement existing among them on account of what they considered an oppressive law has been quieted and that there is every reason to believe that a majority of them will conform with it in time.

As part of his report on the problems of enforcing the Potlatch Law, the Superintendent enclosed some statements made by the Indians when Mr. Lomas had talked with them on his field trip. Eleven Indians of the Cowichan Band appreciated the intepretation of the law made by the Superintendent as it would give them an opportunity to pay their debts. The leading statement was made by Lohah, Chief of the Comeakin.

My son Benoir, before he died, begged me to return all property that he owed—as well as my own debts.

If I do not do it my heart will always cry. I will die of grief.

You know I listened to what you told us, and would have had my Potlach over before the law came in force, but for the death of my son.

At every village, I have visited to invite guests—friends came to cry with me at the loss of my son. I told every one this was the last I would attend that I only wished to pay back what I owed, not to lend more.

If I am allowed to entertain my friends, I will see that no more property is lent, only our debts paid.

If any one do more than this, let him be punished for breaking the law. It cannot be wrong to pay what we owe and this is the only way to do it. We are not like white people. And it is one of our laws that these payments shall be done in public.

If I am not allowed to hold this gathering, the disgrace will be greater than I can bear. I should be sneered at by every Indian. They all know I have always supported the Government and Dr. Powell, often against the whole of the Cowichan Bands, and now I am likely to be the first to be punished.

I owe over 800 blankets and nearly as many dollars for other property. Food is already bought for the potlach. It will spoil. What must we do? The stores will not take back what we have.

Following this report of Chief Lohah, the widow of the late Benoir reported her preparations for potlatching.

I have 20 bales of blankets; they are not mine but what my late husband owed. I have also 4 horses and 2 yoke of cattle to pay for.

I have also 400 yards of printed calico to pay my own debts, 1 barrel of sugar, 10 boxes of biscuits, 300 salt water ducks, $20 spent in powder and shot to get them with.

Chief Baptiste, of the Somenos, stated:

I wish to keep the law. I am not interested in Lohah's Potlach. He owes me nothing, but I say let him pay back what he owes. Other Chiefs are bringing goods to pay their debts. Let this be a final gathering. Let us have no more after this.

Doctos, of the Chemainus, claimed that:

My friends have spent money and time to get food together to help me to entertain my friends while I pay my debts. What are they to do with the food? And what must I do with the property I owe?

I owe 170 Indians goods, some of them as much as 100 blankets. How can I pay my debts unless they are all here to witness? Tell me what I must do.

Another Comeakin, Skehalem, was of the opinion, according to Mr. Lomas, that:

We have come to talk to you, for if Dr. Powell were to hear all we had to say his head would ache. You can put it in a few words and he will know our hearts better than if he listened to all our words. You have known us long, and I want to ask you, Is it not Comeakin who have always done what you told them? Did they not stop dancing? Is not Lohah head of the Tribes? Are not your constables Comeakin? Do not you find Comeakin men the best for your canoe? If this is true help us that we may be allowed to pay our debts, but punish those who lend more property.

One Mr. Gates called attention to "these sticks" which represent 250 Indians to whom he is indebted. His question was simple: "Am I to go to the American side to call them there to pay my debts?" Since he only wanted to pay his debts, he wanted instructions on how to do it. Then Seelempton, also a Comeakin, reported that he owed 240 single blankets, $20 worth of print, $100 in cash, and 2 bales of blankets. In addition to this his friends and relatives were out shooting ducks in preparation for the potlatch. Another, Charley, claimed that he owed 250 blankets. "We don't want to break the law but are quite willing to keep it, if only our debts were off our minds." Tummeen, Lohah's son, stated a much longer case:

I am not a chief, only a boy, but I owe nearly $200 worth of property. My father has always tried to keep the law and teach us to do so. But if he is not allowed to return his debts, in public, the disgrace will be more than he can bear. My father, Lohah, has always helped white men even against the old or bad Indians, and if Mr. Powell does not help him now he will always be laughed at. When he came back on Monday from seeing Dr. Powell, the other Chiefs laughed at him, saying he was like a baby or slave, doing always as his white masters said, and they never did anything for him.

Now if Dr. Powell will try to get permission for him to hold his return Potlach, Lohah will be lifted up above the others, and they will see that the Doctor thinks well of his conduct. You know we should have held our return potlach last year, but my brother was taken ill and died, so now the law has caught us. We were the only tribe who listened to your words, and this is why our friends have so many bales of blankets and other property on hand now.[2]

One woman, Cehamilawet, indicated that she owed 150 blankets and that her sick husband owed 200 more. She said that the "white chief does not understand our ways. We are willing to give up the potlatch, but the Chief's son died so we did not get it over in time." She reported other women who owed many yards of calico which the stores would not take back. And finally Antoine Seseawon of the Somenos stated emphatically that he was always against the potlatch.

I have no interest in Lohah's. I know if I join the Potlach party, I shall be poor, my children will be poor and suffer, but I feel for Lohah. He has always tried to help white men and now the law is against him, and all the Indians are sneering at him. It will kill him and I would like to see him raised up for he is a good man.

Cannot Dr. Powell ask the Chief at Ottawa to give him a little time to pay what he owes, it is as if he asked for a minute.

I was with Benoir when he died and promised to assist his wife to pay his debts, and this can only be done in public.

Dr. Powell also explained in his report that he had gained the impression from reading the *Debates* that the law was to be applied gradually. Apparently he had gained this impression from the parlia-

[2]When Tummeen in the last line of the first paragraph refers to "baby" and "slave," he is using the most opprobrious terms which the Northwest Indians knew. See Ruth Benedict, *Patterns of Culture*, p. 204.

mentary situation in which Sir John was dealing with the Opposition when debating Bill 87: the point of sudden enforcement was raised by Mr. Blake; he cautioned the Government "in attempting suddenly to stop . . . the known customs and habits of these tribes." Because of his confidence in his interpretation of the intent of Parliament, Dr. Powell had told the Indians in his speech of April 13 that any meeting "intended to witness a return of gifts made on some former occasion" would not be interfered with. And in good faith he had accepted from the Indians the promise that when an Indian had paid his debts he would quit potlatching. It did not occur to him that so-called potlatching might be an extensive system in which Indians not only wanted to pay debts but also wanted to create and to assume them. He did not suspect that potlatching had a greater number of purposes than those of debt creation and payment.

Dr. Powell's interpretation of the *Debates* also led him to issue a circular to agents and others indicating that he intended to follow as far as possible a course of conciliation in the enforcement of the law. This circular of April 21, 1885, became the focal point of the ensuing controversy over the application of the Potlatch Law. The circular reads in full as follows:

Will you be good enough to acquaint the Indians in your locality that a Law was passed last year by the Dominion Parliamente which came into force the 1st January, this year, enacting among other things, That any person who engages directly or indirectly in celebrating the Indian Festival, known as "Potlach" or in the Indian Dance, known as the "Tamanawas," is guilty of misdemeanor, and shall be liable to be imprisoned therefor, for a term of six months.

It is not intended to prevent Indians from assembling to return property which they owe on account of previous festivals, but Indians should be warned that any repetition of the Potlach is hereafter illegal. The term "Tamanawas" refers to the Medicine Dance, customary among many of the coast tribes.

The first allegations of improper enforcement of the Potlatch Law came in 1886 from up north, in the Nass River country, where the Methodist missionary Mr. A. E. Green was still stationed. He was concerned about Dr. Powell's policy of conciliation, and in stating his concern, he gives further evidence of the confusion, of the differences of opinion, of the charges and counter-charges which persisted even to 1938 when in the House of Commons it was claimed that the potlatch was "practised clandestinely," at least at Alert Bay in 1936.[3]

[3]House of Commons, *Debates*, June 13, 1938, the statement of Mr. Taylor (Nanaimo).

Only part of Mr. Green's letter of April 3, 1886, is in the Potlatch File. It was apparently addressed to the Deputy Superintendent-General of Indian Affairs. Mr. Green wrote:

. . . I wish to refer to the abuse of the Potlach law, and the degrading influences of the Potlach itself. A year ago I received a letter from Judge Elliott, asking me to read the law on this question to the Indians who still engaged in the nefarious practice. The majority received the law kindly, and would abide by it. Afterwards a circular from Dr. Powell announcing that the law was not intended to restrict potlaching for the return of presents received. This is really the vital point of the potlach, for, as at each time they meet, they give presents, this potlaching must go on forever. I hold Dr. Powell responsible for the terrible state of affairs existing in that region [Nass River] during the last year, for had he not sent that circular, the whole thing would have died out. As it is the Indians state openly in their feasts that they have the authority of Dr. Powell for their actions, and furthermore, when complaints are made to Judge Elliott, he will not take action in the matter (shielding himself with Dr. Powell's circular). It is thus the law of the land is openly violated and ignored, and respect for the government greatly lessened in the hearts of the Indians. For the welfare of the tribes and the good of the country I pray that such steps shall be taken, as that the law shall be in the future strictly enforced. And I fear that Judge Elliott is not the man to administer the law in that country, as he has by his brazen partiality, utterly failed to gain the confidence of the Indians. Furthermore they wish me to emphasize that they desire to have no Indian agent at all.

Such a letter as Mr. Green had written was sufficient to stir up Ottawa. It gave rise to inquiries and correspondence regarding enforcement by the field staff. On May 7, 1886, Dr. Powell replied that he had been informed that some missionaries tried to induce Indians not to acknowledge the authority of the agents. He also reported that "One inducement said to be held out by these Missionaries to Indians to join the church is, that they need not afterwards repay the amounts they have received in this way, and one of the complaints made to me by a Chief . . . during my visit was that many Indians joined the Mission so that they might repudiate their debts. . . ." The Superintendent called attention to the fact that the missionaries were competent to appeal to proper authority by reporting the holding of potlatches. Dr. Powell was certain, as he had stated before, that the potlatch was dying out "as fast as is possible under the circumstances of a large Indian population, with no means to enforce this or any other law of the kind."

Except for Mr. Lomas, agents were in centres rather far removed from the main area where facilities for enforcement were available.

The west coast of Vancouver Island as well as the Nass River has always been remote from Victoria and Vancouver. Today when one takes a Canadian Pacific steamer trip around the Island stopping at a number of the west coast ports, one feels that, although the distances are not great, the remotest parts of the province have been reached. This was even truer in 1886. On the east coast, the area which is now so heavily urbanized, travel was slow. A few years before 1886, as reported by Mr. Crosby, it took eight days to travel 73 miles from Victoria to Nanaimo by sloop. In July of 1886 Mr. Harry Guillod, an agent located on the west coast at Ucluelet, described the conditions under which he was expected to enforce the Potlatch Law.

. . . Under present circumstances I do not see my way to successfully enforcing the law. In my Agency there are 20 tribes consisting of about 3,500 Indians, one white settlement at Alberni, of Trading posts along the coast and three Roman Catholic Missions. As you are aware the Provincial Government refuses to help us with regard to this law.

The only help I have in preserving order in most of these tribes are the Chiefs and the Policemen.

The Chiefs are all strongly in favor of the continuance of the Potlach; the Policemen who are neither paid nor uniformed by the Department I could not depend upon to act in this case and are besides mostly subordinate to the local Chiefs, and I have not as may be the case in other Agencies a party on my side, as with the exception of a few, all are in favor of the potlach, old and young, the old as one of their customs from times back and a bond of amity between the Tribes, the young as an occasion of mirth and amusement. . . .

To carry out the law at once I should have a jail built, a paid white constable and further allowance for travelling expenses, with the surety of help from Victoria in case I meet resistance.

In submitting to Ottawa this report of the agent from the remoter part of the Island, Dr. Powell again stated his own belief that the custom was gradually dying out. He was firm in his view that the chiefs of the Cowichan, at least, would confine their future assemblies merely to returning the property which they owed on account of previous potlatches. It is in this letter that we find for the first time reference to the "social natures" of the custom, that is, defining the potlatch as something more than the payment of debts. The Superintendent was of the opinion that where the potlatch was not carried to excess, "there is not more harm or injury in it than the prevalence of the custom among ourselves of making presents."

The error over the year of grace in regard to the application of the law was in some respects one from which an administrator could recover with dignity and possibly with some grace, but the indecision about the policy of conciliation was more fundamental and thus more embarrassing. Although the field staff had favoured the law, they now faced a number of problems with respect to its application. Some of these were practical ones, namely the costs involved in enforcing the law—salaries and uniforms for constables, funds for the building of jails, and the costs of lawyers and court actions. These expenses were related directly to the conflict between the federal and provincial government as to which one of them would enforce the Potlatch Law.

In all the correspondence regarding the Potlatch Law and in all of the *Debates* of the House of Commons, the first mention of costs for applying the law is found in the major report of Dr. Powell cited above. Since funds had not been especially voted by Parliament nor planned in the estimates of the Department (admitted in a letter of November 23, 1886, when attention was called to the fact that "the Department has no means at its disposal"), Superintendent Powell and his agents were in fact helpless until an agreement could be negotiated with the provincial government; then the province would pay the police costs of the administration of the law. As an example we may note that in reply to the difficulties reported by Mr. Guillod from the West Coast agency, an officer in Ottawa informed Dr. Powell on August 3, 1886, that "potlaching is a misdemeanor and . . . enforcement of the criminal law rests with the Provincial Authorities. It appears to me, therefore, to be plainly your duty to notify the Government of British Columbia of the difficulties encountered by Mr. Guillod. . . . "

Mr. Pidcock, the agent in the Alert Bay area, wrote to his superior in Victoria that the Indians in that area were defiant of the law, especially the "Malimalillekullah and the Fort Rupert groups." Mr. Pidcock reported that all of the Indians had been warned of the "consequences attending their refusal to obey the law, and are now in defiance preparing to hold a Potlatch here and at Malimalillekullah." He concluded with the remark that "I would respectfully advise that the law should be put in force. . . . " For that purpose the agent had looked into the costs of building a small jail. One 14′ × 14′ × 10′ in size would cost about $100, and the ironwork for it would be an additional $25. The distance from Victoria seemed in the agent's view to justify the expenditure. His letter was forwarded to Ottawa by Dr. Powell who indicated that since there was no magistrate in the Kwawkewlth agency, the jail would be of little service to him and that the estimate of costs was too low. Further, according to Dr. Powell, "it is to be regretted that there is no understanding between the Dominion and Local authorities as to the preservation of Peace in Indian districts." Yet, even though late in the fall of 1886 the Deputy Superintendent-

General of Indian Affairs took up these questions of enforcement with Prime Minister Macdonald, asking that some understanding be arrived at between the Dominion and provincial governments "on this most important matter at an early date," it was not to be arranged quickly between the two governments. It was Sir John who had been responsible for the Proclamation and for the legislation of 1884. Now in his hands was the question of enforcement involving principles which one suspects had not received the slightest attention before this important question was raised by the field staff.[4]

The Ottawa file materials can be interpreted as representing increasing frustration for Dr. Powell and his staff. With Mr. Pidcock's earlier letter regarding his inability to enforce the law apparently in mind, the Deputy Superintendent-General in Ottawa noted in Dr. Powell's annual report for 1886 the reference to the "prevalence of medicine and potlach feasts." In reply he informed his field superintendent that "I have to remind you that it is your duty to cause such measures to be adopted as will effectually prevent the Indians from celebrating." To such end, the Deputy in Ottawa continued, the agent in the Kwawkewlth agency should be given a firm hand. To this Dr. Powell answered with a discussion of his inadequate means, in phrases, which, though courteous, were rather strong for a civil servant. "There must," he said, "be some misapprehension as to my ability or power in this matter."

In searching for solutions to his problems of enforcement, he had turned directly to the Provincial Secretary in March, 1887, to see if any steps could be taken by his department, as "some of the Acts for the improvement and control of Indians are virtually inoperative and the Agents are helpless to carry out their provisions." In reporting that action to Ottawa, he called his superiors' attention to the fact that arrangements had already been made whereby the Provincial Treasury was to receive the fines collected from violations of the liquor law. Superintendent Powell could, furthermore, report to Ottawa that he had called the attention of the provincial government to this inability to enforce the law. Finally he informed headquarters in Ottawa that he had by then arrived at the inference that:

[Since] it is not the intention of this Department to provide lock-ups or

---

[4]Perhaps this is one of the examples of the young Dominion acting maladroitly. With hindsight some seventy years long, one would be disposed to think in this kind of a problem it was fortunate that enforcement had to work in part through conciliation and in part through adminstrative confusion. Still there are Canadian Christians who feel today that the Potlatch Law was a "good" law, that it was never "properly" enforced, and that it should still be on the statute books of the Dominion.

constables in any of the Agencies, and if no steps of such a character are taken by the Local Authorities, manifestly the adoption of measures for preventing Indians from celebrating heathen feasts is out of my power, and further than the influence of moral suasion which I need scarcely add is of little account among Indians with no exhibition of power to sustain it. It was for this reason that I conceived it to be my duty to refer to the subject in my Annual Report.

He enclosed another letter from Mr. Pidcock describing further the conditions under which the law had to be enforced.

I cannot secure the services of Indians as constables, so afraid are they of others of their own tribe, and also, I am without any place to secure prisoners in, should I make any arrests. This is a matter which it will not do to undertake unless I am prepared to follow it up without risk of failure, and the determination, with which they cling to the custom, makes me think that the opposition at first will be very strong. At a meeting which I recently held here, and at which I told them that I had instructions from you to put a stop to the "Potlach", Sukwele, the Chief of the Kwawkewlths, and whose word in some matters is almost law, said, would the Government pay him for his "Coppers" which he has been buying for several years, and for which he has paid a great many blankets, because if they would he would give up the Potlach; if he was to give up now, he would have to lose many hundred blankets, and he could not be expected to do that.

I told him I did not think the Government would help him, but I would mention the matter to you.

With a jail and a white constable and what help I can obtain here I might be able to carry out the law.

In April, 1888, four years after the Potlatch Law had gained assent, the Deputy Superintendent-General of Indian Affairs, Mr. Van-koughnet, wrote to Hon. Thomas White, the Superintendent-General of Indian Affairs, in order to point out the desirability of immediate negotiations with the government of British Columbia for the lock-ups and constables on the mainland coast and on Vancouver Island necessary to enforce the law. Six months later the Under-Secretary of State of Canada, G. Powell, Esq., was in correspondence with the government of British Columbia; he emphasized that the problem was especially urgent with the "Kwawkewlth Indians and the Indians of the Skeena and Nass Rivers," and hoped that an agreement could be arrived at so that the "Provincial Government would undertake the administration of the said laws and the erection of lock-ups and the appointment of constables. . . . " The provincial government finally agreed that it would assume such responsibility. By the beginning of 1889 one knotty problem of enforcement had been settled and some factors of confusion had been eliminated.

But even before the two governments reached agreement as to the responsibilities of enforcement, the long campaign for the repeal of the law was initiated. The circumstances of this period of settlement in British Columbia were such that efforts to legislate a morality for the Indian could lead only to confusion. Earlier, it will be recalled, Dr. Powell had thought the whole policy of wardship should be abandoned. Now the emerging differences of perspective and the gradual Canadianization of the Indians gave rise to enough confusion that the history of the law's enforcement remains episodic—a series of petitions, court cases, allegations of abuse, and spectacular newspaper stories. These episodes were a sign, however, that public opinion was forming about the Potlatch Law and its application. More than the members of the Department of Indian Affairs or the missionaries were henceforth involved—those interested now included settlers, teachers, journalists, anthropologists, magistrates, and lawyers. Each of these early episodes contributed to the formulation of a public issue about the Potlatch Law, an issue which eventually fizzled out and was resolved formally and appropriately by omission of the prohibiting clause from the Indian Act of 1951.

In February, 1887, Sir John Macdonald received a petition for the repeal of the law.

We the undersigned Indians of the Cowichan agency beg respectfully to ask you to use your influence to have the clause of the Indian Act forbidding the "Potlach" and "Tamanawas" Dances repealed.

In asking this we would point out that these are two of our oldest customs, and by them we do not injure anyone.

We cannot read like white people and the dances are our winter amusements.

When our children grow up and are educated they perhaps will not wish to dance.

Some only of us dance now, and we do not wish to teach others, but when one is seized with the ("Quellish") dance he cannot help himself and we believe would die unless he danced. On Saturdays and Sundays we will not dance as this offends the Christian Indians.

The lands of our fathers are occupied by white men and we say nothing. We have given up fighting with each other.

We have given up stealing and many old habits, but we want to be allowed to continue the "Potlach" and the Dance. We know the hearts of most of the Coast Indians are with us in this. We therefore ask you to have the law amended, that we may not be breaking it when we follow customs that are dear to us.

This petition had twenty-four marks and signatures at the bottom, and possibly there were others, for the original is mutilated. The signatures were witnessed by one of the Indian agents. Submitting the petition to Ottawa, the Superintendent indicated that although the missionary-clergy-teacher group were very eager to have the law enforced, "the settlers think that much interference with their [the Indians'] native customs would provoke considerable trouble." And again he stated the point of view that the young Indians were making progress and that "it is a question of time until the demoralizing customs referred to will be superseded by advancing forces of civilization." Ottawa forwarded the petition and the Superintendent's comments to Prime Minister Macdonald with the statement that "the Superintendent General approves of his [Dr. Powell's] letter and that he cannot see his way to recommend the repeal of the law referred to."

Although five years had passed since the law became a statute, no arrest had been made and no fine imposed; it was already becoming uncertain that it was a good procedure in any case. On January 22, 1889, an acting Indian agent at Metlakatla, B.C., called attention to the fact that the law had not yet been enforced:

. . . and it proves a great stumbling block to the Indian Agent in the Northwest Coast Agency inasmuch as a great majority of the tribes express a determination to stick to what they term "the oldest and best of their festivals."

The Indians are ready to give up any other old custom when it is shown to be harmful.

They contend that there is but "what is good" in the Potlach and refuse to give it up.

A minority of these Indians led on by certain missionaries clamor for the enforcement of the law against the Potlach and shout shame at the Government and the Agent for having a law and not carrying it out. The Indians of Kitkatla and some other settlements are a unit in favor of the Potlach and so are a majority of Indians in many other places.

I think that as the Indians learn other ways of amusing themselves during the winter season the Potlach will die out altogether.

It seems at present almost useless to attempt to abolish it by law especially as no Indian Agent has sufficient force at his command to do it against the will and determination of the Indians, most of whom are in other respects good Indians and law abiding.

I would most respectfully suggest the advisability of repealing that clause of the Act, or else make its enforcement dependent upon the pleasure of a majority of the Indians of any Indian settlement.

In reply the Department in Ottawa informed the agent of the arrangements which had been made with the provincial government and rejected as inadvisable his recommendation for the repeal of the law. This was on February 26, 1889.

ENFORCEMENT AND THE EMERGENCE OF THE POTLATCH LAW AS A PUBLIC ISSUE

No evidence readily available suggests that there was any general public interest in the potlatch legislation before 1889. Until the time of the first arrest, the only people concerned were the missionaries, the Indian agents, and the officials in Ottawa. Residents of the province had some notions about Indian customs; some rather early letters and official submissions indicate that settlers helped to make up the audiences at a good number of Indian festivals; and of course the traders knew considerable about the Indian rhythm of life and its ceremonial features. But apparently it was not until the first arrest was made and reported in the newspapers that the episodic character of the law's enforcement was started. And years later newspapers continued to refer to the decision of Judge Begbie in this first test case of the Potlatch Law.

About the first of August, 1889, a Kwakiutl known as Hemasak, a member of the Malimalillekulla band, was arrested by Mr. Pidcock, who was a justice of the peace as well as an Indian agent, and sentenced to serve six months in jail—the maximum sentence, two months being the minimum. The case was appealed. (Who sponsored this appeal has not been determined as it was noted merely that "friends of the Indians" did.) Hemasak was released on a writ of *habeas corpus*. When he heard the case on August 21, 1889, Justice M. B. Begbie, who had arrived from England in 1859, supported his decision with some important points regarding legal procedure as well as the nature of the potlatch.

In his "Bench Notes," now in the archives of the Supreme Court of British Columbia,[5] Justice Begbie first made reference to some published citations pertinent to the legal problems involved:

I have some difficulty here; but I think on the whole the prisoner is entitled to his discharge. It appears that the prisoner was charged on the 1 August for the offence of celebrating the Indian festival known as a potlatch and on the same day committed for trial at Victoria on that charge. Being brought up before me on the Speedy Trials Act, a day was fixed for his trial. But before that time it became known that the J.P. at Alert Bay had already tried and convicted the prisoner of the offence.

Thereupon upon Saturday 17th inst. a Rule Nisi for a Habeas Corpus was granted for it seemed improper to hold a man here for a trial which could never come on, as it had already been held.

On Monday 19 August another warrant of commitment was delivered to

---

[5]Copy of Justice Begbie's "Bench Notes" made available through the courtesy of Willard S. Ireland, Provincial Librarian and Archivist, Victoria.

the jailer here, reciting a conviction and sentence for six months' imprisonment and ordering the jailer to hold the prisoner for six months only. There is no evidence to show how this warrant came to the hands of the jailer nor whether it is intended to be substituted for the other, nor when such substitution was determined on. The information is dated the 30th July. All the other 3 documents were dated the 1st August.

For though no certiorare was issued a 3rd document (viz: a memorandum of what took place at the hearing) has been shown to me; by which it appears that no evidence was called but the charge being read over to the prisoner with a woman interpreter, he was asked guilty or not guilty, and pleaded guilty and was immediately sentenced to six months' imprisonment, being the supreme punishment allowed.

It is not alleged that the nature of the charge was explained to the prisoner and from all I know of the gathering, I think it would be very hard to explain.

Different people appear to have very different notions as to what the word means.

At this point Judge Begbie discussed the origin of the word "potlatch," the idea that it might not be ancient but recent, perhaps even due to "the white purveyors of blankets and clothes." He was of the opinion that it was an acceptable practice unless liquor, rioting, and debauchery were involved. Quite obviously the judge claimed to know a great deal about Indians. He continued with some points of legal procedure:

If the Legislature had intended to prohibit any meeting announced by the name of a potlach, they should have said so. But if it be desired to create an offence previously unknown to the law there ought to be some definition of it in the Statute.

Of course it may be said all difficulty is eliminated in the present case where a defendant pleads guilty. But it seems an abuse of the forms of justice to take advantage of that plea against an ignorant Indian who speaks no word of English and allege that he has pleaded guilty to an offence, the facts constituting which we should ourselves be unable to set forth.

The dance Tamanawas for instance referred to in the same section is utterly unknown here, and it may well be that an Indian who had taken part in some quite innocent performance of dancing which the Legislature never intended to ban, might plead guilty to a charge of having danced.

A plea of guilty means guilty of the Act forbidden by the Statute.

It is by no means clear that it was fully explained to the defendant what the Statute forbids. It would seem the Statute should set out what acts constitute the forbidden festival. Until a defendant knows what those forbidden acts are, how can he say whether he has committed them or not?

. . . I think these considerations show that there would be some difficulty in convicting at all under the Statute but I discharge the prisoner on the simple ground that he was not, when the rule issued, held on a proper warrant of Committal.

And as to the proceedings which have been brought forward since the rule issued, (viz.) the conviction, and the 2nd warrant of Committal (the 2 warrants of the conviction are all dated the 1st August), there is no evidence when that conviction was had (i.e., before or after his commitment for trial here) nor any evidence whether the 2nd warrant is intended to be substituted for the first, nor how the jailer comes to have it now in his possession.

Shortly before the hearing by Judge Begbie, the Indians in the Alert Bay area had prepared a typewritten statement of the case for Lieutenant-Governor Nelson. A good portion of it was a recital of complaints against the Indian agent Mr. Pidcock who had arrested Hemasak, claiming that the agent had broken down the door of his house. It was claimed that "Ha-Mer-cee-lue" [Hemasak] had been arrested because of his connection with a marriage between his niece and one of their men; the agent had been falsely informed by two of the Indians at Fort Rupert who had apparently been made constables. The two Indians were described as

. . . walking about our village saying they have power to arrest us for almost anything that we do and making us live in dread all the time. It is our nature to fear the law. When we are imprisoned we feel it so that many die. Several of our families have left us in fear. We do not know where they have gone. They have done nothing that they know is against the Law. If Potlatching is unlawful, why do we not receive such notice. . . . [the Agent] has never said anything about it to us, in fact we very seldom see him and when he does come, he only counts the people or makes an arrest. . . . We are willing to give up all such doings but then we should be allowed something to help us live. Formerly we had plenty but now everything is being taken from us. Our rivers, our trees, our lands, even our fish are scarce among us, yet we are trying to live in peace and want to be friendly to all, but why should we be threatened with arrest all the time, when we do not know what is required of us. We beg protection that we may live in peace unless we break the law.

This petition was signed by a long list of Indians.

In a number of ways the reply which the Department in Ottawa received from Mr. Pidcock, after the Lieutenant-Governor had forwarded the petition, is hardly relevant at this particular point of the inquiry. Any agent would of course justify his actions, particularly when attempting to enforce a law which had been a statute for five years, yet had occasioned no arrests. His answer to the bill of complaints does point directly to the problem of establishing evidence of what was in fact done and the difficulties of evaluating a claim made by an Indian; the Indian version as compared with an agent's version has for almost a century been a main theme in the administration of

Indian affairs. Mr. Pidcock attempted to answer each itemized complaint; his long answer can be summarized under these five major points:

(1) Hemasak was arrested for having on two separate occasions called Indians of various tribes to his village for the purpose of potlatching, contrary to law.

(2) Mr. Pidcock had given notice that the law would be enforced; at the trial Hemasak had admitted that he had heard so.

(3) Hemasak was at home when he was arrested; no door of any house was broken open.

(4) Mr. Pidcock had visited and stayed with the tribe for several days, vaccinating them, calling on the sick, and giving them medicine; he had never refused them "anything when they have asked for it."

(5) Although the petition said that "we are afraid to go and speak to him for fear of arrest," Mr. Pidcock claimed that many Indians had been to see him since Hemasak was arrested.

After reading the petition carefully, the agent drew the conclusion that "the petition was not written at their request or were they aware of its contents, for I am certain they would not have signed their mark. . . . They are no doubt troubled over this man's arrest as they see in it the end of this iniquitous system."

The petition referred to economic scarcities, yet the agent pointed out that this band of all bands had good timber and good fishing. Moreover, Mr. Pidcock claimed that the younger men were in bondage to the older. He concluded with a rebuttal of the Indians' appeal that he be replaced as agent.

Possibly there are some who do not want me here as Agent, but they are not Indians or at best but few Indians, but a white man or two and their wives who are half-breeds and who have used their influence, which undoubtedly is great, in opposing any reforms which might benefit these people. The arrest of this man [Hemasak] caused a marked improvement in the behavior of these Indians, and his release from custody was a blow both to me as agent and to a number of younger men who were in hopes, so they told me, that they were about to be released from the thraldom so long exercised by the older men.

A full report of the Hemasak case, including the petitions from the Alert Bay Indians and the results of the investigation of the agent of the Department of Indian Affairs, was submitted October 3, 1889, to the Privy Council. Any resultant action is unreported; but on November 2, 1889, the complete case was submitted to the Deputy Minister of Justice, for officials in Ottawa were just beginning to learn that the legal entanglements, left unconsidered and undiscussed at the time the legislation had been passed, were numerous. The judgment of Chief Justice Begbie of the Supreme Court of British Columbia, so the Department of Justice was informed, had given a great deal of dissatisfaction to respectable white people and had also weakened the position of the agents. The officials of the Department of Indian Affairs asked if the Hemasak case could be appealed. If so, were there any chances of success? The reply of the Department of Justice was direct: the law made no provision for appeal; and the Deputy Minister opined, if Justice Begbie's statements regarding the meaning of the word "potlatch" were well founded, it would be difficult, almost impossible, to sustain a conviction under the statute; the same opinion applied to the prohibition of the dances. This document is dated December 13, 1889, and appears to close the first of the potlatch cases.

This case and those that followed attracted the interest of the public and what had been hitherto a controversy only among those directly concerned became a general public issue. The issue revolved around the question of whether a plan of conciliation was to be followed or whether there was to be complete and effective enforcement of the law. The passage of the law had been uncontested; the purposes of the government of Sir John A. Macdonald were in accord with those of the missionaries and they had been the two groups with an effective voice at the time. In the early stages of the enforcement controversy, peaceful penetration had not gone sufficiently far to enlist settlers on the side of the Indian, thereby identifying them as anti-missionary and anti-government. Furthermore, some of the consequences of missionary work had not emerged fully when the law was passed; namely, that the work of the missionaries was one of several factors contributing to the disorganization of Indian life. In addition, it was not at first clear to the administrators or the general public that the missionaries in their competition for converts were compelled to try to explain the profound subtleties of the relation of the church to the state, the nature of law and its enforcement, and the Christian tenets of the Dominion. But as the settlers and residents increased in number, there were some who took issue with the missionary tactics, who were concerned about the disorganized Indian, who considered the conciliatory plan of Dr. Powell as the only one which could be followed, and who desired that the ancient English tradition of fair play be upheld. Thus the issue of the potlatch took on a new light. The Fitzstubbs episode demonstrates the foregoing points.

While the legality of enforcement and the ability of the province to punish potlatching as a misdemeanour were being questioned, letters from the Upper Skeena country reached Ottawa about a stipendary magistrate, Mr. Fitzstubbs, who lived at Hazelton. A missionary, Rev. H. K. A. Pocock, of the Church Missionary Society had written expressing doubt not only of Mr. Fitzstubbs' ability but of his interest in enforcing the Potlatch Law. Mr. Fitzstubbs, after learning this from Ottawa and considering the letter a challenge, wrote a note to Rev. Pocock, asking him to relate the experience they had shared when Mr. Fitzstubbs attempted to stop potlatching. Mr. Pocock did so:

After the troubles of 1888, I undertook to reorganize the Mission of Kitwangak of the Church Missionary Society, that village having been the center of the disturbance. Shortly after my arrival you came to the village, while visiting the several tribes to prohibit the Potlatch.

On 7th November a Council was held at Lott's house at which you were the only white man present.

You addressed the Indians, telling them that they must desist from the "Potlatching." They replied, that the law was a weak baby, and in several speeches defied you, and the Government. One man also threatened your life. For over two hours I expected an attack, but your courage and good humor surprised and awed the people, and we left the house unmolested.

I was told afterwards that most of those who were present thought you would be killed.

As part of the Fitzstubbs episode, a very long letter was received in Ottawa from a Mr. Clifford. His identity remains unknown, but his letter revealed the intense feelings apparently held by an increasing number of residents, regarding the Potlatch Law and the policy of acculturation of the Indians. Mr. Clifford did more than refer to the "folly of attempting to stop it." It was his contention that "it is inconsistent to forbid Indians giving feasts to their friends while living, and to encourage them to purchase costly ornaments and tombstones to place over their graves when dead." To him it was very clear that any attempt to put down potlatching forcibly would prove "disastrous to the tranquility now prevailing"; for it remained to be demonstrated whether the suppression of potlatching was a prerequisite for civilizing the Indian as the Methodist missionaries contended. Mr. Clifford felt that this was not the case; rather that the missionaries had taken advantage of the opportunity provided by the existence of the law to make the Indians think that the law was "backing them up in all their monstrous claims and assertions." He claimed that the converted natives were known principally for their "insolence, extortion, and their openly expressed contempt for the law and its administration. . . . " Because of the notion of the conflict between the "law of the Bible and Civil law," the "native teachers without exception are the greatest scoundrels in the tribes, indolent, and hypocritical."

Fitzstubbs submitted to the attorney-general of British Columbia a comprehensive analysis of the nature of the potlatch and his view of the kind of enforcement policy that was needed. As usual the potlatch was defined as "a great obstacle to the hoped for progress." But even so the Indians cherished it, and from their point of view it was a "charitable institution. . . . They invariably ask 'what do the white men propose to substitute for this ancient and popular institution?'" Mr. Fitzstubbs then specified seven major points in support of the maintenance of the potlatch:

(1) It is a fair at which various products are exchanged.

(2) It provides enlarged opportunities for arranging marriages.

(3) At the meetings, questions of property and rank are adjusted.

(4) Although blankets and property are given away, it is with the eye of utility, "and not a shred of the blanket so torn is lost or destroyed."

(5) It serves as publicity for trivial affairs.

(6) The "potlach" is an assurance or benefit society, having its rules by which its members are governed and its property distributed to those entitled.

(7) The "ostentation of the 'Potlach' is not without attendant festivities and displays of hospitality, is not without counterpart in civilized life, is harmless, and gives pleasure to the Indians who do not see why in their case it should be suppressed."

Fitzstubbs pointed out that as there were few white residents on the Upper Skeena but many Indians, "the attempt to enforce the law . . . in too summary fashion might not produce the effect desired, but rather, might defer the good results hoped for, causing disquiet, and a disinclination to obey the law on other points." He also maintained that it would be a mistake to suppose that the opposition of the Indians to the "summary suppression of the potlach implied any disloyalty the Government."

The Lieutenant-Governor of British Columbia forwarded Mr. Fitzstubbs' submission to the Under-Secretary of State in Ottawa, and from that office it was sent to the Department of Justice. The enforcement of the law rested with the provincial government and its officers, but the opinion had been expressed that, because the federal parliament had passed the law, the Department of Indian Affairs should initiate the prosecution of any parties violating it. The Department of Justice pointed out that according to the British North America Act it was the responsibility of the provincial government; but if the provincial government failed in its duty, then it was up to the department to decide whether to incur any expenses or "allow the law to become a dead letter."

By 1890, seven years after the Proclamation, there had been apparently some clarification of the administrative procedure and responsibility for expediting the programme of the federal government in civilizing the Indians. There could no longer be any talk about a year of grace; the question in 1890 was whether the provincial government was or was not to initiate court action; obviously, that government was taking little interest in prosecuting under the law. Furthermore, its chief justice had raised the problem of a legal definition of a potlatch since there was none in the statute. A reaction to the missionary's belief in the importance of the repeal of the Potlatch Law for the progress of the Indian had set in. Finally, after consultation with various legal authorities, officials in the Department of Indian Affairs in Ottawa had come to the conclusion that provincial officers should confer with the Indian agents before interfering with the celebration of the potlatch. Problems of enforcement are placed in an even better perspective when it is recalled that there were tens of thousands of Indians scattered along the coast. Although so-called potlatching was not continuous, yet there must have been enough of it occurring to have made enforcement less conspicuously episodic. But it appears from the records that from 1890 to 1893 the potlatch issue was at a standstill.

The question was renewed in February, 1893, when the Toronto *Empire* published an article entitled "The Evil Potlach" and subtitled "The Season When the Red Man Gives Away His Blankets." The article was a report from a group of missionaries who had gone from Comox to Cape Mudge, directly across Discovery Passage from Campbell River. Upon arrival they found 1,200 Indians gathered from within a radius of 100 miles. The article describes what the missionaries saw:

Their tents were made some of white cotton, some of cedar bark, some of cedar slabs. Into these places hordes were huddled until there was scarcely room to step. Strewn about in all directions were pieces of refuse, food, and other filth, in which the young children were rolling, some of them entirely nude, others with a mere rag of clothing on them. To make the mixture complete, were scores of Indian dogs lying about with the children, others in their beds, or nosing about their foods, licking out pots and kettles until The Scene was Disgusting in the extreme. This is a meagre sketch of the scene by daylight, when a great many of the family were out.

Under the cover of darkness this seething mass of corruption puts on another aspect. Morality among the Indians themselves, under these circumstances, is at a very low ebb; but when a score of white men come in with a few gallons of "fire water," and spend the night with the Indians, the scene become Indescribable. . . .

The article told of the ill health and impoverishment of the aged, the neglect of children for the sake of throwing away blankets, and of course the practice of prostitution to secure funds for potlatching. It ended with criticism of the non-enforcement of the Potlatch Law.

A few years ago a law was passed prohibiting the potlatch. This was as good as winked at by some of the officials; and when a certain tribe asked permission to hold "just one more potlatch" and that permission was granted, the Indians said, "If one tribe can break the law by permission, we will try breaking it without permission." The law remains on the Dominion Statutes, but is practically a dead letter; and the Indians, instead of being an upright and an industrious people, are a filthy, indolent, degraded set, a disgrace and a curse to our country.

The small extent of public and official interest as a result of the *Empire* article can be gauged from the lack of response to it. The Ottawa office asked the agent for a report; the comparison of the article with the agent's report undoubtedly roused the suspicion that there was selected distortion, either by the missionaries or by the writer of the article. And of course it was clear that the decision of Judge Begbie made it impossible to obtain a conviction under the law simply because the law did not define a potlatch. But some people still felt they knew what it was: Hell on Earth.

The descriptive material provided by the *Empire* article and its interpretation of the potlatch were of a character to support a claim that the Northwest Coast Indian was still in need of civilizing. The giving away of property, the conditions of sanitation, the standard of living, the care of children and the aged, the waste of time—these were lively demonstrations of a need for the continuance of the Potlatch Law and a reiteration of the original reasons for its passage in 1884. Although the detailed effects of the *Empire* article may not be worth tracing, there was still sufficient pressure on Parliament for the retention of a potlatch prohibitory clause in the Indian Act; there was even enough pressure, either from special interest groups such as the churches or from the civil servants, to force an amendment (assented to on July 22, 1895)[6] so that successful prosecution could be anticipated if a court action were instituted.

[6]Indian Act, 1895, 58–9 Vic., c. 35, s. 6.

But the pressure was by no means all on one side. The 1895 session of Parliament was considering the amendment when one Mr. Woolsey read of it in a paper and wrote immediately to Hon. Sir MacKenzie Bowell to give his opinion on the legislation. Mr. Woolsey explained that he had lived in British Columbia between 1859 and 1868 and during that period had been well acquainted with Father Fouquet, one of the leading Roman Catholic missionaries. The purpose of his letter was "to caution you against the danger of attempting to stop this by Act of Parliament and force. The probable result would be a repetition of the Indian Mutiny on a smaller scale, the murder of out-lying settlers and the useless shedding of innocent blood." According to Mr. Woolsey, it would "require several generations to abolish the practices and tradition of the centuries."

The potlatch was thus, apparently, a point of interest to people here and there; occasionally something would give rise to a series of letters, charges, and countercharges. But on the whole peaceful pene-tration was going along quietly.

The Indians also made their point of view known. Early in the fall of 1895, the Indian Commissioner of British Columbia, a relatively new officer superior to the Superintendent, forwarded to Ottawa a protest from the Nass River Indians.[7] They petitioned that clergymen be prevented from interfering "with our people in the holding of pot-latches as the Rev. J. A. McCullagh of Nass River has. . . . " The Indians stated that the potlatch was a "method that we have of show-ing our good will toward one another, and we believe that it is our right just as much as it is the right of our white brethren to make presents to each other." The Indians assured the Indian Commissioner that the potlatches were conducted in an orderly manner and that they did observe the law of "Our Great and Good Mother Queen Victoria." The protest closed with the comment that "we know that it is the opinion of many intelligent and good white men that the clergymen meddling in our affairs is very uncalled for and creates a feeling against them amongst us which prevents the accomplishment of an amount of good that might be realized to our advantage."

When the Commissioner, A. W. Vowell, sent the petition to Ottawa, he included further information, giving the background for the im-mediate cause of the protest. When the Indians had held their last dance, "the Rev. Mr. McCullagh j.p. sent his constables to arrest two

[7]Collison, in his *In the Wake of the War Canoe*, gives one the impression that he was of the opinion that the "battle against heathenism" was won by 1890. The Nass River Indians are located in the area to which he is referring.

of the Indians who were put in Gaol and to serve summons on 12 others." The Indians said that "if the parties who wish to prevent the Potlach will give to those who have claims for what they have given heretofore then the people would be willing to relinquish the practice." About $5,000 was estimated as the amount required. The Commissioner, in answering the Indians, promised to investigate the actions of the missionary and praised them for their efforts to help the aged. But in his letter to Ottawa he said, "I have written so much already to the Department on the above subject that it is useless for me to attempt to throw any additional light on the question. . . . "

Just a few months later another missionary, Rev. C. M. Tate, charged the agent, Lomas, with laxity in enforcing the Potlatch Law. In his letter the missionary made five specific points which were essentially the same as all other petitioners had made. But Mr. Tate stated that he was placing a formal charge against Mr. Lomas "for exceeding his duty in telling the Nanaimo Indians to go on with their potlatch, and no one would interfere with them." In the last paragraph of his letter, the missionary stated what had become a commonly accepted interpretation of the attitude of the Indian agents: they did not want to enforce the law.

I trust this matter will be pushed until we get men into these Agencies who will do their utmost to elevate the people under their care. It is an injustice to the Government and to Missionary societies who are spending their money to make a better people of the Indians, to have these demoralizing practices propagated, and that in the face of a law, which if enforced, would speedily terminate all such proceedings.

As in previous cases, an official in the Department of Indian Affairs in Ottawa wrote a letter of inquiry, received a reply from the appropriate agent, and then closed the file of correspondence. Departmental policy in fact supported the notion that there was considerable reason to permit a final settlement of outstanding obligations, but "it would be advisable when possible, to exact in return for any concessions made, a promise to discontinue such festivals hereafter."

Ten weeks later an arrest was made. In January, 1896, agent Devlin in the Fraser Valley advised the Commissioner in British Columbia that one of the Indians had held a potlatch.

The Indian mentioned . . . Bill Uslick . . . is one of those Indians that is very hard to manage. He still wishes to keep up the old habits and customs, and would like to be a leader among the Indians of the neighborhood. The Potlatch given by Bill Uslick was simply a Potlatch. I am not aware that any human, or animal bodies, were mutilated, or anything of that kind occurred. There certainly was a great waste. He practically left himself destitute, having given everything away that he had in the world. I am of the opinion if he was brought before the Court and got a couple of months in prison, that it would have a good effect, and would deter others from following his example. . . .

Upon receiving the file from the Commissioner, the Department of Indian Affairs indicated that if there was certainty of securing a conviction, then prosecution should be initiated, "unless he promises to obey the law in the future." All the Indians of the district were at the court, and the agent explained to them that every Indian who went to the potlatch was liable to the same punishment, but "as he was the principal offender I would only punish him this time, but should a repetition occur I would punish every Indian who was guilty. I feel certain the steps taken will have the effect of stopping the Potlatch in Chilliwack." On February 4 a newspaper, identity undetermined, carried this short statement concerning Uslick's potlatch— "An Indian recently left his wife to starve near Chilliwack and held a hiyu skookum potlatch for his friends. Indian Agent Devlin and Mr. Millard sentenced the unnatural husband to two months in jail."

The arrest and imprisonment of Uslick triggered a renewed and wider interest in the potlatch; newspapers printed letters and petitions about it for several months. Letters from Indians by then, however, indicated distinct changes in their arguments. For example, on February 24, 1896, the *Victoria Colonist* published a petition from the Nass River tribes to Mr. G. E. Courbould, a member of Parliament, and the clippings were sent to Ottawa by Mr. C. M. Tate, who had placed the formal charge against Mr. Lomas. The theme of the petition was that they saw a

. . . contradictory state of affairs adorning your civilization. Churches are numerous; the theatres are located in the various sections of the town; and saloons multiply in numbers; all of which are in conformity with your laws, consequently we wish to know whether the ministers of the gospel have annihilated the rights of white men in these pleasures leading to heaven and hell exactly in different directions. They have kindly forced us out, as we are "not in it."

The petition mentioned Christmas, "Fourth of July," and "24th of May" celebrations, where "money is spent in squandrous profusion with no benefits to the poor of your race," and compared European and Indian funeral rights:

We see in your graveyards the white marble and granite monuments which cost money in testimony of your grief for your dead. When our people die we erect a large pole, call our people together, distribute our personal property with them in payment for their sympathy, and condolence; comfort to us in the sad hours of our affliction. This is what is called a potlach— the privilege denied us. It is a chimera that under the British flag slavery does not exist.

A prominent missionary responded with a personal account of the iniquities of the potlatch. Rev. Alfred H. Hall had arrived in the Alert Bay area in 1877 or 1878.[8] This was the centre of the Kwakiutl country and only twenty miles from Fort Rupert where Boas did considerable field work. Village Island, Turnour Island, and Gilford Island, as well as Kingcome Inlet, are easily accessible by boat. And of course the Nimpkish group were even at that time living mostly at Alert Bay, just across the channel from the Nimpkish River on Vancouver Island. Hall was a master of the native language; he had prepared a grammar and translated hymns, the Gospels, and portions of the Book of Common Prayer. When he wrote to the *Victoria Weekly Colonist*, after twenty years among the Kwakiutl, he was already known for his work as a missionary. His letter on the evils of the potlatch, published in the *Weekly Colonist* on March 19, 1896, was calculated to support the enforcement of the Potlatch Law. Dealing first with prostitution, he told of counting "thirty-two women in one month who embarked by the steamers to bring back the coveted blankets. In my time about fifty women under 25 years of age have died, all of whom have been sacrificed to maintain the potlach. Whenever the tribe ceased to potlach the life of shame, which some of these women lead, practically ceases." Moreover, because of the potlatch, tribes left their villages and remained away for three to five months, leaving the aged and infirm behind to their fate—"once in a deserted village I found an old woman frozen to death and as hard as a stone. I have been applied to for poison to put such out of the way, because their friends (?) wished to follow those who had gone to the potlatch. There can be no real progress while this system flourishes. . . . " The missionary praised the efforts of the Indian Department, however. "It is school versus potlach." He concluded that "the law which forbids the potlatch is not against liberty but licence. It is to the interests of this province that we keep our Indians alive; they are worth preserving. . . . They occupy land the white man does not require. They love the white

[8]Some writers have said 1878. Collison states that Mr. Hall "Joined the North Pacific Mission in 1877 and laboured amongst the Quagulth tribes for some thirty-two years, reducing their language to writing and making translations." (p. 37)

man, and their ultimate future must be absorption and assimilation to the whites."

Two days later the *Province*, in Vancouver, published two letters written in response to the petition of February 24, one from William Dwyer of Cowichan and the other from R. G. Sidley of Osoyoos, located in the interior about 150 miles east of Vancouver. These two letters went over the usual controversial points, and even took up the question of potlatching as a cause of impoverishment. Mr. Dwyer called attention to the fact that "white people give wedding and Christmas presents often to an extent that they can ill-afford." He had attended potlatches and was familiar with them. Mr. Sidley closed his letter with a resounding paragraph against the missionaries:

. . . But just to show you how opinions differ, I heard Chief Tonasket, of the Colvilles, at a potlatch held at the foot of Osoyoos Lake about eleven years ago attribute the decay of the Okanagans to the fact that Chief Scoolatkin had adopted Methodism.

It is however a demonstrable fact that the decay of the tribes mentioned is not due to the "potlatch."

During this particular period, newspaper editors must have felt that their readers were interested in the nature of the potlatch and in the questions regarding its enforcement. The Nass River petition was published by the *Daily Columbian* on February 26, 1896, entitled "Indignant Indians." And the letter of Mr. A. J. Hall appeared in the *Daily Colonist* on March 1. The Indian Commissioner of British Columbia, still located at Victoria, called the attention of the appropriate agent, Mr. Pidcock, to this letter, indicating that the original legislation had been amended and suggesting that the ringleaders be tried. But in so doing, "the greatest discretion must be used to avoid raising a spirit of antagonism." In response to this public discussion, Mr. McCullagh sent a very long statement, essentially a history of enforcement in the Nass River area, to the Commissioner. In this latest analysis, Mr. McCullagh gave a new version of the conflicting interests and groups.

It is generally supposed that this question of the potlatch is one of Christian against heathen and vice versa.

This is not the case. The ringleaders of the potlatch are Christians. The delegation which went to Victoria last Summer was composed partly of Christians, viz.: Amos Gosling, William Jeffry, and Moses Gagwilen; the aforementioned Quksho, alias Mathew Nass, who assaulted Nish-yek, is Christian; Stephen Laklaub, who incited the Indians to disobey the summons, is a Christian; of the seven potlatch cases dealt with by me this winter four are Christians. To emphasize this point I have several times in the course of this report indicated whether the men were heathen or Christian.

Thus it is that in enforcing Sec. 114 of the Indian Act the Government will not be taking the part of Christians against heathens. Left to themselves the heathen Chiefs would give no trouble; it is when two or more evil-disposed Christians, who profess to know everything, gain an influence over them that they go astray. Of course the Chiefs are not without blame, for they leave no stone unturned to surround themselves with such characters.

The burden of Mr. McCullagh's analysis was simply that the laws had fallen into disrespect among the Indians.

Lomas sent a report to the Commissioner about the Nanaimo potlatch which had taken place the previous fall. Before it was given, he wrote, the "Indians came to me and promised that this should be the last one in their village, and that they would do their utmost to prevent the introduction of liquor. Owing to a delay in the arrival of the Musqueam Band the gathering was not over for about twelve days, but the whole affair passed off without any friction, there was no drunkenness, quarrelling, or fighting." This potlatch was visited by hundreds of white people, "both Ladies and Gentlemen and even little children." Mr. Lomas himself had gone several times and reported that "they one and all pledged themselves that this should be the last gathering of the kind that should be held in their village, stating that Victoria [Songhees] and Nanaimo had made the same pledges which all understood and intended to keep."

The same agent a few days later submitted a report of a gathering of 1,500 Indians on Kuper Island.

One day was devoted to sports at which I and others were invited to be present, the prizes being provided by the hosts, who did not compete themselves. The boat sailing, canoe and foot races were well worth seeing. A large number of ladies and gentlemen resident on adjacent islands were present, holding picnic parties on the shore, many photographs being taken. One gentleman was present during the whole gathering, obtaining information and views for an English magazine. There were no Provincial Police present at any time. The Penelkut have promised that this should be their last Potlach; every member of the band appeared to be on their mettle to show the white people that as regards their village the articles written against the gatherings were false. . . .

This particular flurry of public interest closed with two letters, one from a Nootka Chief and the other from Franz Boas who by that time was well known to many people in British Columbia. On April 1, 1896, the *Daily Colonist* published "The Nootka Chief Speaks." Chief Maquinna referred to the potlatch system as a bank and drew a parallel to the white method of banking. He called attention to the Indian ways of supporting the aged and to the fact that the Indian agent "does not support the old and poor now." Furthermore, "they say it is the will of the Queen. This is not true. The Queen knows nothing about our potlach feasts. She must have been put up to make a law by people who know us." And then he pointed out a number of other white-native parallels:

. . . a white man told me one day that the white people have also sometimes masquerade balls and white women have feathers on their bonnets and the white chiefs give prizes for those who imitate best, birds or animals. And this is all good when white men do it but very bad when Indians do the same thing. The white chiefs should leave us alone; they have their games and we have ours. . . .
      . . . The potlach is not a pagan rite; the first Christians used to have their goods in common as a consequence must have given "potlaches" and now I am astonished that Christians persecute us and put us in jail for doing as the first Christians.

In the last paragraph Chief Maquinna said, "I am sorry to hear the news about the potlach and that my friends of the North were put in jail." (We suppose that these convictions were made in the Nass River country by Mr. McCullagh.)

The letter from Franz Boas was addressed to a private person who in turn sent it to the editor of the Vancouver *Daily Province*; it was published March 6, 1897. The letter was a very long one and was essentially the same as his article in the 1898 volume of the *British Association for the Advancement of Science*. This same material was later used by Dr. E. Sapir, in writing to Mr. Scott, the Deputy Superintendent of Indian Affairs. Boas's first major point was that the meaning of the potlatch had been misunderstood by the whites; otherwise, he believed, they would not have tried to suppress it. In expanding this statement, he too drew the parallel with our own banking and credit system.

It must be clearly understood that an Indian who invites all his friends and neighbors to a great potlatch, and apparently squanders all the accumulated results of long years of labor has two things in mind which we cannot but acknowledge as wise and worthy of praise. His first object is to pay his debts. . . . His second object is to invest the fruits of his labor so that the greatest benefit will accrue from them for his own benefit as well as for his children. . . .

With reference to the cruel ceremonies, he did not consider it advisable to interfere with them as "forced discontinuance will tend to destroy what moral steadiness is left to him." In addition

. . . the cruelty of the ceremonial exists alone in the fancy of those who know of it only by the exaggerated descriptions of travellers. In olden times it was a war ceremony and captives were killed and even devoured. But with the encroachment of civilization the horrors of the old ceremonies have died out. . . .
. . . The lingering survivals of the old ceremonies will die out quickly, and the remainder is a harmless amusement that we should be slow to take away from the native who is struggling against the overpowerful influence of civilization.

Shortly before the Boas letter appeared in the press, the newspapers again played up a case. According to the reports, the Salmon River case was one in which the officers appeared to handle the Indians rather roughly while trying to make an arrest. Official communications said that "alarming reports" were circulating in the newspapers, "owing to suppression of the potlatch." Along with Ottawa, the attorney-general of British Columbia, in collaboration with the agent, took immediate steps to "restore harmony."

To some extent the 1895 amendment marked a turning point in the enforcement of the Potlatch Law. After Mr. Corbould had received Mr. Tate's letter and referred it to the Department in Ottawa, an official wrote and explained to Commissioner Vowell in British Columbia that "the law, until amended last Session, was, however, practically inoperative, and it was useless to endeavour to enforce it." Mr. Vowell's attention was called to the fact that two or three convictions had been secured since the passage of the amendment. However it was still basic policy to "proceed very cautiously in order to guard against evoking a mutinous spirit among the Indians." Agents were to use "great circumspection, exhausting every means of bringing the Indians to abandon the custom, through moral suasion, before instituting prosecution. . . . " It is interesting to note that the amendment to the Act does not mention the word potlatch. It was clear that the Department in Ottawa wanted a legally effective law, and that it intended to stand in a conciliatory position between the missionaries, the general public, and the Indians while at the same time supporting the agents. The agents, it was obvious by now, were responsible for the initiation of prosecutions—not the provincial authorities. The legal and administrative position of the Department of Indian Affairs and its officers was clear.

Within a year's time, however, strong pressure to repeal the amended law was put upon Ottawa; and within four years, there was strong pressure from the Christianized Indians to enforce the law. These actions were accompanied, moreover, by changes in the tactics both of the Indians and of the provincial government. We have seen that even before the law changed the explanations of the nature of a potlatch had changed considerably; reports indicated further that in some places, especially the Victoria-Nanaimo area, what had been called potlatching had altered radically. Training in mission schools, a longer period of contact with friendly settlers, the influence of the trader, and the expansion of the economic system could only mean that by 1895 the Indian had had a greater opportunity to learn from the white man. These changes soon appeared in the conflict of the Indian and his guardians as the Indians adopted more and more of the white man's methods.

ENFORCEMENT AND NATIVE RIGHTS

When the Proclamation was issued in 1883 and the Potlatch Law passed in 1884, Canadian officials and legislators believed that the behaviour called potlatching was absolutely immoral. There could be no question of the rights of the Indians except insofar as the problems of the administration of justice in the Canadian legal system might be involved. It was, furthermore, then assumed that it would take only a few years for the Indians to see the individual and collective harm caused by their persistent potlatching. The various consequences of the law were unanticipated: the controversies among natives and experts about the morality of potlatching and the nature of the in-stitution; the detailed comparisons of the Indian and European ways of life in which similarities in such things as totem poles and tomb-stones, or potlatches and cocktail parties, led to unfavourable con-clusions about the Canadians; and the experience and growing sophisti-cation of the Indians in Canadian modes of trial procedure and political manipulation. These uncalculated developments were salient features of a renewed period of controversy about the potlatch, mani-fested, as they were, in local village politics by the organized efforts of the proponents of potlatching to have the law amended or repealed and by the organized efforts of the native opponents to have it enforced.

For unknown generations, northern Indians have been going south. The earliest expeditions were chiefly war-making trips; later, after the establishment of white settlements, they went as seasonal agricultural workers or as labourers in the fishing industry. They of course responded to the emerging urban areas of Victoria and Vancouver which provided not only occupational opportunities but also the glittering lure of the big city. In addition the coastal Indians rather early discovered Victoria's role as the capital—a city where representatives and delegations could go in their efforts to secure individual or collective goals. Not only were provincial officials located there but also the main office of the Indian Commissioner of the federal government before it was moved to Vancouver.

It was the Nass River petition, published in the *Victoria Daily Colonist*, February 24, 1896, that gave the first clue about how the Indian and his guardians as the Indians adopted more and more of ment and regional development, thus changing the social context of the potlatch issue. There was a shift from a mere explanation of the potlatch and a request for permission to engage in the ancient ceremony to a protest against the law and a demand for the right to undisturbed celebrations of the potlatch. An aspect of this shift was the use of lawyers for direction in public discussion and by Indians charged with offences. A sentence in the petition of February 24 which appeared in the *Colonist*, and two days later in the *Columbian*, showed this new orientation: "We came to Victoria to obtain our natural rights." The "petition of rights," according to the articles, was to be sent to Ottawa by the "indignant Indians."

On March 20 Commissioner Vowell sent a number of documents to the Ottawa office, among them the clippings of these newspaper articles, the long analysis of Mr. McCullagh presenting evidence that it was the Christianized natives who were the potlatchers, and materials from Mr. Lomas. Several of Mr. Vowell's comments were of unusual significance. The Indians from the Kwawkewlth agency, he said, "have proved themselves non-progressive, lazy, idle, and indifferent to the advice constantly given them and leading towards their advancement and welfare." This description of the Kwakiutl convinced the Commissioner that missionary and departmental work was unsuccessful among migrant Indian groups. In report after report, for decades, agents and commissioners had made such statements about the Indians from the Kwawkewlth agency, the same agency which later was to become the focal point of police and court action as a result of firm efforts to enforce the Potlatch Law.

The second comment of Commissioner Vowell must have seemed, at the time it was written, only casual in nature; he said that Indians had made inquiries from several court officials after the law had been amended. What the inquiries were about, he does not say, but we may presume that they were concerned with natural rights, for the papers reported that after their visit with the Superintendent of Indian Affairs, the Indians had consulted with a city lawyer about their complaints.

If the opponents of the Potlatch Law were organizing their protest, making a search for a legal basis rooted in a European philosophy of the natural rights of man, and in addition interpreting the potlatch in terms of Canadian values and sentiments, the Indian proponents of the law were also organizing. Their charge was simply that the law on the books was not being enforced. Three years after the petition of rights was formulated in Victoria and sent to Ottawa, a delegation of Indians from the Nass River in opposition to the potlatch visited Victoria in order to call upon Attorney-General Martin. Their case was essentially the well-established view of civilization *versus* savagery. But in addition they submitted claims to support the statement that putting the potlatch in terms of Western values and sentiments was a misrepresentation; and they made it clear that almost annually deputations had gone to Victoria to try to secure by misrepresentation the maintenance of the potlatch system. The potlatch was defined by this delegation as a heathen government, and as such "it is a government in opposition to all that would tend to the furtherance of our best interests.[9]

The news writer who composed the report of the delegation's visit to Victoria chose as his leading sentence, "To potlatch or not to potlatch is the question which is agitating the minds of Indians of Nass River district. . . . " Not only were individual Indians making a personal choice and thus choosing sides, but groups were organizing petitions and, when it seemed that petitions were not effective, delegations were being sent to Victoria. The delegation in support of the law, as noted above, was the response to several disappointing years of work with petitions. While these petitions were being prepared there must have been considerable discussion among supporters of the law about possible amendment. Its repeal was under discussion too, for the printed petition of March 22, 1898, to Indian Affairs in Ottawa contained in its last paragraph a reference to that kind of action.

When Attorney-General Martin wrote from Victoria to the Superintendent-General of Indian Affairs in Ottawa after the visit in 1899, he enclosed a petition signed by 138 Indians who referred to themselves as Christian Indians. This petition argued several major points.

[9]*Victoria Daily Times*, May 1, 1899.

It claimed that a majority of Indians were opposed to potlatching, and that when a similar situation occurred among the whites, the law was then enforced. After mentioning the fact that the Tsimshian and the Haida had given up potlatching, the petitioners, of the Nishga tribe from Aiyansh, said:

We do not wish to be behind them in civilization and progress. So long as a few of our people are permitted to go back to it, and we are burdened with its weight, which keeps us back. . . . We had confidence in the law and believed it would be put in force and so we waited. We did not know that there could be a dead law on the Law Book. . . . We have got several good cases of Potlatching now ready for trial where much property was destroyed. We have witnesses ready and are prepared to pay a lawyer. Mr. Todd has taken down some of the facts. Let the law be put in force. . . .

After this period of activity by petitioners and delegations, there was a decade with few ostensible Indian actions and little official or public attention to potlatching. In 1901, on January 4, a Vancouver newspaper announced a "squaw sold for $1,400." On April 23, 1904, the *Victoria Daily Times* carried a large spread of story and pictures about "Winter Festivals of the Indians of British Columbia," the "ancient customs of a peculiar race: the potlach, cedar bark dance and the hamatsa"; it was written by Thomas Deasey, a speaker of the Chinook jargon who had toured some Indian villages and who was later to become an Indian agent. Although he claimed to have witnessed potlatching, there was no report of any arrests or court cases. The *Colonist*, December 24, 1905, reported "the potlatch season." After describing the preparations, such as the collection of "blankets of all colors and sizes, sugar, beans, flour, pilot bread and other staple provisions," the article ended with an interesting item which, if accurate, suggested acculturation.

A feature of this potlatch will be the music to be supplied by Indian bands. A large cash prize is offered for the best, and it is said there will be at least three bands in attendance. This will guarantee a high old time, and dancing will probably be kept up day and night, one band taking a rest while another discourses the discordant strains to which the Indians will attempt to keep time.

The day of the big potlatch is gradually passing away, and people living in the North believe it will not be very long before that custom is dropped entirely.

Then in 1906 it was announced by an unidentified paper that five Indian girls had been sold during a recent potlatch, although "it has been supposed that the Dominion government had succeeded in putting an end to potlatching among the Indians of this province." All was apparently quiet until 1910 when the *Victoria Daily Times* reported a "potlatch at Quamichan." Three years later, on January 29, it announced "Fourth Big Potlatch of Year Held." In perspective the absence of official attention and the few newspaper reports make the period between 1905 and 1914 seem like the conspicuous calm before a great storm.

During this time Halliday, the Indian agent at Alert Bay, expressed concern about persistent potlatching in his agency, that is, among the Kwakiutl. The Deputy Superintendent-General published Halliday's reports in his *Annual Reports* for 1911, 1912, and 1913. In view of the significance of the actions of Mr. Halliday in succeeding years, his "General Remarks," in the *Annual Report* for 1913 are given in full.

The work amongst the Indians in this agency is on the whole discouraging. The missionaries of both Anglican and Methodist denominations have laboured for years, and laboured faithfully, but the result seems to be negative. The chief source of difficulty seems to be the apathy of the Indians themselves. They are wrapped up in their old customs to a great extent, particularly with regard to the potlatch and its ramifications. All their ideas centre on the potlatch. Their buildings, more particularly the older buildings, have been built entirely with that end in view. They are huge, barn-like structures without floors and made of a frame of huge cedar logs covered in with usually split cedar boards and with the exception of the front, which is usually made of rustic siding and painted. In these houses they can entertain their friends and give away their gifts. These buildings are heated by open fires in the centre and the smoke finds its way out through a hole in the roof and through the various crevices between the boards. There is always smoke in the houses and it has a bad effect on their eyes, the majority of the older people being more or less affected in their sight and many of them quite blind.

Education will in time change these old customs, but it requires time and patience, and it is questionable whether the changes will take place in time to save them as a race. The birth-rate for the past year was 22.76 per thousand, while the death-rate was 42.15, with a total decrease of thirteen. (p. 229)

Because of his concern about apathy, the lack of progress, and the persistence of potlatching, Mr. Halliday charged two Indians, Chief Ned Harris and Chief George Bagwany, with potlatching and brought them to trial on May 7, 1914. The two Indians were of the Nimpkish band, Kwakiutl tribe. The Vancouver *Daily Province* described the trial as the first of its kind since the decision of Chief Justice Begbie, twenty years earlier. It reported that Mr. Halliday had warned Harris and Bagwany against potlatching. Counsel for the defence, Mr. D. E. McTaggert, claimed that Agent Halliday had admitted that:

. . . the only gifts had been those of blankets and that no pernicious effects could follow from a distribution of blankets. He further admitted that the potlatch had not been attended by any of the flesh cutting or voluntary tortures that used to attend the potlatching of the olden days, and that it was a recognized custom among the Indians to pay their debts publicly in the presence of tribes as witnesses.

The trial was held in Assizes Court in Vancouver on May 7 and can be said to have set into motion a whole new phase of enforcement. According to the newspaper accounts, "a large number of men from the Nimpkish tribe are present in court as witnesses and spectators." The two defendants were found guilty but given a suspended sentence. It became known that Mr. Justice Gregory who presided at the trial was aware that it was the first case under the revised statute and felt, therefore, that a suspended sentence ought to be allowed. Bagwany and Harris were released under bond. The trial generated a great deal of activity in the form of petitions and letters to the Department of Indian Affairs and other offices in Ottawa:

September, 1914. A four-page petition was sent by Indians from Port Hammond asking for the maintenance of the old customs without alteration. These were Musqueam Indians of the Squamish band.

December, 1914. A seven-page petition from the Nootka Indians on the west coast of Vancouver Island, was sent to Indian Affairs, asking that the Potlatch Law be repealed. This petition referred to Dr. E. Sapir, the first time that the name of this anthropologist appeared in the discussions.

December, 1914. A one-page petition was sent from the Indians at Sechelt, B.C., in favour of maintaining the Potlatch Law. It said that the potlatch was "opposed to civilization" and wanted to support the Fraser River Indian petition to stop the potlatch.

December, 1914. A petition from the Indians at Coquitlam, B.C., stating six major points, asked that the Potlatch Law be amended so as to prevent potlatching.

January, 1915. Charles Nowell, a Kwakiutl of Alert Bay, sent a list of names of each copper to Mr. Clements, a member of the House of Commons, with the symbolic potlatching value of each sheet of copper metal indicated, the coppers varying in value as do banknotes. It had been suggested that the Canadian government might purchase the coppers so as to stop potlatching thus killing motives of acquisition and accumulation. Almost forty years later Charles Nowell was the informant for *Smoke from Their Fires*, by Clelland Ford.

February, 1915. A letter from Dr. Sapir to Deputy Superintendent-General Scott quoted at length from article of Franz Boas in *British Association for Advancement of Science*, 1898, pp. 54–5.

March 2, 1915. Fort Rupert Indians, of the Kwakiutl group, sent a petition to the Deputy Superintendent-General through Agent Halliday, complaining of arrests and trials, pleading for understanding and asking that commissioners be sent out, "for we are sure that these judges and lawyers do not understand what the potlatch is but they have to go by the law." This petition was sent after several meetings among themselves and a conference with their agent, Mr. Halliday.

May, 1915. In his report to Ottawa, Agent Halliday reported another trial but indicated that a grand jury dismissed the potlatch case of Klakwagila, for "they did not see any offence."

March 27, 1919. Court case: *Rex* v. *Kwostestros; Rex* v. *Lakosa.* Verdict: guilty, sentence suspended.

May, 1919. Inspector Ditchburn, of the Royal Canadian Mounted Police, reported on the cost of redeeming coppers.

February, 1920. Charles Nowell again wrote to Mr. Clements, M.P., appealing for his influence to be used in stopping arrests and prosecutions.

February, 1920. Indians of Village Island, near Alert Bay, wrote to Mr. Clements, M.P., appealing for "understanding" in potlatch activities and thus stopping court actions.

March, 1920. Attorney Lyon, of Vancouver, wrote to Deputy Superintendent-General Scott, asking for an investigation of arrests and court cases. There is evidence to suppose that he was retained by a group of Indians, possibly those at Alert Bay.

January, 1921. Ahousat chiefs, on the west coast of Vancouver Island, sent a petition to Ottawa, with seventeen signatures, explaining the potlatch and asking its retention.

This list suggests the amount of activity. Missionaries were apparently working chiefly through the Christian, non-potlatching Indians, although there was an occasional direct statement. Barristers became prominent through their correspondence with officials in Ottawa; they thought that the statute was too severe and needed some amelioration. The activities summarized above set the stage for the greatest single, persistent effort made by the Canadian government to enforce the Potlatch Law, as it had been amended in 1906. It was a complex affair, for by now there were numerous protagonists, resistance to the law had become organized, and a new generation of missionaries, Indians, and British Columbians were in important positions. Moreover, the evidence suggests that competitive potlatches, although having been held for some years, were by the 1920's considered to be extraordinarily symbolic of the Indian, as compared with the Canadian, way of life.

Mr. Halliday made his first prosecutions in 1914, and it could be argued that they represent the beginning of the Alert Bay cases. But there was no sustained effort on the part of the federal government until January, 1920, and Mr. Halliday himself considered this the beginning of the campaign. In chapter seven of *Potlatch and Totem*, Mr. Halliday expresses the opinion that potlatching was getting worse, apparently between 1914 and 1920. And when he reports that it was assuming greater proportions, we may assume that he is referring to the fact that any one affair was greater in attendance with more property exchanged was well as destroyed—sewing machines, flour, and other modern trade goods which to the non-Indians were consumable goods or equipment to be used for domestic purposes. Mr. Halliday received from the Department of Indian Affairs instructions to enforce the regulations and "to see that this custom is done away with entirely." Therefore he sent notice to every Indian village about the law and the fact that it was, at that time, an indictable offence. Although he does not identify them, he does report that the provincial police initiated prosecutions against two Indians in his agency, although in all other respects the Indians were quite worthwhile fellows. The two Indians pleaded guilty, and Mr. Halliday testified before Judge Gregory that they were "good fellows" and "law-abiding in every other way." As a result Judge Gregory reprimanded them, asked them to warn the other Indians, and gave them a suspended sentence.

For our purpose it will suffice to present in calendrical form the several court actions and activities of Indians, lawyers, and other interested parties.[10]

January, 1921. Two Kwakiutls, one Mrs. McDougall and one Munday, prosecuted for alleged potlatching in December, 1920; case dismissed for want of evidence.

May, 1921. Mr. E. K. DeBeck, lawyer for the Alert Bay Kwakiutls, instructed by his clients to petition Ottawa for revision of section 149 of the Indian Act.

December 9, 1921. Five Indians charged with potlatching at Kingcome Inlet, October 15, 1921; convicted.

[10]This summary statement is not based upon exhaustive examination of court records and is therefore undoubtedly somewhat incomplete. It has been compiled from the statements of William Halliday in *Potlatch and Totem*, newspaper reports and comments, notes in the file of Dr. Marius Barbeau, anthropologist then in Mines and Resources Branch, Ottawa, and several entries in the Ottawa Potlatch File, as well as *Hansard.*

December 15, 1921. Circular letter from Ottawa to all agents, regarding the increase in potlatching. Instructions reinstated.

January 20, 1922. Appeal of five Kwakiutl Indians convicted December 9 heard before Chief Justice Hunter of the Supreme Court of British Columbia; appeal dismissed.

January, 22, 1922. Five Indians arrive at Oakalla Penitentiary.

February 16, 1922. Vancouver barrister wrote to Ottawa regarding revision of section 149; stated belief of Indians in the imminent revision of the section.

March, first week, 1922. Twenty-nine Kwakiutls tried; seventeen found guilty; sentence delayed until March 31, to provide defendants with an opportunity to accept or reject the plan of R. W. Ellis, a barrister, namely to sign an agreement for no more potlatching and to surrender potlatching paraphernalia, to be paid for by the National Museum. Ottawa.

March 4, 1922. Mr. DeBeck sent to Ottawa three formal petitions protesting against section 149; these were signed by almost all older members of the Kwakiutl group.

March 13, 1922. Petition from seventy Cloyoquot (west central coast of Vancouver Island; not Kwakiutl) Indians asking for continuance of potlatch.

March 31, 1922. Indians, tried earlier in the month, sentenced: one given six months, second offence; twelve given two months; four given suspended sentence, two for taking only minor roles, two for signing agreement.

April 19, 1922. Mrs. Dick Mountain and Billy Moon charged with potlatching; both guilty. Mrs. Mountain given suspended sentence; Moon given two months at Oakalla.

April 28, 1922. Questions in the House of Commons about Alert Bay cases by Mr. Leon Ladner, a member from British Columbia.

April 29, 1922. Questions of Mr. Ladner replied to by Minister of Interior who reported that there were fifty convictions and at that time four were serving sentences, of whom three were being considered for parole by the Department of Justice.

May 10, 1922. A letter to Ottawa by Mr. James A. Teit, an early resident of British Columbia, assistant to Franz Boas, and special agent of the Allied Tribes of British Columbia referred to section 149 as "standing injustice."

May 11, 1922. Mr. Leon Ladner, M.P., asked Indian Affairs for a change in section 149.

May 19, 1922. Amos Dawson charged with perjury in trial of January,

1921; sentenced to three months in Oakalla; Bob Harris sentenced to four months in Oakalla for perjury in trial of January, 1921.

June 19, 1922. Debate in the House of Commons.

July, 1922. The Deputy Superintendent-General of Indian Affairs visited Vancouver and interviewed Indians and others.

August, 1922. Potlatch question discussed at the annual meeting of Allied Indian Tribes; special committee appointed. Mr. Andrew Paull, of the Squamish band, and Mr. James A. Teit constituted the committee.

August 30, 1922. Franz Boas lectured before the National Historical Society and discussed the potlatch; reported in *Victoria Colonist.*

February, 16, 1923. Formal petition received in Ottawa for either a revision of section 149 or appointment of an investigating committee. Petition claimed that prosecutions were being carried on only at Alert Bay while there was still potlatching in other agencies; sentences were harsh treatment as conviction required jail sentence.

August 13, 1923. Vancouver Daily Province reported three of the ten of the Nakwato band, of Blunden Harbor, released from Oakalla because of clerical error. Convictions reported by Halliday in *Potlatch and Totem* but date unascertained.

August 30, 1923. Letter of Mr. Andrew Paull to Mr. Stewart, Superintendent-General of Indian Affairs, setting down the major points of Mr. Stewart's July interview with Indians.

May 14, 1923. Inventory and evaluation by Dr. E. Sapir of the potlatch paraphernalia surrendered and shipped to Ottawa; value: $1,415.

October 31, 1924. Law firm of Dickie and DeBeck sued Alert Bay Indians in Supreme Court of British Columbia for non-payment for professional services rendered; total unpaid: $3,370.57.

May 22, 1925. Vancouver Daily Province editorial, "The Potlatch Question."

In discussing the trials of 1922 in *Potlatch and Totem*, Halliday stated that potlatches were assuming greater and greater proportions, and appraised the significance of the trials and convictions listed above:

Since that time the potlatch has been gradually dying away, and in no instance has it been done openly. Under the statute it has to be proved that it is an Indian festival, dance, or ceremony, and also it must be proved that at this Indian festival, dance, or ceremony the giving away of money, goods, or articles of any sort formed a part or was a feature. There have been a number of instances where people who felt they must give away have done it surreptitiously. They would travel in a boat to the village where they felt it was incumbent on them to give something away, and, while there, call the people individually to the boat and give them what they intended. This method, of course, freed them from any prosecution, as there was neither ceremony, dance, nor festival in connection with it; but on the other hand, . . . the affair would fall very flat. (p. 194)

Halliday claimed further that the prosecutions were quite timely as many of the younger men, "conscious of the evils of the system," wanted to break away from it; but they were held by the "older men," who, in fact, "had even gone so far as to warn them that if they carried out their intention they would be obliged to sever all connections with the Indians living on the reserves. At Alert Bay, in 1946, the late Mrs. Stephen Cook reported to the writer that "my sons have been chased from the fishing grounds because they would not potlatch." In the local politics of the villages, the differences between the "younger" and the "older" appears to be one of the recurring ways in which the issue was drawn. Quite naturally the enforcement of the act and the trials supported the intentions of the "younger men."

Another statement of Mr. Halliday's in the same context may be noted here. Althought it was public policy to prohibit the potlatch, and Ottawa insisted upon enforcement, yet it was also the policy to be lenient, as "it was thought that education and missionary training amongst the Indians would so open their minds to the folly of the custom that the custom itself would die a natural death without any legal prosecutions having to be taken to compel it." (p. 188) The leniency of the policy may be observed in the number of suspended sentences and of agreements whereby the Indians promised to give up potlatching and to surrender their paraphernalia.

There are some data available for appraising the prediction of Mr. Halliday that "the potlatch has been gradually dying away," but not for his assertion that "it has not been done openly." There are in fact some data which would tend to contradict this statement. For example, a number of anthropologists in personal conversation have reported potlatches; several informants have told the writer of potlatches such as the one held in the Alert Bay area in the spring of 1950, at which it is claimed $15,000 changed hands. But then Mr. Halliday at only one agency was not in a position to judge the trends within other tribal groups of the Northwest Coast.

This particular phase of enforcement was, as the brief calendar of events suggests, marked by the extensive use of lawyers by the Indians. It was of course necessary to use defence lawyers; but Mr. E. K. DeBeck had lived in Alert Bay while his father was an Indian agent there, and knowing something of Indian languages and customs, he served as an informal adviser as well as a barrister in court for the Indians. There is even evidence that the lawyers advised the Indians how to potlatch without risking a charge of potlatching as defined by the Indian Act. One plan became known as "disjointing the potlatch," a system whereby debts and gifts would be made six months after the meeting.[11] This interest of the lawyers, as professional specialists in the ways of the law, apparently gave rise to the belief among the Indians that the law would be amended. But in fact, except for an effort in 1936 to make the law more stringent, nothing was done until Ottawa omitted it from the new legislation of 1950, proclaimed September 4, 1951.

In 1922 when a member of Parliament, Mr. Ladner, had raised questions on the floor of the House of Commons regarding the Alert Bay Cases, public policy for the first time became subjected to the scrutiny of locally elected representatives, and not only to the mere formalities of Opposition questions. As far as the potlatch is concerned, the Indians, although wards of Ottawa, now had informal representation in Parliament.

It will be noted that Dr. Boas was listed as having given a speech to the National Historical Society, August 30, 1922. Now for the first time in the history of the controversy, a cultural anthropologist was officially consulted. Indian Affairs at Ottawa engaged Dr. Marius Barbeau, then of the Department of Mines and Resources, Anthropology Section, to prepare a formal description of the potlatch. This statement was of course designed only for the advice of the Deputy Superintendent-General and the responsible cabinet minister. In some way information regarding work on such a report got into circulation; it was said by Mr. DeBeck and Mr. Andrew Paull that the "Anthro-

[11]For example, the potlatch of Dan Cranmer, just before Christmas, 1921, was referred to by Mr. Cranmer and his associates as "The Christmas Tree Potlatch," so he informed the author in 1946. Mr. Cranmer was involved in the Alert Bay trials of 1922. In the listing of "potlatch goods" turned in to the National Museum, Dr. E. Sapir, in writing to Dr. D. C. Scott, Deputy Superintendent-General of Indian Affairs, on May 14, 1923, includes the items and their value which were turned in by Mr. Cranmer. Mr. Cranmer informed the writer that he had made two trips to Columbia University in order to record for Franz Boas potlatch speeches and songs of a chief. He was known among the Kwakiutl as a creator of songs and held what Canadians would call copyrights on them.

For readers who are interested in acculturation, Moeran in *McCullagh of Aiyansh*, pp. 59–60, reports Mr. McCullagh as stating that "the winter I returned to England [1890] they made a clay figure, covered it with dough, and ate that as a substitute for flesh." This is some of the behaviour which was supposed to have been outlawed by the "potlatch law" in 1884.

pological Society" was making a study and a report. As far as it can be determined there was no such society, and it may be inferred that the Barbeau Report was what Mr. Ladner had in mind when he placed questions in the House, including one about this "society."[12] In addition to Drs. Boas and Barbeau, James A. Teit, who served as an adviser to the Indians, became involved in activities dealing with public policy. Thus legal experts, the lawyers and parliamentarians, and experts on cultural systems appeared as important participants in the potlatch issue.

Contrary to the hopes of many Indians, and possibly without their awareness of it, the process of acculturation was changing the nature of the potlatch. But this was not the crucial point for the traditionalists. The significant point then and today was and is that of maintaining an Indian way of life as compared with a white way of life. There are almost no sources of data to use for describing or analyzing another important group of Indians—those who wished to have the law repealed so that they could follow without interference what they thought to be the Indian way of life. Charles Nowell, raised in the tradition of potlatching and on several occasions indicted for potlatching, was very active in attempting to have the law changed; he was discussed by Helen Codere in *Fighting with Property*: "Charles Nowell in his later years remains serenely confident of the propriety and glory of the system he entered as a young man. He and many others, as the agency reports reveal, felt that a law as unjust and uninformed as the Indian Act would surely be repealed, and they acted accordingly."

About the time that Charles Nowell was born, Franz Boas did his first field work on the Northwest Coast, among the Kwakiutl. It is characteristic of human relations that the stranger, the unknown person, must validate himself; this is particularly true if the stranger is a social scientist interested in describing social relations and organization as was Franz Boas. And this validation is even more necessary if a person is a member of a majority group. Hence, Codere quotes in the same context what Boas published in 1896 as part of his first experiences as an ethnographer among the Kwakiutl. They said to him:

We want to know whether you have come to stop our dances and feasts, as the missionaries and agents who live among our neighbors try to do. We

---

[12]The first writing of Dr. Barbeau on the potlatch is found in "The Totemic System of the North Western Indian Tribes of North America," unpublished thesis presented at Oxford University. For the Ladner discussion with Minister of Interior Stewart, see House of Commons, *Debates*, June 19, 1922, pp. 3191–2. Mr. Ladner wanted to know if the "Society has made a report favourable to the lessening of these restrictions and giving back to the Indians some of their rights?"

do not want anybody here who will interfere with our customs. We were told that a man-of-war would come if we should continue to do as our grandfathers and great-grandfathers have done. But we do not mind such words. Is this the white man's land? We are told it is the Queen's land; but no! it is mine! Where was the Queen when our God gave the land to my grandfather and told him, "This will be thine"? My father owned the land and was a mighty chief; now it is mine. And when your man-of-war comes let him destroy our houses. Do you see yon woods? Do you see yon trees? We shall cut them down and build new houses and live as our fathers did. We will dance when our laws command us to dance, we will feast when our hearts desire to feast. Do we ask the white man, "Do as the Indian does?" No, we do not. Why then do you ask us, "Do as the white man does?" It is a strict law that bids us dance. It is a strict law that bids us distribute our property among our friends and neighbors. It is a good law. Let the white man observe his law, we shall observe ours. And now, if you are come to forbid us to dance, begone, if not, you will be welcome to us. (p. 89)

It is quite obvious that Boas underwent the trial in a more than satisfactory manner, for he worked among the Kwakiutl on later occasions and found a number of them to be of invaluable assistance.

He emerged with the honor of the name, Heiltsakuls or "The one who says the right things." He owed this honor, and undoubtedly the success of his work to his response to the absolutely unequivocal and uncompromising statement of the Kwakiutl position as expressed by one of their chiefs in this council. . . .

The high level of excitement and activity evident in the period of the prosecutions was apparently not maintained. Essentially what happened at this time was a distinct shift in tactics on the part of the Indians wanting to perpetuate the potlatch system and a loss of interest by the other parties. During the rest of his term as agent at Alert Bay, Mr. Halliday apparently pressed no other cases. The experience of the trials demonstrated the critical position of the agent in his efforts to enforce section 149. As the active guardian of the Indians, the agent was a prosecutor of a group, although as a Canadian he thought he was prosecuting individuals—the basis on which the legal system operated. Furthermore, if the agent failed to secure convictions, he was looked upon by Ottawa as lacking discretion and by the Indians as a failure as well as being a prosecutor. In addition, the trials were costly, especially during the period that potlatching was an indictable offence. For the trials of 1922 Crown prosecutors had to be paid, and it cost the federal government $1,415.50 to reimburse the owners of potlatching paraphernalia. The efforts at enforcement must have absorbed an unusual amount of time and energy from the routine administrative work of the whole agency; in fact, the law could not be strictly enforced without a significant increase in the agency's costs of operation. Although Ottawa could never admit an unwillingness to expend funds for potlatch cases, yet the assumption was that potlatching would pass away, and it was only sensible to ask why funds should be spent for prosecutions.

But the Indians considered the potlatch prosecutions from an entirely different position. The fact that Dickie and DeBeck had to sue the Indians for legal fees suggests several attitudes on the part of the Indians. The law firm sued individual Indians, but the whole group was involved. They had paid some $900 to the lawyers, and in the 1920's this was undoubtedly a large sum of money for Indians. In spite of the lawyers, the Indians went to jail and the statute was not changed. Then, too, many Indians had been discommoded and there were no allowances for witness fees or expenses. Perhaps even more central to the Indian interests was the discovery of a way to potlatch in spite of the law. It could be done through private potlatches[13] and by disjointing the potlatch. Furthermore the geographic features of the area aided surreptitious potlatching; it need not be strictly private. It was easy for the agent at Alert Bay to look out over the moorage and count the fishing boats at home during off-season periods; but it was another matter for him or the provincial or federal police to arrive at Village Island, Turnour Island or Kingcome Inlet, and secure evidence of potlatching. A lookout could give warning too easily. Whereas earlier potlatchers travelled only in canoes, and storms did create problems, the increased use of the gasoline engine provided easier access to isolated villages. And finally an Indian's orientation towards time is basically different from that of the white man; they could wait, and although the adaptations of the potlatch were not entirely satisfactory, they were adequate substitutes for the time being.

[13]Codere quotes Charles Nowell from Ford, *Smoke from Their Fires*: "Beatrice was my next oldest daughter. She married Jimmy Wadhams from the Tlowitsis. He came here with his near relatives to give me the money. All came to my house. They gave me $450 to marry my daughter and $100 to Big Sam who is one of my wife's relatives. When Jimmy Wadhams want that to be paid back, I and those three will work together and pay him. The next day they went to the church and got married. Jimmy is waiting for the time when the Indian Act is amended—for the Indian Agents are promising all the time that it will be amended—so the potlatch and payment can be done in the right way. . . . I gave a potlatch at her first monthly too. This was done privately—not publicly like Jane's. My wife gave the potlatch for my third daughter, Agnes, when she first got the monthly. That was done privately too. When Violet got her monthly, her mother also gave one for her that was done privately. That was done by sending people out to go around with money. One is carrying the money, and one is carrying a book where the names are written and how much is coming to them, and the one who is carrying the book tells the other how much is to be given." *Fighting with Property*, p. 88. Quoted with permission of the author.

One more factor entered into the change in the tactics of the Indian traditionalists. For reasons we are unable to determine, it appears that in the 1920's a split occurred among the missionaries regarding the potlatch and public policy. Mr. Duncan and those who followed for decades represented for all denominations, especially the Protestant ones, the explosion of missionaries into the benighted world of heathenism. But shortly after the turn of the century, missions were being "rethought." Although the exact date cannot be specified when this new orientation impinged upon the missionaries of British Columbia, the Indians sensed the split and turned their attention from the lawyers to the "new" missionaries. And surprisingly enough some missionaries began to see the "injustice" of the Potlatch Law.

For many years the Church Missionary Society and the United Church of Canada have used fairly adequate boats for their superintendents to travel from one landing to another or between towns. In fact, these boats have been more than a means of travel, for they carried an ordained minister-missionary who was also licensed as a boat captain. Life along the Northwest Coast is rugged, and these boats have carried medical aid and rendered many services for Indian and white alike. As visitors to many sections, the missionaries and superintendents on these boats undoubtedly had opportunities to gather much information about Indian attitudes toward the Potlatch Law. The churches had taken an active interest in the passage of the law, and they had representatives at many conferences with Indians about the modification or repeal of the law.

When Rev. John Antle was the missionary captain of the M.S. *Columbia,* Superintendent Green went with him on an inspection trip and prepared a report dealing with the northern half of the mission area under his jurisdiction. His comments on the potlatch reveal a new attitude on the part of some missionaries.

I visited Chief Johnnie Scow, an old Tillicum of mine. I found him well but unhappy about the arbitrary way in which one of their old tribal customs, the Potlatch, has been swept away. He admits that the Indians could do without some things in the Potlatch, but as it was the back bone of the social life of the Indians, they are left without joy or pleasure. When all is said and done, the Indian has borne with a great deal of patience an outrageous attack upon his liberty, scarcely equalled in the annals of British colonialism. The Indian is asking for a modification of the law which will allow him to use such of his old customs which are not contrary to what we call our Civilization, and I am on the side of the Indian and will do my best to see that he gets what he is asking for.

Superintendent Green's article was printed in the October, 1931, issue of the *Log of the Columbia,* published in Vancouver, a monthly report to the communicants of the Anglican Church on Pacific Coast mission problems and missionary activites which circulates to thousands of Canadians. Five months after Green's statement appeared, one Rene Duncan wrote, for the *Log*, a fairly long article: "The Potlatch: A Plea for the Modification of the Law Prohibiting Potlatches." But between the statement of Superintendent Green in October and the article by Duncan in February the explanation below appeared:

Not often in the history of missionary work in this district have we had the Bishop of the Diocese meeting the representatives of the Indians in a friendly talk about their old tribal customs which, as we mentioned in this paper some time ago, had been swept away by the law "at one fell swoop."

Perhaps if there had been more heart to heart talks of this kind in the past, there would not be so many non-Christian Indians in the Quagutl tribes as there are at the present time. Of course the Bishop was accused by the goody ones of favoring the Potlatch, as they have also accused me, which shows how wide they are of the mark. Neither Bishop Schofield nor myself want to see the Potlatch back again as it used to be, but we both realize that intolerance and the use of the big stick never yet advanced the cause of Christ, nor helped to spread the message. . . .

The Potlatch would pass away in time anyway and no one knows this better than the Indians, but why outrage and embitter a people whose only crime is to love their own people. . . .

And so the Bishop met the Indians with a Christian tolerance and sympathy which will, I believe, do much to sooth and heal the wounded and embittered spirits of a people, who deserve of the White man, who is fast absorbing the country which was once all theirs, at least a square deal.[14]

The significance of this change in the missionaries' point of view was not to become clear for another ten years.

Meanwhile, in the parliamentary session of 1936, the House of Commons was notified that the government intended to tighten up on the strictures of section 140 of the Indian Act, formerly designated as 149. The Government did not proceed with the amendment, "owing almost entirely to the efforts of the honourable member for Comox-Alberni (Mr. Neill)," but the effort at amendment was noted as far east as Montreal where the *Gazette*, on February 26, 1936, ran an editorial stressing the "socialistic features" of the potlatch and comparing it with cocktail parties of the white man. Wide press coverage was given to those opposed to increasing the strictures. If the single editorial is representative, the year 1936 when the amendment was proposed marked the beginning of a significant trend in public opinion

[14]*Log of the Columbia*, November, 1931, possibly written by the editor, Rev. John Antle.

which later supported the post-war changes in administrative policy and the unparalleled increases in the annual budget for Indian Affairs. Church officials played a central role in this reappraisal of the problems of the Indians and of the legislation which concerned their welfare. But still, when the Synod of the Anglican Church in British Columbia convened in 1935, Anglican opinion had not shifted sufficiently for its Committee Considering the Indian Potlatch to recommend amendment or repeal of the law. It was admitted that the early missionaries might have assumed a "harmful attitude" by classifying everything as either Christian or heathen. Thus the potlatch, not being the former, automatically became the latter.

Before Mr. Neill became a member of the House of Commons, he had served as an Indian agent in British Columbia. Along with Mr. Ladner, he became the informal political representative of the unenfranchised coastal Indians. Since he had, as publicly acknowledged, been the person chiefly responsible for maintaining the status quo when revision of the potlatch legislation was considered, the Indians quite naturally turned to him. It was his point of view, later expressed in the House, that Canadians were trying "to make imitation white men out of them instead of Christian Indians." The Indians were appealing through him for permission to hold potlatches, but this permission could not be and was not granted. Nevertheless, there is evidence that the Indians continued to potlatch; Codere, for example, stated that a 33,000 blanket potlach took place in 1933.[15] Yet it was the belief of responsible officials that potlatching was confined chiefly to one agency, Alert Bay.

Although potlatching seemed to be continuing, officials were also aware that the statute could not be enforced phrased as it was. For example, there was not only the provision of the first paragraph which dealt with the celebrating of an Indian festival, dance, or other ceremony and the giving of gifts, but there was also paragraph three which prohibited the Indians from participating in such affairs on reserves other than their own. With respect to the first, the trial cases for some decades had proved ineffective: potlatching still occurred and some of the Indians were applying pressure for permission to carry on their traditional customs. And it was impossible to prevent the Indians from travelling from reserve to reserve, not only because of the geography of the coast but also because the Indians were con-

[15]It is the suspicion of the author that its more traditional and vigorous forms will, even today, be found on the west coast of Vancouver Island among the Nootka.

tinually moving to new places of residence. Also, the Indians in any one band of an agency might be living, quite properly, in several different places. Alert Bay was chiefly for the Nimpkish at first, but later Indians from Kingcome Inlet, Fort Rupert, Village Island, and Turnour Island were living there.[16] Thus any Indian agent who had to place charges and plan prosecutions was placed in a more difficult position. Moreover, he had lost the support of public opinion; the federal administration and the cabinet did not see fit to revise the statute so that it could be enforced; and at least one church was no longer fully in support of continued efforts to suppress Indian customs by police and legal action, for as the extracts from the *Log of Columbia* stated, the Indians were embittered and there were not very many active Christians, at least within the Kwawkewlth agency.

The final debate on the potlatch issue in Parliament occurred in the session of 1938. Mr. Taylor, the member from Nanaimo, presented a very long case against "the heathen custom." The central issue he chose to emphasize was the use of the potlatch in celebrating Indian marriages; "marriages could be solemnized for Christian members of Christian churches, but do not let us perpetuate this evil of the potlatch, as it is now being perpetuated."[17] Mr. Taylor was answered by Mr. Neill who pointed out that Mr. Taylor was investigating affairs in a district which he did not represent and that he was presenting the old point of view, supported by quotations from a book of 1876 and by correspondence with an elderly, retired missionary. Mr. Neill then quoted from a letter he had received from a missionary:

The mistake we have been making is in trying to make of the Indian what he was never intended to be—a white man. The church by adopting compulsory measures, may succeed in suppressing the potlatch but she will never win the Indian.

He will respond, as he has always done, to sound leadership, wise counsel, and above all consistent example.

The two methods were summarized by Mr. Neill, as reported in the *Debates* of the House: "The policeman with his revolver in his hand saying, you shall not do that, or the kindly moral suasion of the church,

[16]When the writer was in Alert Bay in 1946, Indian informants claimed that the agent had divided the reserve into two major sections: the area for "potlatchers" to live and the area for "non-potlatchers." This was not confirmed. The more likely explanation is that more residential area had to be opened up because of Indians wanting to take up residence there. This movement is of course an indication that Indians are becoming more fully integrated into the new economic system, especially logging and commercial fishing.

[17]House of Commons, *Debates*, June 13, 1938, pp. 3806–11.

leading the Indian step by step." Parliamentary records do not report any further discussion of the potlatch. In the spring of 1940, responsible officials of the government and the Anglican Church held a meeting with various Indian representatives regarding modification of the potlatch which by then had changed significantly. But this meeting at Kingcome Inlet, in the Kwawkewlth Agency, did not bring any changes in the Potlatch Law. The dilemma of the government was unchanged, and the dilemma of the churches, so aptly described in the missionary's letter above, remained.

It was true that the churches had failed, if they meant by making a white man out of the Indian the complete and effective imposition and acceptance of Anglo-Saxon morality and Christian theological principles. But no one could specify exactly what a Christian Indian was in his moral attributes. For the churches, marriage is a sacrament, and as in the days of Mr. Duncan and his conflict with the Church of England over matters of ecclesiasticism, Indian marriages continue to be an issue among churchmen. Ceremonial cannibalism appeared to be gone, as were self-torture and the cutting of the flesh of animals. But the making of marriages in a somewhat traditional manner was important to the Indians, and many of them were known to have both the traditional Indian and the church ceremonies. When the writer was in the Alert Bay area in 1946, a Kwakiutl church wedding was held. To the observer it appeared to be the same as any other Canadian Christian wedding. But informants claimed that it was merely a "show for the white man." The "real wedding" took place earlier. No effort was made to confirm this claim but it is heard often from white people who "know the Indians."

Seven years later thousands of pages of reports on the Indians were published as *Proceedings and Evidence* of the Joint Committee of the Senate and the House of Commons, and in those many pages, recorded between 1947 and 1949, not a word is said about the potlatch. The Potlatch Law was simply omitted from the new legislation, and efforts to legislate that kind of morality were at an end. The whole potlatch issue just disappeared.

Peaceful Penetration and Enforced Acculturation

It was inevitable with settlement developing the way it did that the Indian social system would be placed under considerable strain. The technological change consequent to settlement has been for them as well as non-Indians a revolutionary one. The whole structure of their lives had changed—their occupations, their housing, their diet, clothing, and prospects for health, their places of residence, their education needs. In fact it has made it possible, for those who wish, to cease being Indians, that is, to get away from legal Indian status.

Enforced acculturation, and by this it is clear that statutory law with police action and legal prosecution was involved, was not conceived as a means of facilitating the development of a new social organization to fit the technological change which had occurred. It was conceived in terms of a collaboration between Church and State for the administration of wardship. Not only was wardship to protect the Indians but it was to protect the non-Indians; and with Indians who were ceremonial cannibals, who practiced the blood-feud, who wasted time, who destroyed property, and who did not recognize the legal and religious contractual scheme of European marriage-making, it was necessary at least to try to substitute an Indian system of morality for the religious and secular forms of the Protestant Ethic in particular and Christian morality in general. Although there is no way by which we can compare the intensity of Canadian attitudes toward cannibalism, blood-feuds, the destruction of property, and a rhythm of life in which time seemed to be unoccupied, it is probably safe to say that Canadians, both English and French, felt Indian procedures to be highly repugnant. The mores of the Canadian system define property quite differently, even if there are tombstones for the dead, debutante and cocktail parties, and wealthy people who seem to be on continuous vacation.

Strictly legal procedures were used, although it was not clear whether the offence should be summary or indictable, both of which were tried. Furthermore, there was the policy of leniency—suspended sentences, paroles, the long periods of non-enforcement, and so on. As public opinion changed the law could not be made more stringent, and due to the inimitable political sense of Mr. Mackenzie King, it was simply left out of the 1951 revision. Whereas Sir John A. Macdonald had started with unbounded faith and hope for subduing the Indians, Mr. King and his responsible officers felt that the public policy in this matter had gone far enough. Perhaps it is a principle of Anglo-Saxons that when a law cannot be enforced even after revision, then remove it; that is what some of the better-informed Canadians thought about the Potlatch Law.

It is true that the Indian learned something from efforts at enforced acculturation. In attempting to suppress the potlatch, the Canadian government through its agents and by collaboration with Christian denominations was unable to provide a satisfactory substitute, or as anthropologists term it, a functional equivalent for the potlatch. The system of wardship and the legal procedures as experienced by the accused Indians and by the surreptitious and private potlatchers could bring about no satisfactory redress in grievances for the Indians. The goals of the two groups were far apart, and justice was administered from the Canadian rather than from the Indian point of view. Enforced acculturation resulted in a schism among the Indians, dividing them into two categories: potlatchers and non-potlatchers. In the first category were the traditionalists, people who were said to be the creditors, and individuals who were looked upon as backward and non-progressive, and in some instances, as drunkards and ne'er-do-wells. In spite of lenient enforcement across the generations, the public policy in maintaining the Potlatch Law came to be considered a form of persecution rather than of prosecution; the contrast conception of white-Indian became a working orientation for all Indians as a result of their differential treatment in employment, income, the opportunities for acquiring capital and credit, and their use of natural resources for themselves and commercial development. Thus the Potlatch Law became a major factor in the emergence of a sense of injustice and a knowledge of what Indian status means in the contemporary social organization of British Columbia. In reaction, a sense of unity, of being Indian, emerged among those groups which found it possible to maintain vitality and continuity in their changing social system. The contemporary Indian and his conception of continuity points to the larger social context, unkown to the white man, within which an Indian, descended from the old Northwest Culture system, lives today. In what way the potlatch has been culturally transmitted but changed by acculturation we do not know, for as Justice Holmes wrote in one of his decisions, "A word is not a crystal, transparent and unchanged; it is the skin of a living thought and may vary greatly in color and content according to the circumstances and the time in which it is used."[18]

[18]Quoted by John F. Harding, "Libel and Right of Privacy Problems Involved in the Publication of National Magazines," *Conference Series No. 10*, p. 44.

4. The Land Title Question

WHEN PARLIAMENT passed the Potlatch Law in 1884, there were about 17,765 Indians in the coastal region directly affected by it. The Indian population of the province was declining at the time, and it continued to decline until 1929 when it reached its lowest point—an estimated 12,366 in that part of the province. In 1938, the year that Parliament directed its attention to the potlatch issue for the last time, the population trend had just been reversed, and by 1939 the Indian population had increased to 13,303. The Southern Kwakiutl group, of the central Coast region, though only a relatively small portion of the total Indian population, provided the leaders who mobilized and sustained the opposition to the law and its enforcement. Figures for 1917 (the closest year to the first arrest in the Alert Bay trials, 1914–22, for which there are available figures) show an estimated 1,890 in the total Kwakiutl population, and by 1929, the next year for which figures are available, there were only 1,088 in the Southern group.[1] Although the Southern Kwakiutls were the focus of the prosecutions between 1914 and 1922, the Potlatch Law controversy became, for all coastal Indians, a memorable experience. It is reported by Hawthorn and his associates that "a number of current [1958] beliefs and attitudes had their origin in the long struggle around this institution [the potlatch] and have survived today with something of a life of their own."[2] What these beliefs and attitudes are, they do not specify. The evidence suggests, however, that particular experiences during the potlatch issue developed a general sense of injustice. Even the missionaries had recognized that the potlatch was central to the social organization of the Indians. The Indians came to consider the missionaries' efforts to eliminate this basic institution along with court and police actions, as an unjust denial of the Indian past. William Scow, one of the Kwakiutl potlatchers convicted in 1922, now Chief Scow and several times president of the Native Brotherhood of British Columbia, is considered to be one of the outstanding Indian

[1]The best population statistics for Indians in the whole province have been prepared by Wilson Duff and published in Hawthorn, Belshaw, and Jamieson, *Indians of British Columbia*, chapter III.

[2]Hawthorn, *et al.*, p. 38.

leaders in all Canada; he expressed the Indian view when speaking to Mr. R. A. Hoey, then Deputy Superintendent-General of Indian Affairs, that "when you took the potlatch away from us, you gave us nothing to take its place." Chief Scow's statement means that the whites were unable to create a substitute institution which would continue the past and provide a basis for the anticipation of the future as did the potlatch.

The Potlatch Law experiences were not the sole factor responsible for developing the Indians' sense of injustice; there were many others also related to the settlement process. One gains some notion of the Indians' feelings resulting from the European invasion, the conflict, and the subordination as well as the cultural change, in this letter of Chief Billy Assu, a Kwakiutl of the Cape Mudge band and a defendant in the 1922 potlatch trials.

Editor "Fisherman"
DEAR SIR:

In reply to the letter that was published "You have the Floor," October 3, as an Indian Chief, 75 years old who has lived all through the changes that our people have had since the coming of the white man, I would like to reply.

I would like to say first of all that the letter is just one example of what is always being thrown at us. Most of it is said because the writer does not know anything about it.

Then about Indian health. . . . I remember when there were 75,000 Indians in B.C. Now there are a little over 25,000. What has happened to the old people? Diseases we never had before were brought here. My father went north to visit the people in the villages around Alert Bay and could hardly land because of the dead bodies lying all around from smallpox. This was long ago and the first time we knew that disease. There are many other diseases the white men gave us too that we never had before. At our meetings I used to see all the old people around, half and half. I saw my grandparents and my grandfather's mother. The young boys today don't often see their grandparents. I am the only one of my generation left here now. White man's whiskey and diseases have done the rest. At one time, maybe 40 years ago, I had lots of trouble to keep the white bootleggers away from my people.

One other thing that this man says that is all wrong is about our being able to "take liberties with the law." Such as spearing, netting, and trapping spawning fish. If we were to do any of these things, including shooting game out of season, we would soon be arrested. There have been many arrests for such things in B.C. One of the men here went to fish offices for permit to fish in the river to cure for winter for his family. He got a permit for only 50 fish. Not much for a large family.

He talks about the filth of our communities. I wonder if he has visited many reserves. We can say that our Reserve and homes are as clean as any white homes in B.C. There are some who do not come right up to the mark but that is true with white people too. We do not judge everybody by that few.

He talks about us having too many rights for conquered people. There was no trouble or bloodshed when the white people came. There could have been but we made treaties instead of fighting because we did not want to make any trouble. When the white people first came there was a law in Victoria that when we needed cedar for canoes or fish or anything like that we could take it without trouble. Queen Victoria also said that if they wanted land on the Reserve they had to buy it, not just take it. Now it is not like that.

One thing about income tax and so on. Why should we pay taxes in so that the white people can keep members in Ottawa? We have no vote, we have no member in Ottawa to speak for us and to help us.

At the first time when God gave land to the people, he gave some to the English, French, Japanese, Chinese, Indians, too. Now the white people change God's work and take our place from us and think we have no place or anything.

When we had this country there was lots of timber, lots of fish, lots of gold. Then companies came along and took much of this away and they paid money to the government for royalties. That is what the government pays to us as relief ($4.00) per month and for the few other things they buy for us. They give $30.00 a month to the white people and not from their own money. We have no widows pension or anything like that. There are no old women and old men's homes for us, yet we pay taxes to keep them up for others. That's why my people kick about the tax. If I ask for a road from our place to the government road we don't get it. I have seen where a road is put in for two white people living a little ways off and a wharf for just a few. We can't get government jobs. These are the reasons we kick about taxes everywhere we go. . . .[3]

Unavoidably of course, the policies of the federal and provincial governments relating to land and reserves involved displacement and resettlement for the Indian. The Indians of today manifest feelings of suspicion and distrust not only about the (to them) unwarranted negation of their traditions but also about the reserve system. This reserve "psychosis" a term first employed by John Dewey and used again in the same sense by Kenneth Burke in *Permanence and Change* (footnote 67) refers to a particular frame of mind, a rigidly integrated complex of attitudes which makes the Indians over-defensive about the management of their reserves and resources and about their rights in relation to the reserves. The reserve psychosis was a product of many actions. As in the case of the potlatch, general social unrest gradually became focused around a claim to the ownership of the whole province, and the protest grew from a simple expression of

[3]From the typescript made available by Mr. Moore, a missionary at Cape Mudge, in June, 1946.

belief to a complex legal case. Hawthorn reports that there is a contemporary "aftermath of the potlatch." This apt phrase could be even more readily applied to the consequences of the land title question.

It has been established by several historical studies that in British Columbia the land policy of the Imperial government effectively restrained the actions of the colonials and their local officials. When this restraint was removed by Confederation, which British Columbia joined in 1871, the progress of settlement and the change in policy created the conditions for a protest over the land title and agitation continued for more than fifty years. Both the federal and provincial governments were deeply involved and the formal settlement left the Indians with a feeling of defeat. This, in conjunction with the trade union movement, gave rise to the Native Brotherhood of British Columbia. The middle and older generations still harbour their resentment and it may continue as part of the Indian personality in British Columbia and of the pattern of interactions between whites and Indians.

THE REVERSAL OF IMPERIAL POLICY

Canada, upon becoming a dominion, inherited the Imperial policy with respect to the Indian title to the land. The basic point about this inheritance was the fact that as long as the British were in control in North America, they never dispossessed the Indians of their land. In a report prepared for the Department of Indian Affairs regarding the land title, Mr. MacInnes, a barrister of British Columbia, pointed out six main reasons for that policy, and in so doing, he contrasted it with policy in Mexico, Central America, and Peru. (1) The northern Indians could resist aggression more effectively than could the Peruvians and Mexicans as they were warriors. (2) There were so few Indians in that vast area that the needs of the colonists could be fulfilled without entirely displacing the Indians. (3) The Indians did not possess any of the coveted precious metals or stones that the Mexicans and Peruvians had in quantity. (4) It was to the interest of the French and English to maintain conditions which facilitated the fur trade in those early days, and this involved maintaining the Indians in their lands. (5) Mr. MacInnes submits four paragraphs of historical evidence to show that the fervour for converting Indians to Christianity was related to securing areas for settlement, but it is not this motivation that continued into the decades in which the movement of agitation and protest took place in British Columbia. (6) North of Mexico there were not just one or two Indian nations, "the overthrow of which could by international law be held to vest in the conquerors the title to any vast territory."[4] After making these points, Mr. MacInnes calls attention to the fact that there was no necessity for dispossession; it was possible for the first colonists to enter into peaceful possession of sufficient land.

British imperial principles were applied in the early days in British Columbia. As the MacInnes report stated, "the Indian Title was impliedly and specifically recognized in British Columbia by the Imperial Government, the Hudson's Bay Company, and the Colonial Governments, from the very first advent of whites to that Province."[5] Two years after the organization of a colonial government for Vancouver Island in 1849, James Douglas was appointed the second governor. Under his rule, the Indians continued to be recognized and treated as the owners of the land, and in 1850, 1851, and 1852, Douglas took the first steps in purchasing land and setting aside Indian reserves. As a person who had spent his life with the Hudson's Bay Company, the governor did not find it difficult to accept Imperial policy. Even though based upon different motives, the policies of the Company and the government were essentially the same. But as a responsible public official on the frontier, Governor Douglas was faced with the necessity of facilitating peaceful penetration, and this meant maintaining security for a relatively few Europeans among a large group of hostile Indians. Mr. MacInnes claimed that the policy of granting reserves even after the administration of Governor Douglas was based upon the fear of an Indian war.[6]

At the same time that Governor Douglas was implementing Imperial policy in British Columbia, the Province of Canada was making treaties with the Indians in what is now Ontario. On September 7, 1850, the Robinson Superior Treaty was made with the Ojibway Indians of the northern shore and hinterland of Lake Superior; the area ceded to

[4]T. R. E. MacInnes, "Report on the Indian Title in Canada with Special Reference to British Columbia," House of Commons, Sessional Paper No. 47, 1914, unpublished, pp. 3–12; typescript made available through courtesy of Major D. M. MacKay, Director, Indian Affairs Branch, Department of Citizenship and Immigration. Reference to this sessional paper is henceforth by name of author MacInnes.

[5]MacInnes, p. 2.

[6]Ibid., p. 17. Later, on page 59 MacInnes quotes the somewhat different view of Commissioner Powell, made in 1874: "If there has not been an Indian war, it is not because there has been no injustice to the Indians but because the Indians have not been sufficiently united." From British Columbia Papers connected with the Indian Land Question 1850–1875, p. 153, henceforth referred to as B.C. Papers.

the Province of Canada was 16,700 square miles. Another 35,700 square miles of the northern shore and hinterland of Lake Huron was ceded in the Robinson Huron Treaty of September 9, 1850. About twelve years later, a treaty was signed between the Province of Canada and the Ottawa, Chippewa, and other Indians for all of Great Manitoulin Island except the land to be set aside as reserves. These and later treaties were looked upon as necessary for the elimination of Indian title to the land. They were a continuation of the policy followed in the treaties of 1786–1836 when the Crown signed treaties with various Chippewa and Mississagua Indians in the southwestern part of the province.

Five years after Confederation, Treaty No. 1 with the Chippewa and Swampy Cree in southern Manitoba was signed, followed eighteen days later, August 21, 1871, by Treaty No. 2 with the Chippewa and others in central and southwestern Manitoba and what is now southeastern Saskatchewan. Two years later Treaty No. 3 was signed with the Ojibway Indians in southwestern Ontario, and in 1874, Treaty No. 4 with the Indians of southern Saskatchewan. As settlement continued westward, and the government felt it necessary to settle the land title problem, treaties were signed at various intervals from 1875 to 1923. But of all the treaties signed, the only ones negotiated with the Indians of British Columbia were the Hudson's Bay purchases of 1850, 1851, and 1852 and Treaty No. 8 in 1899 covering only the Indians of northeastern British Columbia who were grouped with the Cree, Beaver, Chipewyan, and others of northern Alberta and the Northwest Territories. The Indians of coastal British Columbia, to whom payments had been made and for whom the reserves had been established in 1850, 1851, and 1852, were thus left to watch the continued expansion of the Dominion of Canada by treaty while making no further agreements of their own. Later in 1927 this was to be the peg on which the British Columbian Indians hung their legal case. In respect to this, Rev. P. R. Kelly stated at the hearings in 1927:

It is quite true that that is a matter of fact, and we do not question it for a moment, that the Indians of British Columbia have been treated as generously as other Indian tribes throughout the rest of the Dominion. But within recent years, shall I say during the past twenty-five to thirty years, Indian tribes have been curtailed in their activities. You know as well as I do, Senator Barnard, that they were a law unto themselves . . . and upon consulting advisers here and there, even as white men do, it came to the surface that their title had not been ceded.

If it had not been ceded, then in view of the fact that their ancient rights were taken away, why should not a formal recognition be made and a consideration equivalent to that conceded to other tribes of Indians in other parts of the Dominion be granted to the Indians of British Columbia? That was at the back of all this trouble. . . .[7]

At the same time they watched settlement in their homeland expand conspicuously, they experienced a reversal of policy on the part of the colonial, and later the provincial, officials in 1865 after Governor Douglas left office. Before this reversal by local action, Imperial policy was based upon a conception of the Indians as the owners of the land; tribal groups were considered to be independent nations. But the Colonial Office, although aware of the land abuses perpetrated by settlers, was quite powerless to exercise local control. Abuses had been taken note of much earlier in the Royal Proclamation of 1763, when the purchase of reserved lands from Indians by private persons was forbidden, and squatters on reserved lands were ordered "to remove themselves from such settlements."[8] This document, furthermore, looked upon the Indians as allies and instructed Governor Murray, on December 7, 1763, to "treat with the said Indians, promising and assuring them Protection and Friendship on our Part." Sir James Douglas was to follow these instructions in his turn. In a dispatch of 1859 to the Secretary of State for the Colonies, he said:

As friends and allies the Native races are capable of rendering the most valuable assistance to the Colony (This, in part, would have been military service if the "fifty-four or fight" attitude of the Americans had been maintained as regards the boundary of British Columbia.) while their enmity would entail on the settlers a greater amount of wretchedness and physical suffering, and more seriously retard the growth and material development of the Colony, than any other calamity to which, in the ordinary course of events, it would be exposed.[9]

An additional facet of the Douglas policy was that the title of the reserved lands of the Indians remained with the Crown and was inalienable. This meant that white people could not purchase the lands, and also that no single Indian could sell tribal lands. Sir James went even a step beyond this: proceeds from the land were to be used exclusively for Indian purposes.

A crucial part of the Douglas policy for establishing reserves was to

[7]Special Joint Committee of the Senate and House of Commons,*Claims*, p. 224.

[8]Five relevant paragraphs of the Proclamation are quoted in full by MacInnes, p. 29; more extensive quotations are found in *Claims*, pp. 40–2. In talking with Indians in British Columbia, the writer was impressed by the number of them who knew about the Royal Proclamation of 1763.

[9]Quoted by MacInnes, p. 43, from *B.C. Papers*. Parenthetic comment is that of Mr. MacInnes.

let the Indians fix the boundaries. In a letter to Ottawa after his retirement, Douglas stated his procedure for locating boundaries:

14th October, 1874

To this enquiry I may briefly rejoin that in laying out Indian reserves no specific number of acres was insisted upon. The principles followed in all cases was to leave the extent and selection of the lands entirely optional with the Indians who were immediately interested in the reserves; the surveying officers having instruction to meet their wishes in every particular. . . . This was done with the object of securing their natural or acquired rights. . . . It was never intended that they should be limited or restricted to a possession of ten acres of land, on the contrary we are prepared, if such had been their wish, to have made for their use more extensive grants. These latter reserves were necessarily laid out on a large scale, commensurate with the wants of these tribes.

This letter may be regarded and treated as an official communication.[10]

In view of the fact that the Secretary of State for the Colonies had given Governor Douglas a *carte blanche* for dealing with the Indians and the land problem, his decisions were in effect Imperial policy. Three years before his retirement in 1864, Governor Douglas transmitted from the House of Assembly of Vancouver Island to the Secretary a petition for three thousand pounds for the purpose of purchasing lands from the Indians. The petition, dated March 25, 1861, was denied by the Secretary although he was "fully sensible of the great importance of purchasing, without loss of time, the Native Title to the soil of Vancouver Island." It was his advice that the colony should provide the funds as "it is essential to the interests of the people of Vancouver Island . . . and trifling in the charge it would entail." According to the historical evidence, neither the colony nor the Dominion government ever took the recommended steps for settling the land title question.[11]

In the petition for funds to extinguish the native title on Vancouver Island, Sir James stated the Indian conception of title to their lands:

As the native Indian population of Vancouver Island have distinct ideas of property in land, and mutually recognize their several exclusive possessory rights in certain districts, they would not fail to regard the occupation of such portions of the Colony by white settlers unless with the full consent of the proprietary tribes as national wrongs; and the sense of injury might produce a feeling of irritation against the settlers and perhaps disaffection to the Government that would endanger the peace of the country.[12]

[10]MacInnes, p. 65.
[11]The petition and reply are published in full in *Claims*, pp. 236–8.
[12]Quoted in MacInnes, p. 45.

As much as the Governor may have recognized and respected the Indians' conception of property, about the time of his retirement from office the vagueness of this native conception or their ulterior motives (possibly those of displaced hostility), began to conflict with the settlers' eagerness for land. For example, in April, 1863, the following exchange of letters took place between Governor Douglas and the Chief Commissioner of Lands and Works, R. C. Moody:

An application has been made to me this morning by the Native inhabitants of Coquitlan River for an additional grant of land contiguous to the Indian Reserve immediately opposite Mr. Atkinson's premises.

That reserve, it appears, is so small, not exceeding 50 acres of land, as to be altogether insufficient to raise vegetables enough for their own use.

I beg that you will, therefore, immediately cause the existing reserve to be extended in conformity with the wishes of the natives, and to include therein an area so large as to remove from their minds all causes of dissatisfaction.

Notwithstanding my particular instructions to you, that in laying out Indian Reserves the wishes of the Natives themselves, with respect to boundaries, should in all cases be complied with, I hear very general complaints of the smallness of the areas set apart for their use.

I beg that you will take instant measures to inquire into such complaints, and to enlarge all the Indian Reserves between New Westminister and the mouth of the Harrison River before the contiguous lands are occupied by other persons.

Moody's reply on the following day stated:

I have the honor to acknowledge the receipt of a communication from Your Excellency, dated 27th instant, respecting an application from the Indians on the Coquitlan for an additional grant of land. . . .The reserve in question was most carefully laid out, the Indians being present, and after they had themselves marked according to their own wishes the bounds, the area was further enlarged. I resisted the appeal of the neighboring settlers, and acceded the amplest request of the Indians. . . . In every case the wishes of the Indians are carefully consulted and the bounds are widely extended beyond the limits marked out by themselves. Any statement contrary to the above, made to Your Excellency from whatsoever quarter, is absolutely without foundation. The Interests of the Indian population are scrupulously, I may say jealously regarded by myself and every officer and man under my command. . . . Several full reserves have already been made, but I hear incidentally that there are other Indian villages and potato grounds with the sites of which Lands and Works Department is not acquainted.[13]

At the time that Colonel Moody was given command of the Royal

[13]These two letters are part of a series, in B.C. Papers, used by MacInnes, p. 56, to show Governor Douglas' recognition of the title.

Engineers stationed in British Columbia, he had also been appointed the Chief Commissioner of Lands and Works. His instructions of appointment stated explicitly that "the governor is the supreme authority in the colony." Furthermore, that "Her Majesty's Government count on the immediate raising of large revenues from the land sales" and that the Colonel was to afford the Governor "the benefits of your talents and experience in any suggestions for ensuring . . . this paramount object."[14] In short, the Imperial government was providing Governor Douglas with a highly skilled surveyor and road builder but, as a military officer, Colonel Moody was excluded from the formation of governmental policy. Although his appointment was for one year, he remained on succeeding appointments until the summer of 1863, at which time the Royal Engineers were disbanded and some twenty-five to thirty of his staff returned to England with him. After the departure of Colonel Moody, civilians henceforth occupied the post of Chief Commissioner, a post which was apparently becoming more extensive in function; for in 1864, two offices were created—Mr. Walter Moberly was appointed Assistant Surveyor-General and Sir Joseph Trutch became the Chief Commissioner of Lands and Works. It was these two new officers in the colonial administration who initiated the change in basic policy, and it was they who appear to have been obsessed with the idea that the Indian was an obstruction to settlement and progress.

The complaints of settlers about Indians were given official attention as in the case of a Mr. Nind, who in July, 1865, in a letter to the Colonial Secretary, called attention to Indian claims and obstructing tactics.

I have the honor to address you on the subject of Indian land claims above Kamloops and in its vicinity.

That branch of the Shuswap tribe, . . . numbering, I am informed, less than five hundred souls, claim the undisputed possession of all the land on the north side, between the foot of the Great Shuswap Lake and the North River, a distance of nearly fifty miles where lie thousands of acres of good arable and pasture land, admirably adapted for settlement. I have heard of one cattle-owner who paid their Chief, Nisquaimlth, a monthly rent for the privilege of turning his cattle on these lands.

Another branch of the same tribe, not so numerous as the first, claim all the available land on the North River, extending northward many miles above the mouth, which also possesses attraction to the settler. These Indians do nothing more with their land than cultivate a few small patches of potatoes here and there; they are a vagrant people who live by fishing, hunting, and bartering skins; and the cultivation of their ground contributes

---

[14]Begg, *History of British Columbia*, p. 231.

no more to their livelihood than a few days digging of wild roots; but they are jealous of their possessory rights, and are not likely to permit settlers to challenge them with impunity; nor, such is their spirit and unanimity, would many settlers think it worth while to encounter their undisguised opposition. This, then has the effect of putting a stop to settlement in these parts. Already complaints have arisen from persons who have wished to take up land in some of this Indian territory, but who have been deterred by Indian claims.

In September Chief Commissioner Trutch was asked to make a report on the letter quoted above. In his reply Trutch indicated the pressing nature of the problem and recommended a rather thorough investigation to ascertain what the Indians claimed, what had been assigned to them, and "to what extent such reserves can be modified with the concurrence of the Indians interested in them—either with or without money or other equivalent." In his final paragraph, Trutch stated that he was "satisfied from my own observation that the claims of Indians over tracts of land, on which they assume to exercise ownership, but of which they make no real use, operate very materially to prevent settlement and cultivation in many instances . . . and I should advise that these claims should be as soon as practicable, enquired into and defined."[15] The Colonial Secretary was not prepared to undertake a general investigation as proposed, but he did request that Mr. Moberly, a civil engineer, be authorized "to make enquires on his way down and to reduce these reserves if he is of the opinion that it can be effected without dissatisfaction of the Indians."

Shortly before the difficulty in the Kamloops area developed, the reserves along the Fraser between Harrison River and New Westminster had become problems. A Mr. McColl was sent out under instructions from Sir James Douglas to handle the complaints. McColl marked out reserves which ranged from 50 to 109 acres, and in one case as many as 200, for each adult man. In reporting to Governor Seymour through the Colonial Secretary in 1867 about these acreages and boundaries, Mr. Trutch said, in part:

. . . He seems to have merely walked over the ground claimed by the Indians, setting up stakes at the corners pointed out by them, including the lands they chose to ask for, and then to have estimated the acreage contained therein. These figures, therefore, cannot be relied on, but it is certain that the extent of some of the reserves staked out by McColl is out of all proportion to the numbers or requirements of the tribes to which they are assigned. The Indians regard these extensive tracts of land as their individual property; but of by far the greater portion thereof they make

---

[15]B. C. Papers, p. 30.

no use whatever, and are not likely to do so; and thus the land, much of which is either rich pasture or available for cultivation, and greatly desired for immediate settlement, remains in an unproductive condition—is of no real value to the Indians, and utterly unprofitable to the public interests. . . . Two methods of effecting this reduction may be suggested either (1) to disavow absolutely McColl's authority to make these reserves . . . or (2) to negotiate with the Indians for the relinquishment of the greater portion of these lands which they now consider their own. . . .

The former of these systems was carried out last year in the reduction of the Kamloops and Shuswap Indian Reserves, where tracts of land of most unreasonable extent were claimed . . . and I think that a similar course may be very fairly and expediently adopted in this case.

The Indians have really no right to the lands they claim, nor are they of any actual value or utility to them, and I cannot see why they should either retain these lands to the prejudice of the general interests of the Colony, or be allowed to make a market of them either to Government or to Individuals.[16]

The Colonial Secretary replied that Governor Seymour had had this subject under consideration and that "it is apprehended that Mr. McColl entirely misinterpreted Governor Douglas' wishes." In November, 1867, Mr. Trutch reported that he "in Company with Captain Ball, the Magistrate of the District, visited all but four of the Indian reserves on the lower Fraser which were laid out by the late Sargeant McColl. . . . I took occasion at each village to inform the Indians that McColl had no authority for laying off the excessive amount of land included by him in these reserves, and that his action in this respect was entirely disavowed." In making his analysis of the legal status of the Indian title, MacInnes stated that "there can be no question that Sir Joseph Trutch deliberately misinformed them—he knew quite well that Sergeant McColl did have authority from Governor Douglas to lay off what he is pleased to call 'excessive amounts of land' for Indian reserves." (p. 65)

It is obvious that the new colonial administration had three basic criteria in carrying out their duties—a fixed conception of the Indian's needs and his limited use of the land which determined the quantity and the locations of the reserves in relation to expanding settlements. The new policy was developed prior to the entrance of British Columbia into Confederation, and it led to a complete denial of the Indian title, even before the Terms of Union had been ratified by British Columbia.

In a memorandum prepared to refute the allegations of the mistreatment of the Indians by the colonial government—allegations made

[16]*Ibid.*, p. 41.

by the Aborigines Protective Society—Mr. Trutch stated, and stated incorrectly, to the Secretary of State for the Colonies, Earl Granville, on January 29, 1870, that

. . . the title of the Indians in the fee of the public lands, or of any portion thereof, has never been acknowledged by the Government, but, on the contrary is distinctly denied. In no case has any special agreement been made with any of the tribes of the Mainland for the extinction of their claims of possession; but these claims have been held to have been fully satisfied by securing to each tribe, as the progress of the settlement of the country seemed to require, the use of sufficient tracts of land for their wants for agricultural and pastoral purposes.[17]

This statement of policy and, surprisingly enough, of Indian satisfaction was reiterated in 1872 when, as first Lieutenant-Governor of the province of British Columbia, Hon. Mr. Trutch wrote to Sir John A. Macdonald, the Prime Minister, a fairly extensive statement on the problems of setting up an administration for the Indians in the province. Referring to the larger portion of forty to fifty thousand as "utter savages," he spoke of the need for calling in naval vessels to control them, the need for experienced personnel, and the desirability of possibly placing administrative responsibility in the office of the Lieutenant-Governor, who then was Mr. Trutch. Later, he went on to say:

. . . Then as to Indian policy I am fully satisfied that for the present the wisest course would be to continue the system which has prevailed hitherto only providing increased means for educating the Indians and generally improving their condition moral and physical.

The Canadian system as I understand it will hardly work here. We have never bought out any Indian claims or lands, nor do they expect we should, but we reserve for their use and benefit from time to time tracts of sufficient extent to fulfill all their reasonable requirements for cultivation or grazing. If you now commence to buy out Indian title to the lands of B.C. you would go back of all that has been done here for 30 years past and would be equitably bound to compensate the tribes who inhabited the districts now settled farmed by white people equally with those in remote and uncultivated portions. Our Indians are sufficiently satisfied and had better be left alone as far as a new system towards them is concerned only give us the means of educating them by teachers employed directly by the Government as well as by aiding the efforts of the missionaries now working among them.[18]

---

[17]The complete memorandum is given in testimony by Dr. Duncan C. Scott, *Claims*, p. 5, originally published in *B.C. Papers*. In citing this memorandum, MacInnes, p. 35, states that "Governor Musgrave detailed Mr. Trutch . . . to make an official reply to these complaints."

[18]Reported by Dr. Scott, *Claims*, p. 6.

This reversal in policy is in no way to be interpreted as clarifying the problem or as ending the dissatisfaction of either the natives or the settlers. There were only a few settlers scattered among the Indians and they had very little if any military power available; and there was developing an increasing inclination among the Indians to violate the laws. Two governors of the colony of British Columbia seem to have done nothing about conditions in the colony, which, as Shankel points out, demanded a well-defined policy. Governor Seymour had told the Legislative Council at his first session that he had "no Bible to introduce on Indian policy." Shankel comments on this lack of action:

Half-hearted attempts were made between the years 1866 and 1870 to bring some uniformity of practice into Indian policy, but expression of dissatisfaction over the lack of system was frequent, both from the Indians and whites during these years. Delegations of Indians waited on the Governor, urging vigorous measures, and urging something more than "Captain Kennedy" had done. The *Colonist* urged an end to what it termed "chaotic conditions." The position became such that early in 1869 the Legislative Council requested the Governor to issue a Commission to inquire into and report upon the best system of administering Indian Affairs and of managing the reserves. Mr. Alston in speaking of the resolution declared that in every civilized country where aborigines were dispossessed of land, a policy of protection was inaugurated and a special department created to care for their interests. The revenue contributed by Indians, he continued, amounted to one-fourth of the Colonial revenues and "to show our gratitude we put them down on the estimates for $500 for every purpose." Trutch and Ball and Helmcken opposed the resolution, declaring that justice had been done to the Indians of British Columbia over any other colony.[19]

The view expressed by Trutch and Ball and Helmcken is one which many British Columbians have continued to hold. In the Terms of Union the idea became the now famous thirteenth clause: "liberal policy as that hitherto pursued by the British Columbian Government shall be continued by the Dominion Government after the Union." By having this conception of colonial policy regarding Indian affairs incorporated into the Terms of Union, the advocates of the Trutch-Ball-Helmcken point of view strengthened the province's hand in dealing with the Dominion government as it perpetuated the idea that justice had been properly attended to when the Indians were assigned what enterprising white men deemed to be sufficient land for the purposes of an Indian family. This policy was more than the expression of the settlers' desires through their political leaders; it was a major stroke

[19]Shankel, "The Development of Indian Policy in British Columbia," pp. 80–1. Quoted with permission of the author.

by which the Indian was denied the opportunity to share or participate in the appreciation of land values as a result of settlement. White men could pre-empt 320 acres and buy as many more. Some Indians were assigned as little as nine acres, almost none were acquainted with pre-emption laws, and in any case few had the necessary capital for purchasing land. In a different perspective, it could be said that again the white man visualized no future for the Indian.

THE INDIAN PROTEST: BEFORE 1875

When Rev. P. R. Kelly appeared before the Joint Committee of Parliament in 1927, he declared:

I want to say this, speaking on behalf of the Indians of British Columbia, that this, I take it, is the culmination of about fifty years of endeavour on the part of the Indian tribes of British Columbia to obtain a hearing. I say this to bring before you the importance of the effort made by the Indian tribes of British Columbia.[20]

Undoubtedly Dr. Kelly had the petition of 1874 in mind as the beginning of the endeavour. Still, prior to 1874 sufficient preliminary activities had occurred to indicate the earlier development of the Indian protest movement, characterized by the jealousy and the general resentment which had accrued from thousands of incidents between Indians and settlers and between Indians and officials during the gold mining period. Soon this resentment was organized into the action represented in the petitions and deputations directed to local officials. The Indian was trying to do something about local, specific abuses and was depending upon local authorities. He was reacting, as before, directly to the settlers and their attitudes but now he had learned to write, or more likely to have had written, formal petitions. The settlers' reactions to the organized protest of the Indians were summarized in this document:

I cannot get wood off my land except by a sort of permission. I cannot build as I intended to do. Everybody says "Sure what the devil is the good of a Government that can't put a few siwashes off a man's land." I said always "I'm waiting for Powell." Now Powell [Commissioner of Indian Affairs, Victoria] has not fixed it, nor is there even a probability that he can or will. The idea that I have had from the first in this affair is that you must make the Indians respect your power. They have a hundred times more respect for a gunboat than all the talk in creation.[21]

[20]*Claims*, p. 147.

[21]*B. C. Papers*, p. 133. Note the use of the term *siwash*. At least on the coastal areas of the northwest portion of Canada and the United States, and to some ex-

The *B.C. Papers* also published another letter regarding the ownership of land which shows the general resentment of the Indians.

Maple Bay, April 27, 1869

In the case of dispute between Mr. Rogers and the Indians, I summoned Te-cha-malt on a charge of trespass, but as I found it was a case of dispute, as to the ownership of the land, and on the Indian promising not to interfere until I received further instructions from the Government, Mr. Rogers also agreeing to let the matter stand over, I have taken no further action. . . . Te-cha-malt made use of very improper language, and was very insolent. He said he was the Chief, and that the land was his. He also said that Governor Seymour could not take the land from him, that if the Governor sent his gunboat he would fetch his friends from all parts, and hold the land against him. He also said the Governor was a liar, and had not fulfilled his promise to pay for the land he had taken. And they told me that he did not care for me or the prison either, that I had no power over the Indians.

JOHN MORLEY

We have seen from the potlatch controversy that the whole of native life in the northwest was becoming unsettled. Because social control had broken down, it became possible for Indians who had never before had the sanctioned right to potlatch to secure trade goods and engage in the ceremonial practices. In earlier days raiding parties from the north had ventured into the southern region; but in the colonial period thousands went to Victoria and later, Vancouver. Governor Douglas even found it necessary in 1860 to use a gunboat to tow canoes away from the settlement. Begg records, "the northern Indians at Victoria were so numerous at Victoria [sic] in March, that on the 16th of that month H.M.S. Tribune was commissioned to tow the Indians and their canoes out as far as Johnson's Pass, in charge of Sheriff Heaton, whence they must shift for themselves." (p. 309) Father Fouquet referred to Governor Seymour's speaking to sixty chiefs and 4,000 Indians in the area that is now New Westminster.[22] While increased mobility resulted in the accentuation of certain aspects of tribal organization and the

---

tent in the interior, one often hears *siwash* also used as an adjective, meaning "no good." It is applied to Indians in that sense as well as dogs, coffee, and a variety of other things. Some westerners believe that a tribe of *siwash* Indians actually did exist, and in some cases it is used as a neutral designation for Indian. But Indians consider it derogatory and opprobrious. However, just outside the harbour of Vancouver, there is a pinnacle rock known as Siwash Rock. Several Indians talked about it without being disturbed by the term *siwash*. There are legends about this rock, some of which have been published. In the Indian Village programme for the Diamond Jubilee of the founding of Vancouver, in 1946, Siwash Rock is stated to be "a monument to Clean Fatherhood." Some scholars are of the opinion that the term *siwash* is a corruption of the French *sauvage*.

[22]*Claims*, XVIII.

eventual disintegration of others, the settler's problem impinged upon that of the natives over the questions of pasture for stock, especially horses, potato grounds, and the location and size of reserves. There is no longer any precise way to trace the emergence of the Indians' resentment and the increase in violence. The few documents which we assume to be valid indices are characterized by individualized hostility rather than any group action.

General resentment could be expressed before a magistrate or directly to a surveyor or a settler, but it took on a different character when converted into action in the form of petitions and delegations to colonial, later provincial, officials. From the outcome of the Te-cha-malt case, the Indians involved may have learned the importance and effectiveness of protest and the role of the government in such actions. In May, 1869, the Lands and Works Department reported as follows on the dispute:

In reference to the dispute between Mr. Rogers and the Cowichan Indians as to the section of land (Section 14, Range 7) Quamichan District, reported in your letter dated April 27th, I have the honour to inform you that this matter had already, before your report was received, been brought under the consideration of His Excellency the Governor on the complaint of the Chiefs of the tribes residing on the Cowichan Reserves, that the section of land above named having formerly been part of the land reserved for their use, had been cut off by Mr. Pearse without their concurrence or knowledge.

His Excellency granted these Chiefs an opportunity of stating their case at a personal interview with himself, from which statement corroborated to some extent by the evidence of Mr. Robertson, who was one of Mr. Pearse's surveying party when the reserves were laid out in 1867, it appeared that there must have been a misunderstanding between Mr. Pearse and these Indians as to the exact limits of the lands to be held in reserve for them, and being willing to take a favourable view of the claim of the Indians to the land in the dispute, His Excellency has directed me to hold the section of land in question under reserve for their use, and to notify Mr. Rogers that his Pre-emption Record of this land, having been made by me under the mistaken supposition that the said land was open for pre-emption, must be cancelled.[23]

But even though this case may have provided some political education for the Cowichan Indians, the available evidence indicates that in several areas the missionaries quite likely played a central role in organizing the resentment into a demand for the recognition of Indian rights and the restitution or adjustment of the reserved lands. Though they were anxious to change the cultural values and systems of the

[23]B.C. Papers, p. 60.

natives, the missionaries also resented, and some protested, the actions of the settlers and the nature of government policy. It was possible for the missionaries, and later other white people, to play the role of organizer shortly after the reversal of policy was initiated and important colonial officials became provincial appointees. By this time Mr. Duncan controlled a whole village and was well established among the Tsimshian as were a number of Roman Catholic missionaries and others in the Fraser Valley and along the lower Coast. The continued success of the missionaries appeared to be based upon their alignment of their political actions with Indian interests; thus they served the Indians in more roles than that of go-between in Indian-white relations or Indian-government actions. Although we do not know which missionaries or other white people were instrumental in framing the following petition of protest addressed to Indian Commissioner Powell, it is obviously a more sophisticated document than the Indians by themselves could produce:

The petition of the undersigned, chiefs of Douglas Portage, of Lower Fraser, and of the other tribes on the seashore of the mainland to Bute Inlet, humbly sheweth:

1. That your petitioners view with a great anxiety the standing question of the quantity of land to be reserved for the use of each Indian family.

2. That we are fully aware that the Government of Canada has always taken good care of the Indians, and treated them liberally, allowing more than 100 acres per family; and we have been at a loss to understand the views of the local government of British Columbia, in curtailing our land so much as to leave in many instances but a few acres of land per family.

3. Our hearts have been wounded by the arbitrary way the local government of British Columbia have dealt with us in locating and dividing our Reserves. Chamiel, ten miles below Hope, is allowed 488 acres of good land for the use of 20 families; at the rate of 24 acres per family; Popkum, eighteen miles below Hope, is allowed 369 acres of good land for the use of four families; at the rate of 90 acres per family; Cheam, twenty miles below Hope, is allowed 375 acres of bad, dry, mountainous land for the use of 27 families; at the rate of 13 acres per family; Yuk-yuk-y-yoose on the Chilliwhack River, with a population of seven families, is allowed forty-two acres, five acres per family [sic]; Sumaas (at the junction of Sumaas River and Fraser) with a population of seventeen families, is allowed 43 acres of meadow for their hay, and 32 acres of dry land; Keatsy, numbering more than 100 inhabitants, is allowed 108 acres of land. Langley and Hope have not yet got land secured to them, and white men are encroaching on them on all sides.

4. For many years we have been complaining of the land left us being too small. We have laid our complaints before the government officials near to us. They sent us to some others; so we had no redress up to the present; and we have felt like men trampled on, and are commencing to believe

that the aim of the white men is to exterminate us as soon as they can, although we have been always quiet, obedient, kind and friendly to the whites.

5. Discouragement and depression have come upon our people. Many of them have given up the cultivation of land because our gardens have not been protected against the encroachments of the whites. Some of our best men have been deprived of the land they have broken and cultivated with long and hard labor, a white man enclosing it in his claim, and no compensation given. Some of our enterprising men have lost a part of their cattle, because white men had taken the place where those cattle were grazing and no other place left but the thickly timbered land, where they die fast. Some of our people are now obliged to cut rushes along the bank of the river with their knives during the winter, to feed their cattle.

6. We are now obliged to clear heavy timbered land, all prairies having been taken from us by white men. We see our white neighbors cultivate wheat, peas, etc., and raise large stocks of cattle on our pasture lands, and we are giving them our money to buy the flour manufactured from the wheat they have grown on same prairies.

7. We are not lazy and roaming-about people, as we used to be. We have worked hard and a long time to spare money to buy agricultural implements, cattle, horses, etc., as nobody has given us assistance. We could point out many of our people who have those past years bought with their own money, ploughs, harrows, yokes of oxen and horses; and now, with your kind assistance, we have a bright hope to enter into the path of civilization.

8. We consider that eighty acres per family is absolutely necessary for our support, and for the future welfare of our children. We declare that 20 or 30 acres of land per family will not give satisfaction, but will create ill feelings, irritation among our people, and we cannot say what will be the consequence.

9. That, in case you cannot obtain from the Local government, the object of our petition, we humbly pray that this, our petition, be forwarded to the Secretary of State for the provinces, at Ottawa.

Therefore, your petitioners humbly pray that you may take this our petition into consideration, and see that justice be done us, and allow each family the quantity of land we ask for.

And your petitioners, as in duty bound, will ever pray.[24]

When this petition of 1874 was entered in the proceedings of the Committee in 1927, Dr. Scott, Deputy Superintendent-General, indicated that as a consequence a royal commission was appointed and that "the Indians and the Government got together, and decided upon what land should be reserved. That was the first real attempt on the part of the Government to adjust the difficulty, with respect to reserves, and to carry out the terms of Article 13."[25] Within twelve years, the petition was the method used by all the Indians who wished to protest about some abuse or other.

[24]*Claims*, pp. 103–4.
[25]*Ibid.*, p. 105.

The protest made in the above petition resulted in the provincial government taking a defensive line. But even on the defensive, the provincial government felt compelled to take action in order to manage the Indians and, if possible, the federal government. The petition had been a consequence of a Dominion Order in Council, passed March 21, 1873, recommending that eighty acres of land be assigned by the provincial government to every family of five persons. The provincial government in turn asked Mr. Duncan for advice on the land issue. There is no evidence that he had any resentment about the general treatment of Indians in the province at that time though the bitterness of the later fight which resulted in his move to Alaska in 1886 certainly indicated that he was a person of principles and determination. In his official statement, Attorney-General Walkem included the advice received from Mr. Duncan.

1. That no basis of acreage for Reserves be fixed for the Province as a whole, but rather that each nation of Indians be dealt with separately on their respective claims.

2. That for the proper adjustment of such claims let the Dominion and the Provincial Governments each provide an agent to visit the Indians and report fully as to the number of pursuits of each nation and the kind of country they severally occupy.

3. That the Provincial Government deal as liberally with the Indians as other Provincial Governments in the Dominion.

My opinion is that a liberal policy will prove the cheapest in the end, but I hold it will not be necessary in the interests of the Indians to grant them only cultivable lands; rather I would recommend that a large portion of their Reserves should be wild and forest lands, and hence may be very extensive without impoverishing the Province, and at the same time so satisfactory to the Indians as to allay all irritation and jealousy towards the whites.

4. I think the Provincial Government might reasonably insist upon this with the Dominion Government: that no Indian shall be allowed to alienate any part of a Reserve, and in case of any Reserve being abandoned, or the Indians on it decreasing, so that its extent is disproportioned to the number of occupants, that such Reserve or part of a Reserve might revert to the Provincial Government.

Mr. Duncan adds: "The existing Reserves are shown to be, by the correspondence, both irregular in quantity and misplaced as to locality, by following tribal divisions, which is no doubt a mistake and fraught with bad consequences.

"My advice would be, in the meantime simply to ignore them, as it certainly would not be wise to regard them as precedent, and it would be impolitic to have two systems of Reserves in the Province, one tribal and the other national."[26]

---

[26]*Ibid.*, p. 47.

The provincial government declared that it would not accede to the recommendation of eighty acres, but that twenty acres would be assigned for each family of five. Since surveying for the reserves was already under way, the disagreement meant a suspension of work. There appeared to be no way of resolving the disputes between settlers and Indians at least for the time being, since the two governments could not even agree. This seeming deadlock called forth a number of comments including Commissioner Powell's statement that the absence of an Indian war was due not to lack of discontent but rather to the fact that the tribes were insufficiently united. It is under these circumstances that Father Grandidier, a missionary in the Okanagan area, made his well-known remarks, published in *B.C. Papers*, used by MacInnes in his report and again by Andrew Paull in his testimony before the Joint Committee in 1927.

. . . Who will wonder at the dissatisfaction that has been growing amongst the Indians? The land was theirs and their forefathers before the whites came; that land has been wrenched from them in virtue of might, not right; not a cent has been given them to extinguish their title to the land. . . . And it is not correct to say that no injustice has been done to the Indians in taking away their land because they did not cultivate it. For they were the owners of the land, and the title to the property is not rendered valueless because the property is left to decay. . . . They had been left to struggle on the parcel of land allotted them, without any encouragement, any help, any agricultural implements from any quarter and because they are forebearing and peacefully disposed, they are to be granted a minimum possible of land. . . . They do not think that when a white man can pre-empt 320 acres, and buy as much more, besides the facility of leasing more, that they are unreasonable in asking 80 acres of their own land per family. But if the Indians are persistently refused their demands, if they are deprived of their father's land without any hope of redress from the proper authorities their dissatisfactions will increase, meetings shall be held again, . . . the end of which I am afraid to foresee. . . . If it is my duty to teach the Indians to keep the commandments of God and obey the just laws of man, it is no less my obligation to spare no effort in order that justice be done to them, and that peace and security be preserved in my adopted country.[27]

According to Andrew Paull's testimony, the land title question had become a "great national question" in 1874 and still was in 1927. While one may not want to give this complex of issues the definition of a "great national question," it is evident that Indians, missionaries, government officials, and settlers were considerably agitated. The continued defensive line of the province in response to Indian protests

[27]*B.C. Papers*, p. 146–8; MacInnes, p. 58; *Claims*, pp. 118–19.

and the actions of the federal government, the increasing political education of the natives, the gradual loss of unrestricted resources for the natives, and the partial urbanization of some tribes—these were just a few of the factors which operated to define the idea of a aboriginal title, a title that could be extinguished only by a "meeting in council" and some kind of settlement. For them, settlement by potlatch was the traditional way, but as white people could not understand the native view of potlatching, the idea of extinguishing the aboriginal title by negotiation was taken up as a substitute. It later acquired a symbolic importance, highly surcharged with emotions, which no one envisaged in 1874.

THE INDIAN PROTEST: 1874–1917

The petition of 1874 was concerned with the acreage being allotted to each Indian. In March of the same year, the legislative assembly passed an act for the purpose of consolidating the laws affecting Crown lands in the province. Because no cession of the Indian title had been obtained, the act was disallowed in March, 1875. The provincial legislature amended it, and after consultation with the Dominion government regarding a procedure for the selection and allotment of reserves, the act went into operation.[28] The federal government had recognized the Indian title by signing treaties with the eastern Indians; its failure to do so in British Columbia resulted in increased jealousy, reported by Commissioner Powell in 1876.[29] In September of this year, Lord Dufferin, Governor-General of Canada, urged the recognition of the aboriginal title.[30] Later high ranking officials from Ottawa, including Sir Wilfrid Laurier, either protested or made promises to do all possible to "get justice done." The argument of the provincial government was simply that justice had been done. None the less continued complaints necessitated the appointment of a commission in 1887, "to Enquire into the Conditions of the Indians of the Northwest Coast."[31] But 1887 appears to have become better known as the year that a fairly large group of delegates went from

[28]Relevant documents are given in *Claims*, Appendix B, p. 39ff.

[29]See Shankel, pp. 168–72, for the development of the system of Indian agents, starting in 1879. A federal order in council, April 3, 1881, provided for the appointment of six agents—two on Vancouver Island, two in the southern interior, one on the Lower Fraser, and one among the Kwakiutl.

[30]MacInnes interprets this as an Imperial protest against provincial injustice, p. 68.

[31]For details see Shankel, p. 189. In his memorandum to the Committee in 1927, Dr. Scott makes no reference to this commission.

Fort Simpson to Victoria to interview the provincial government. Mr. Kelly recalled the feelings of that year, in his submission to the Committee of 1927:

. . . At that time they brought before the Government this fact, that they were not adequately provided for as far as land was concerned, and they became conscious of the fact that in days to come rights which they had inherited from time immemorial would be taken away from them. Even at that early date, forty years ago, they were conscious of that, and it was brought to the notice of the Provincial Government. About that time, when Reserve Commissioners went around and approached the Haida Tribe of the Queen Charlotte Islands, I heard this from the lips of those who were present asking them to state a certain area of land to be set apart for them with which they would be satisfied. The Chiefs who gathered in council together said this, "Why would we ask you to set lands apart for us? This territory is ours and it has been ours as far back as we can remember. Any time any other people claimed our lands we disputed them with force. Why are you coming here and asking us to say what area of land would satisfy us?" . . . They told the Commissioners that they were not prepared to name any area because the whole area of land was theirs.[32]

What had made the Fort Simpson Indians conscious of the land problem were the restrictions regarding the cutting of timber as well as their restricted acreage. One of the Indians at the interview stated that "we want to be free on the top of this land of ours." MacInnes reports part of this interview:

. . . They said: "our reserve is very little; and we have not got any timber land; neither have we got our hunting grounds. These are what we want and what we came for. We want you to cut out a bigger reserve for us, and what we want after that is a treaty."

The Premier told these Indians that there was no such thing as a treaty with Indians, and gave them to understand that certain lands had been given to them as a matter of charity, for which they should be very thankful. I quote the Premier's remark from the report of this conference issued by the Provincial Government, at page 256:

"Hon. Mr. Smithe: 'There is no such law either English or Dominion that I know of, and the Indians or their friends, have been misled on that point. The land all belongs to the Queen. The laws provide that if a white man requires a piece of land he must go to the land office and pay for it, and it is his. The Indian is placed in a better position; a reserve is given to each tribe, and they are not required to pay for it. It is the Queen's land just the same, but the Queen gives it to her Indian children because they do

---

[32]*Claims*, p. 152. In the discussion which followed Mr. Kelly's statement it was uncertain whether this statement of Haida chiefs to a commisson was made in 1876 or 1887.

not know so well how to make their own living, the same as a white man, and special indulgence is extended to them and special care shown.' "[33]

This was a denial of the Indian title as early as 1887, and of course it was a negation of the whole treaty system used before and after 1887 by the Dominion government for the purpose of extinguishing the aboriginal title.

Evidence introduced in the Committee hearings in 1927 made no reference to the problems of Mr. Duncan, problems which he finally solved by moving in 1886 to Annette Island, Alaska, and thus coming under American jurisdiction. The great conflict over Canadian Metlakatla was undoubtedly a factor in the increasing consciousness of the Indians regarding restrictions and the land question. In any study of the Indian agitation and organization, and of provincial and federal policy as well, the establishment of Metlakatla and its removal to Alaska is of central significance. For at least twenty years prior to his move to New Metlakatla, Mr. Duncan was touted by government officials, church officials, and white residents of British Columbia as the ideal, the most successful worker in the mission field. The original mission village of Metlakatla was the paragon of such establishments, and other missionaries tried to emulate Duncan's programme of mission work. Indians, from miles away, also knew about Mr. Duncan even before the question of the land title at Metlakatla arose.[34] To comprehend the intensity of feeling regarding the land question, it is necessary to recognize that this was an issue around which the continual conflict between evangelism and ecclesiasticism could become

[33]MacInnes, p. 66. Shankel gives some interesting data from the interview of this delegation. "The removal of Duncan and his followers to Alaska, coming on the heels of all these troubles, might have been expected to have a settling effect, but it seemed to act as a signal for an outburst of more extensive land claims than ever before. A deputation of Indians from Port Simpson and Nass River visited Victoria. . . . Their complaints were that they were slaves and had no voice, that their reserves were too small, that they had no timber lands nor hunting grounds, and that they desired a treaty. When O'Reilly, Reserve Commissioner, reminded them that the Tsimpseans possessed 73,000 acres for 2,200 people, they still held themselves to be slaves. Some of them declared that they were like white men but not allowed to be. They expressed their fears that their reserves might be sold any time without their consent, and that they deserved a treaty." Pp. 161–2. Quoted by permission of the author. Note the recurring reference to being slaves, one of the lowest terms of contempt that a Northwest Coast Indian could use.

[34]The most extensive history of this issue is found in Henry S. Wellcome, *The Story of Metlakahtla.* Wellcome devotes pp. 169–438, including the appendices, to it, for it was this issue which, according to him, caused Mr. Duncan to negotiate with American authorities and move finally to Alaska.

organized, an issue in which the hostility between a lay missionary and a newly-appointed bishop could become manifest, and an issue within which distant authorities in Britain could make their power felt in a local situation. And further than this, it was an issue in which the provincial authorities could implement their conception of Indian rights by a show of force.

When Attorney-General Walkem in 1874 asked Mr. Duncan for his advice, he was expressing the high esteem held for the success of Mr. Duncan. As discussed in chapter II, Mr. Duncan had developed two basic plans on which his mission was built: first of all, he isolated his converts from the continuing pagans and provided them with a very carefully modified form of Christianity as it was practised by the Church of England; and secondly, in isolating his converts, he set up new lines of economic activity which were completely modern for the times.[35] Until 1881 all apparently worked well. Wellcome expressed this feeling of success and well-being by stating that "Christianity, humanity and civilization seemed to triumph over the whole region." Whether "the storm of persecution" broke as suddenly as he claims, we do not know. But he was undoubtedly correct in saying that it arose from an entirely unexpected quarter.

Mr. Duncan had attempted to secure from the home office of the Church Missionary Society permission to use his modified form of the Lord's Supper; the Society insisted upon the full, unchanged, traditional form. It was not long before Mr. Duncan was suspected of giving to the Indians "mutilated Christianity" and "false teachings." The Society tried replacing Mr. Duncan, but his successor did not work well, and a general demand resulted in Mr. Duncan's return.

. . . Mr. Duncan entirely abdicated the mission at Metlakahtla to an ordained clergyman sent out by the Society, and had only been absent for a few weeks preparing for a new mission, when Metlahkatla was thrown into a state of dreadful confusion; and the organization well nigh wrecked, by the unwise ecclesiastical enthusiasm of the new missionary; the effect of whose methods upon many of the still superstitious minds was to create

---

[35]Begg reports: "In 1882–3 various industries were carried on under Mr. Duncan's management, such as sawing lumber by a watermill under native charge, the manufacture of barrels for fish-curing, blacksmiths' work, and other mechanical arts. A salmon cannery for exportation of the products abroad was established and was successful. A factory for weaving cloth was also established, in which the young Indian women acquired great proficiency. Since Mr. Duncan's departure these industries have become languid, and some of them have entirely ceased. The neatly-built houses are, many of them, vacant, and the once sprightly and prosperous village is sadly dilapidated." P. 503. The Canadian Metlakatla has recovered since Begg published his history.

a sort of fanatical cyclone. Some were led in the fever of their delirium to declare that they had witnessed miracles; beheld, and held converse with the Holy Spirit; and that angels hovered about the village.

This man in his blindness, was actually congratulating himself on the work of the Holy Ghost, but when the news of the foolishness reached Victoria, there was a general demand that Mr. Duncan should instantly return and save his life's work from utter destruction. He did return, but it was with great difficulty that he succeeded in eliminating the results of a few weeks' misdirected, fanatical zeal.[36]

In 1879, not long after this failure at replacement by the Society, the northern part of British Columbia was made into a bishopric, and the village of Metlakatla became the headquarters of the Bishop of Caledonia. The first appointment to the new bishopric was given to Bishop Ridley, who attempted to dissociate Mr. Duncan from the work of the diocese; it was the consequences of the Bishop's efforts which led eventually to the founding of New Metlakatla on Annette Island.

The tactical moves made by Bishop Ridley reveal an all-out effort.[37] He attempted to create a faction of natives loyal to him through the use of "an agent of the Society operating secretly." His attempt to bribe the native teacher, David Leask, by offering to increase his salary from one hundred to one hundred fifty pounds per year, was rejected.[38] When the Bishop made a trip to England, he refused to carry with him a letter of explanation and complaint from the Indian Council, in which it was claimed that the Bishop "corrupted an English school teacher who said that the Government had authorized control of the school to be placed under the Bishop; one hour after school opened, the teacher had deserted to the Bishop's faction, and it was then necessary for Mr. Duncan to conduct the school," and that a "female native teacher" had "been away on the Bishop's yacht"; on being rebuked, she gave up her position and was then employed by the Bishop at an increased salary.

Of course Mr. Duncan was no longer connected with the Church Missionary Society, and thus it was necessary for him to rely upon the profits from his store in order to support the mission. False statements, it was claimed, were published, and the Bishop's adherents were not allowed to trade at the regular store; hence he opened a store in the mission house where goods were sold cheaper. But Mr. Duncan's store weathered this part of the storm.

[36]Wellcome, p. 193.

[37]For the details of the conflict between Duncan and Ridley, see *ibid.*, p. 207ff.

[38]Although a thorough library search has not been made, one gains the impression that no studies have been made of native teachers and preachers.

The Bishop then brought in secular aid. In 1882 he sent a false and alarming report to Victoria. Since no British warship was available, arrangements were made for the U.S. revenue cutter *Oliver Wolcott* to be sent with a magistrate. Upon its arrival Mr. Duncan and others were summoned, but there was no riot. This false alarm cost the government $7,000. There were numerous other incidents, such as trouble over the use and ownership of drums, with an arrest followed by imprisonment; and the Bishop and a white school teacher, equipped with firearms, spent a whole night in the school house expecting an attack. Also, the Bishop attempted to put up a building, but the Indians quietly pulled it down, and not even the Indian agent, endeavouring to impose certain articles of the Indian Act, was able to stop the undoing of the Bishop's work. Attempts were made to establish legally the violations of property, and although the Indians were tried, there was insufficient evidence to convict them. Other incidents followed, including the arrival of a man-of-war with three commissioners.

Gradually knowledge of the true state of affairs reached England and two agents of the Society were sent to the Pacific Coast. They attempted to persuade the Indians of their good intentions and the wealth of the organization. But then the controversy shifted to Mr. Duncan's uses of the Society's funds, uses contrary to the rules. But none of the foregoing conflict appears to have been as intense and as significant as the question of the ownership of Mission Point.

. . . The natives to their dismay, were told, that they had no rights in the land whatsoever; but that the Queen owned, as well as ruled, all the country of British Columbia, not excepting even the village site of Metlakatla! To back up this appalling announcement the Government sent a party of surveyors . . . to survey two acres in the village, to be alienated from the Natives and secure such to their bitter enemy, the Church Missionary Society. The Natives stood amazed at seeing and hearing all this; for had they not heard from the lips of Earl Dufferin, when Governor General of Canada, of the goodness, and sympathy of the Queen—and how safely they might confide their interests to her keeping . . .[39]

The Metlakatla Indians went to Victoria for legal advice and were informed that they held the title; the Provincial Executive Council told them that the two acres would be turned over to them if so requested by the Dominion Government. A delegation went to Ottawa, and it looked as if all were settled. Prime Minister Macdonald promised to communicate with the Church Missionary Society, and the Indians were satisfied. But according to Wellcome's interpretation, Sir John A.

[39]Wellcome, pp. 285-6.

Macdonald, pressed politically, agreed to support the Church Missionary Society in return for votes. The problem of the two acres was never cleared up by Sir John, and consequently the situation deteriorated until only two alternatives remained—to shoot or to move to Alaska. After many negotiations, including a trip by Mr. Duncan to London, the move was made in 1886. Thus the years between 1876, the year that reserve allotment commissioners were operating, and 1886 were ten years of the most acute conflict over principle in the experience of Indians and missionaries.

Since the Fort Simpson Indians are not far removed from Metlakatla, we may assume that their visit to Victoria in 1887 was motivated by concern about the principles for which the conflict had been sustained and the way in which it had been resolved.[40] The Duncan-Ridley fight clearly showed missionary influence and direction. Indian Commissioner Powell reported on it to Ottawa in 1885, and again two years later.

. . . Powell again regretted the deplorable conditions brought about by missionaries who had other interests than spiritual, and had assumed full control of temporal affairs of Indians, even advising them to repel the Indian Agent and prevent the introduction of the Indian Act, and claimed that the attitude of the Tsimpseans, who expressed dissatisfaction with land reserves and demanded payment for the whole country, was entirely due to the advice of those who prevented officers of the Government from controlling

---

[40]Indians were protesting against the appointment of agents. On the one hand government officials thought the appointment of agents would create clarification, and part of the report of the Commission of 1888 stated that "a good deal of friction and trouble amongst Indians would be remedied by the presence . . . of a capable Indian Agent, one who would gain their confidence, and to whom they could look for sensible and trustworthy advice. It is useless to send among them second rate, ill-paid men." After quoting this, Shankel has a footnote saying, "The testimony of several persons interviewed by the writer, men who had spent the greater part of a lifetime on the upper coastal section of the Province, agreed that with few notable exceptions the agents were not interested in the welfare of the Indians." Shankel, p. 180.

On p. 192 Shankel writes: "One of the grievances frequently voiced was that they were not allowed to live as white men. Some asked to be relieved of Indian Agents and to have their own Councils, also to be released from the Indian Act and to live by white man's law."

In the *Annual Report* of the Indian Affairs Branch, 1884, p. lvii, this attitude is reported: "The Indians of Metlahkahtla and of Fort Simpson, over whom as well as over the Indians generally of the northwest coast, an agent was placed, as stated in my last Annual Report, refused to receive or recognize that officer. He accordingly returned to Victoria and, as already stated in the introductory part of this report, a stipendiary magistrate was, on the suggestion of Your Excellency, as expressed in an Order in Council of the 2nd June, subsequently appointed by the Government of British Columbia to administer justice on that coast. . . ."

in temporal affairs, an obvious reference to missionaries. There is no doubt that the attitude of some missionaries toward Indian Agents was antagonistic. One Indian testified that some missionaries frightened Indians with the story that Agents would only oppress them.

The Executive Council of British Columbia, in urging the appointment of an Indian Agent for the upper Skeena River, plainly declared that the Indian unrest was because of aspersions against Government officers by Methodist missionaries. In a recent interview a gentleman resident in British Columbia who as a youth travelled on the Northwest Coast with a Government reserve officer, stated that much of the trouble over Indian claims to land title was because of missionary agitation, and in this respect he considered the Church of England missions only one degree less culpable than the Methodist. In an interview of about the same date with Mr. W. M. Halliday who lived on the Northwest Coast from 1894–1933 . . . [he] said that missionaries played a part in reviving the question of land title claim, and that both Church of England and Methodist missionaries were more or less equally to blame. The report of the commission of 1888 was highly condemnatory of the Methodist missionaries, but it has been rightly pointed out that the entire personnel of the Commission were members of the Church of England.[41]

The land title issue was one that easily maintained a strong bond between a missionary and his congregation, for the penetration of the settlers continued and the negative policy of the government had been by now made quite clear. The evidence suggests that the Indians felt hopelessly trapped and were willing to take more extreme action than before.

As yet no test question had been raised to determine what would happen to the reserved Indian lands if a tribe died out or if a tribe no longer had a use for the land. In Imperial policy it was assumed that the land belonged to the Crown and was inalienable. But British Columbia had taken the point of view that the title should revert to the province. Until 1875 the concern of the Indians had been with acreage and location. Now they had a new conception of their rights, and the provincial reversionary right, admitted by the federal government in the order-in-council of November 5, 1875, became increasingly important to them. There was no final surety for the Indian with respect to the title of his lands; thus one more factor was added to the problems of acreage and location.

Between 1887 and 1906 the agitation continued to grow, but little satisfaction was given. No important clarification of the issues had been accomplished by 1906, and one may suspect that the Indians had become more than dissatisfied; they were now distrustful of provincial and federal policy. In 1906 three important chiefs, including Joe

41Shankel, pp. 151–2. Quoted wth permission of the author.

Capilano, were sent to London in order to call upon His Majesty King Edward VII and place their claims before him. According to Shankel it was in "the spring of the 1906 that at a meeting of the Indians of Cowichan a decision was reached to send a deputation to England to petition the King in the matter of land. The delegates accordingly left in July bearing a petition in which they complained:

1. That the title of their land had never been extinguished,

2. That white men had settled on their land against their wishes,

3. That all appeals to the Canadian Government had proved vain,

4. That they had no vote and were not consulted with respect to Agents."

Shankel's interpretation of this move is a limited and questionable one. He says "it was an ill considered move, to be sure, with no hope whatsoever of any immediate result. Considering their lack of knowledge of Government administration they cannot be censured. However, the very fact that they should undertake such a trip and at such expense is striking evidence in itself how deep were their feelings in the matter."[42] MacInnes has stated that:

The King . . . was always looked upon by the Indians as friendly to their peculiar rights and privileges, first as an Ally and subsequently as a Protector and Great Father. . . . The Indians on the other hand at no time made, and to this day will not make, an appeal to a colonial, provincial, or federal government in Canada as the sovereign power from whom they ask recognition of their title. Their appeal has always been made, and from British Columbia is now being made, direct to the King.[43]

In 1909 British Columbia undertook to dispossess the Skeena Indians, near Prince Rupert, of some land.[44] This action precipitated increased activity on the part of the Indians and their white advisers and friends. In the spring of 1909 a petition was presented to His Majesty by three Indians representing twenty tribes, and quite naturally it was referred to the Government of Canada. Also in 1909 the "Indian Tribes of the Province of British Columbia" was formed

[42]While visiting the Indian Village of the Diamond Jubilee in Vancouver in 1946, the author heard Chief Mathias Joe telling white visitors that his father visited the King regarding the land title. When nothing was done about the title, his father withdrew from the Catholic Church and told his priest and the Bishop when he met him on the street one day, that he would not return to the Church until his land was returned to him.

[43]MacInnes, pp. 13–15.

[44]This was the act which resulted in the Deputy Superintendent-General of Indian Affairs requesting Mr. MacInnes to make the study and report which has been quoted above. See also Shankel, the chapter entitled "The Tsimpian Reserve Issue," pp. 214–17.

for the purpose of stating Indian grievances and promoting a solution of the issues. In 1909 the premier of British Columbia again denied the existence of the Indian title: "Of course it would be madness to think of conceding the Indians' demands. It is too late to discuss the equity of dispossessing the red man in America."[45] The increased tempo of activity carried over into 1910 when the "Friends of the Indians," organized by white folk, became active; they, too, went to Victoria to interview the premier, Sir Richard McBride. In March of 1910 another deputation of Indians went to Victoria and were told by the premier that his government held the opinion that the Indians had no title to the public lands of the province. And it was in the summer of 1910 that Prime Minister Sir Wilfrid Laurier met with groups of Indians at Prince Rupert and at Kamloops. He told the northern Indians at Prince Rupert that "the only way to settle this question that you have agitated for years is by a decision of the Judicial Committee, and I will take steps to help you."[46] The steps taken by the Dominion government included the appointment of J. A. J. McKenna as a special commissioner and the establishment of the Joint Royal Commission on Indian affairs in British Columbia, which sat from 1912 to 1916.

The comments of the commissioners on the responses of some of the Indian groups reveal the attitude of the Indians to the land problem. The Haida Indians at Skidegate, Queen Charlotte Islands, refused to meet with the commissioners, so a description of the reserves had to be secured from the Indian agent: "The representations of the Queen Charlotte Agency Indians for more adequate land allotments were hampered by their identification with the movement for recognition of Aboriginal Title and their fear that applications for additional Reserves might prejudice action in that connection (for which reason the Skidegates declined to discuss their land requirements with the Commission). . . . "[47] In the Hazelton area, east of Prince Rupert, meetings were held on the reserves, "and were well received by all except the Kitwancool, Getanmax, Kispaiox and Glen Vowell Tribes. These men refused to give any information about their reserves and declared their intention of adhering to this attitude until the question of Aboriginal Title had been settled."[48] In the same area the Kuldoes who refused to meet in the office of the Indian agent invited the commissioners to another building. Upon arrival there, "the Indians

[45]Quoted by MacInnes, p. 16, from the *Montreal Star* of July 31, 1909.
[46]*Claims*, p. xx.
[47]*Report of the Royal Commission on Indian Affairs for the Province of British Columbia*, III, p. 726–7.
[48]*Ibid.*, I, p. 172.

refused to answer any questions and would only speak of the aboriginal title to which they laid claim." At Metlakatla the reception was cordial and co-operative, but at Fort Simpson all information was refused. With respect to the Nishga, who presented a petition to Ottawa in 1913, the commission commented that:

During their visit to the home of the ancient Nishga nation, the Commissioners were distinctly impressed by the qualities of intelligence, progressiveness, industry and self-reliance displayed by these Indians, and by their requirement of other lands suitable for profitable use. This requirement the Commission has endeavored to meet by the cutting off of useless allotted lands and the allowance, where available, of other lands applied for by the Indians the potentialities of which render them of greater value to the Indians than the lands so cut off.[49]

These protests reported by the commissioners had by 1916 changed their character. They were no longer general and vague. The general resentment had been converted into a demand for a specific plan of action, namely a settlement of the aboriginal claim. Increased sophistication on the part of the Indians is revealed by the *British Columbia Land Situation: Memorandum for the Government of Canada*, dated May 3, 1911, at Ottawa, and signed by A. E. O'Meara. This was said to be a "statement of facts," made on behalf of the Douglas Portage chiefs. Not only did it incorporate facts of previous actions and attitudes but it also contained an argument leading to a request for governmental action.[50] Similarly a delegation of ninety-six Indians who went to Victoria in 1910 to wait upon the premier of the province was armed with specific demands, with documents of various kinds, and with their plea written down, as was the memorandum of the Douglas Portage chiefs. A record was thus accumulating, and the line of action could be delineated as the protest evolved into the final, complicated action of the 1927 parliamentary joint committee hearing of the Senate and the House of Commons. It was in this *Memorandum* that the aboriginal title claim made its first appearance as a *legal* claim.[51]

[49]*Ibid.*, III, p. 550.
[50]This *Memorandum* is given in full in *Claims*, pp. 53–4.
[51]This point is emphasized by the Deputy Superintendent-General of Indian Affairs in his presentation to the Joint Committee, 1927, *Claims*, p. viii. "The claim then began to take form as one which should be satisfied by a treaty or agreement with the Indians in which conditions and terms put forward by them or on their behalf must be considered and agreed upon before a cession of the alleged title would be granted. . . . The fact was admitted that it was not until about fifteen years ago that aboriginal title was first put forward as a formal legal claim by those who ever since have made it a bone of contention and by some a source of livelihood as well."

As government officials noted later, and with some feelings of animosity, not only was there now the legal claim, but the conditions under which it could be settled were specified.[52] As the claim became a legal conception with specific conditions for settlement, the need for counsel also changed, especially when the land title problem was included in the terms of reference of the Royal Commission of 1912–16. J. A. J. McKenna, the Dominion's special commissioner, in conference with Premier McBride, had set out the terms for the Royal Commission. The preamble stated that "it is desirable to settle all differences between the Governments of The Dominion and the Province respecting Indian lands and Indian Affairs generally. . . . " The commissioners did not attempt to do everything the preamble suggested; specific reference to the land title question was not made in the eight paragraphs of agreement and instruction. The two governments saw the problem, literally, the way the Indians had defined it at first: an acreage-location problem. Even though the Commissioners did a very thorough piece of work and attempted to be liberal, they did nothing but adjust acreages; they assumed no responsibility for the aboriginal title claim or for other aspects of Indian affairs generally.

While the Royal Commission was at work adjusting acreages, pressure group action appears to have been intensified. For this action to have any prospects of success, specialized counsel was necessary. Action had to be directed to the appropriate officials, it had to be couched in the terminology and form of governmental usages, and the action had to be sustained.[53] Most desirable of all, were advisers who were specific functionaries, knowledgable in the law, proper procedures, and grand strategies. For example, in the case of the Nishga petition the federal Department of Justice had become involved, and after this, efforts were made to have the case sent directly to the Judicial Committee of the Privy Council in London. Copies of the

[52]When the ninety-six Indians were discussing the problem with Premier McBride and the provincial Executive Council, they indicated their dissatisfaction with the results of their interview of the previous year. "McBride declared that the issue would never have been raised except through 'pernicious advice of some unscrupulous whites.' He further claimed that so far as the Province was concerned, the matter of dissatisfaction was unknown until a few months previous. Such a view seems quite incredible in view of at least two delegations to the King within the previous five years." Shankel, p. 195. It will be recalled that Indian Commissioner Powell felt that missionaries were participatng too much in political activities instead of "spiritual affairs."

[53]Shankel points out that the Nass River Indians spent $500 for legal advice in Victoria. For the Nishga petition of 1913, Mr. A. E. O'Meara referred to himself as their "honourary advisor."

petition were sent to J. M. Clark, counsel of the Indian Rights Association of British Columbia, to the chairman of the Friends of the Indians of British Columbia, to the Secretary of State for the Colonies, to the Prime Minister of Canada, to the Minister of Indian Affairs, and to the Minister of Justice. In May, 1916, Mr. A. E. O'Meara was retained as professional counsel by the Allied Tribes and worked with them until the end of the hearings in 1927.[54]

The heightened activity of the proponents of the land title claim was paralleled by increased governmental activity as the two governments attempted to resolve the problem. For the federal government it was essentially a legal problem centred around the question: How can the federal government get the provincial government to appear in a court of law? The provincial government continued its defensive policy and refused to appear in court, but the federal government maintained its customary faith in the adequacy of legal and administrative procedures for resolving the problem. For the Indians, the issue became more difficult and more complicated, and they drew increasingly apart from the two governments. While the Indians developed an organization to support their claims of injustice, the two governments claimed their policy to be generous as well as just. The completed work of the Royal Commission resulted in 47,000 acres of land being cut off from the reserves, and the British Columbia Land Act of 1916 returned 2 million acres from other federal land to the province as noted in *Claims of the Allied Tribes of British Columbia*. Even if the rearrangement of reserves had resulted in an increase instead of a net reduction of 47,000 acres, the frame of mind of the Indians was such that the net results had to be rejected by them. In the certainty of injustice, organizational activity through circular letters only confirmed what the Indian already knew for himself.

About this time the Indians began to produce their own leaders. Heretofore chiefs had appeared in the office of Governor Douglas or other governors of the colony or province, or had gone to London, but the evidence seems to show that the leaders at least behind the scenes were often white. However, now Rev. Peter R. Kelly appeared as a leader and remained so until after the hearings in 1927, as did Mr.

[54]In the documents available Mr. O'Meara carries in several places the title of Reverend; in one place he is referred to by Mr. Kelly as barrister. Shankel thinks that he was an unfortunate choice but interestingly enough because "he never understood what the government was trying to do," and not because he did not marshall well a point of view and evidence for a constitutional argument for the aboriginal land title. If he had "understood" what the government was trying to do, from Shankel's point of view, he would not have been retained or there would have been no case.

Andrew Paull. The former was a northern Indian, a member of the Haida group, who went to Victoria for the first time in 1910. Mr. Paull became the secretary of the Allied Tribes, and in that capacity did the work of gathering, collating, and organizing historical facts and experiences, verbal and written, regarding the land title claim. It was they who gave direction to the work of white friends and organizations, and who appeared as the spokesmen of delegates in Victoria and in Ottawa. These two men, supported by other able men, such as Chief Billy Assu of Cape Mudge, gained national attention and respect. Although Mr. Paull was a southern Indian, of the Squamish tribe, the northern ones—the Haida, the Tsimshian, and the Kwakiutl groups— became eventually the chief organizers, managers, and spokesmen through their activities in founding and directing the Native Brotherhood of British Columbia in 1930, just three years after what seemed complete defeat in the hearings of 1927.

In addition to producing their own leaders, the Indians now found it possible to achieve a greater unity of organization. In 1916 the Allied Tribes of British Columbia was formed through the initiative of the coastal Indians. This organization was the one which pursued for eleven years the land title claim by collecting funds, retaining Mr. O'Meara as professional counsel, and eventually securing a hearing in Parliament through the appointment of the Joint Committee in 1926. It managed to hold together, in spite of its struggle with Indians of the interior, enough of the tribes of the province to make the organization acceptable as a representative of Indian claims. Thus when the Allied Tribes rejected the work of the Royal Commission, the rejection was a clear indication that the Indians were more than just dissatisfied over having to accept whatever governmental policy doled out to them. It indicated very definitely that the coastal Indians had become almost completely modernized as a result of the work of the missionaries and the Indian agents, and as a result of their own activities in the struggle for survival in the fishing industry and for the maintenance of their traditional cultural values symbolized and integrated by the potlatch system.

THE INDIAN PROTEST: 1917–1926

In the earlier developments of the protest movement, the desire, on the part of the province, to reverse Imperial policy resulted in an explicit and persistent denial by the province of the aboriginal title to the land. In consequence, the political education of the Indians was extended. Political education involves the ability to appraise the re-

sults of individual and organizational activities in relation to their
influence on the members of the opposition and the colleagues of the
enterprise. For the purposes of delineating the main frame of action
for the final denouement of 1927, the main events of the intervening
years can be discussed in chronological order; in this manner appraisals of past actions and decisions as written or as manifested in
tactics can be presented briefly.

A central problem faced by Canadian Indians who wish to take
political action, and this is true in the United States also, has been to
develop unity among the tribes or regional groups. In 1917, on December 6, a meeting of the tribes of the interior was held at Spence's
Bridge, centrally located at the confluence of the Nicola and Thomp-
son Rivers. It was called in order to protest the results of the work
done between 1912 and 1916 by the Royal Commission. A resolution
passed on that date states succinctly how these Indians felt about the
work of the Commission, and includes a total rejection of the four
years' work. The paragraph following is part of that resolution:

We are sure that the government and a considerable number of white
men have for many years had in their minds a quite wrong idea of the
claims which we make, and the settlement which we desire. We do not
want anything extravagant, and we do not want anything hurtful to the
real interests of the white people. We want that our actual rights be determined and recognized; we want a settlement based upon justice. We want
a full opportunity of making a future for ourselves. We want all this done
in such a way that in the future we shall be able to live and work with the
white people as brothers and fellow-citizens.[55]

Several months later, on May 27, 1918, the Nishga—a Tsimshian
group from the Nass River country which had been politically active
since at least 1887 when representatives went to Victoria and which
had taken independent action in 1915 by sending a delegation to
Ottawa—had their agents send a report to the Lord President of His
Majesty's Privy Council. The Nishga Petition, first received by the
Dominion government on June 19, 1913, became singularly important
in the minds of all Indians. It claimed title to the land on the basis
of the Declaration of 1763, and generally explained the Indian thoughts
on the land title question. Since this Petition was rejected by an Order
in Council in June, 1915, the Nishga group in 1918 sent the report to
London, and from then on Indian action was premised on the assumption that their case was pending before the Privy Council. Administrators later called this assumption a fiction. When the Allied Tribes
presented their claims in the final parliamentary action of 1926–27,

[55]*Claims*, p. 170.

the opening sentence of their statements indicates that "the general view held by us with regard to the report of the Royal Commission was correctly stated . . . by the Agents of the Nishga Tribe . . . on 27th May, 1918."[56] With respect to specific conditions and modes of procedure, the Allied Tribes further used the Nishga proposal that "the matter of lands to be reserved [should] be finally dealt with by the Secretary of State for the Colonies." The Allied Tribes wanted all other matters of business to be attended to by the Parliament of Canada.

In the process of cultural change and in the development of institutions for the new conditions of living, the Tsimshian, Haida, Kwakiutl and Coast Salish have apparently found it more feasible to develop collective action and political solidarity than have other regional groups in British Columbia. These coastal tribes have attempted to secure support from all the Indians in British Columbia, but they have had limited success as is evident from the issues and problems within the Native Brotherhood of British Columbia and in the parliamentary hearings, 1946–49. To solve the problems of collective action which separate interior from coastal Indians, the Executive Committee of the Allied Tribes met in Vancouver, in February, 1919, and "an alliance of tribes [was] formed subsequently," thus bringing more tribal groups into the organization. It is also at this time that more formal action was taken to secure additional assistance from outsiders. James A. Teit, who is famous in anthropological history and literature as an associate of Franz Boas, was appointed to a post known as Special Agent. In this way the Allied Tribes was developing further strength to conduct the campaign.

As part of this campaign, propagandistic features were extended. In November, 1919, what was said to be an "exhaustive" statement of the claims of the Allied Tribes was prepared for the government of British Columbia. The statement was issued in the form of a pamphlet and apparently given wide circulation. It is regrettable that conditions make it difficult to recapture the reception of this pamphlet and its influences, for propaganda and public relations, as well as lawyers and special agents, were by then considered a necessary adjunct to the Indians' campaign. When the Dominion Government asked that a "concrete proposal" be made, the Indians replied that they had already made concrete proposals. These had been first formulated in 1916 and submitted to the government of Canada and the Secretary of State for the Colonies.[57] The pamphlet was, thus, essentially a restatement.

[56]Ibid., pp. 33–4. The Nishga Petition is reproduced in full on p. 58.
[57]See Ibid., pp. xi, xxi, 31ff.

To turn to the results of the Royal Commission's report, on another front, it was necessary, because the changes in reserves were based upon an agreement between the Government of Canada and the provincial government, for Parliament to initiate legislation for the purpose of fulfilling the original agreement with the government at Victoria. Therefore, in the parliamentary session of 1919–1920, Bill 13 was introduced for that purpose. The major reaction of the Allied Tribes was to have Special Agent Teit prepare a memorandum for the Senate. For reasons unknown this was never delivered, and it was not until the hearings of 1926–27 that the Teit document was read into testimony and evidence, but since Teit was expressing the point of view of all the Indians in the province, those north and south as well as interior and coastal groups, the memorandum is quoted here in part:

The Indians see nothing of real value for them in the work of the Royal Commission. Their crying needs have not been met. The Commissioners did not fix up their hunting rights, fishing rights, water rights, and land rights, nor did they deal with the matter of reserves in a satisfactory manner. Their dealing with reserves has been a kind of manipulation to suit the whites, and not the Indians. All they have done is to recommend that about 47,000 acres of generally speaking good lands be taken from the Indians, and about 80,000 acres of generally speaking poor lands, be given in their place. A lot of the land recommended to be taken from the reserves has been coveted by whites for a number of years. Most of the 80,000 acres additional lands is to be provided by the Province, but it seems that the Indians are really paying for these lands. Fifty per cent of the value of the 47,000 acres to be taken from the Indians is to go to the Province, and it seems this amount will come to more than the value of the land the Province is to give the Indians. The Province loses nothing, the Dominion loses nothing, and the Indians are the losers. They get fifty per cent on the 47,000 acres, but, as the 47,000 acres is much more valuable land than the 80,000 they are actually losers by the work of the Commission.[58]

The consideration of Bill 13 was marked by considerable action. For the Indians it was one more basic legislative and legal step against them. From the viewpoint of the province, it was a step in support of the position upon which all strategies had been based for at least a half-century. The Indians sent a delegation to Ottawa; their solicitor appeared and presented their claims. In the course of the debate in the Senate, Senator Bostock expressed the fear that if Bill 13 passed, the Indians might "be entirely put out of Court and be unable to proceed on any question of title." Parliament, however, did pass Bill 13; it became Chapter 51 of Statutes. In this manner the Governor-General-in-Council was authorized to adopt the report of the Commission and

[58]*Ibid.*, p. 125.

to carry out the original agreement with the province of British Columbia.

From the standpoint of responsible officials, the Indians' preoccupation with the land title question was now not only irritating but also useless. The officials, whose approach to the claims of the Indians was a legal one, controlled the right to say whether the case of the Indians could be brought to a test of law in an appropriate court action.

Another special agent for the Indians was Mr. O'Meara (addressed in 1914 by the Minister of Justice, C. J. Doherty, as Reverend Arthur E. O'Meara, B.A.), who seems to have been retained first by the Nishga and later by the Allied Tribes. When the Minister of Justice informed him by letter in 1914 that the Government of Canada had no power or authority to refer anything to the Privy Council, the Minister of Justice was able to state his own recommendations on how to bring clarification into the thinking of the Indians and thus more adequate procedures into their actions. The Nishga Petition had been considered in December, 1913, by the Minister of Justice; in March, 1914, the Deputy Superintendent-General of Indian Affairs had sent a memorandum regarding it to the Minister of the Interior; and as indicated, the Minister of Justice had written to Mr. O'Meara about the way cases are sent to the Privy Council. When the delegation of fifteen Indians went to see Dr. Duncan Scott, the chief administrator of Indian Affairs in Ottawa, Mr. O'Meara was again involved. In September, 1916, the Duke of Connaught, having looked over the correspondence, replied to a letter from the Nishga Indians and interior tribes, suggesting that they wait until the Royal Commission had completed its work—in fact, ordering them to do so. The secretary to the Governor-General informed Mr. O'Meara that His Royal Highness was not prepared to interfere. Then in 1918 the "agents" of Nishga sent to the Lord President of His Majesty's Privy Council their view of the work of the Royal Commission. Finally, on March 17, 1920, the secretary of the Governor-General sent a "final" letter, the last paragraph reading as follows:

You have already been informed on several occasions of the attitude of the Dominion Government towards this claim and there does not appear to be anything further for me to add except the Governor General takes no action nor does he desire to take any action, except upon the advice of his constitutional advisers. Under these circumstances, I must ask you to consider this letter as final.

When Mr. Mackenzie King took office as Prime Minister in 1921, he was apparently interested enough to have his Minister of the Interior, Mr. Stewart, look into the matter, and Mr. Stewart seems to have taken a personal interest in the case. In the summer of 1922, Mr. Stewart met with Indian leaders in Vancouver. Prior to this meeting, in January, the Kelly-Teit Memorandum was prepared, for apparently the "final" letter from the secretary of the Governor-General had raised the question as to whether Mr. O'Meara should be retained as general counsel. This new memorandum stated that he would be retained as counsel for the "newly formed Alliance of Indian Tribes of British Columbia." What Mr. Stewart accomplished in the summer of 1922 is not clear, but he did return to Vancouver in 1923, and on July 27 had a meeting with the Executive Committee and general counsel of the Allied Tribes at which he conceded that the Tribes were entitled to secure a judicial decision on the Indian land controversy and gave assurance that the Dominion of Canada would help them to secure such a decision. Eight years had elapsed since the Minister of Justice had written to Mr. O'Meara for the first time but during those years no official of the Dominion Government had gone as far as Mr. Stewart. The Deputy Superintendent-General of Indian Affairs, Dr. Duncan Scott, went to Victoria and in August met with many Indians and held a comprehensive discussion with them about many issues: fishing rights, hunting licenses, timber rights, funded moneys, pelagic sealing, education, medical care, and hospitals. In his statement regarding this conference, Dr. Scott said, "It became clear that the Indians intended to rely on the claims made by the pamphlet, and in the end it will be found that all the claims made there, with one important addition, are now made conditions for the cession of the Indian Title."[59]

Ever since British Columbia joined the Dominion in 1871, provincial officials have been very circumspect in their official actions. They have, at the same time, been courteous to any group of Indians who would ask for an audience and come to Victoria. The province had no difficulty in accepting the Report of the Royal Commission of 1912–1916; it did not do so however until 1923, and it did so then on the assumption that the two governments had brought about final settlement of all questions. Thus, when the Indians met with the Hon. Mr. Stewart in Victoria, Premier Pattulo refused to send a representative to the meeting, for it was his formal opinion that Indian problems were issues to be settled between the two governments. This policy was followed by provincial officials until the 1940's, at which time Indian labour became important, and a new generation of officials gained control of the provincial government.

As in most of Canada, the Indians in British Columbia have not been

[59]*Ibid.*, p. 67.

particularly wealthy, especially prior to World War II. The development of the campaign for justice had its beginnings in the days when the funds necessary for promoting claims to justice were hard to come by, and as the campaign became more complex and more extensive, the Allied Tribes were apparently short of financial support. In September, 1923, the Executive Committee of the organization reported on the meetings with the Hon. Mr. Stewart and Dr. Duncan Scott, and also appealed for funds, saying that "the Committee must have ample means to take full advantage of any opening to press for success which would make possible the full attainment of the aspirations of the Indian Tribes."

From the available records, it would be presumptuous to attempt an appraisal of the influence of the collective pressure which the Allied Tribes placed upon the federal government. But after the meetings in Vancouver and Victoria, Dr. Duncan Scott reported on October 17, 1923, that he had discussed the problems of the Indians with the Department of Fisheries and with the province and had been "informed by the Chief Inspector for the Province of British Columbia . . . that Mr. J. A. Motherwell, Chief Inspector of Fisheries for the Province, has stated that salmon and herring and seining licenses similar to those which in the past have been issued to resident whites will in future be available to Canadian Indians in their own name."[60] The Indian had had the privilege of catching fish and game on a reserve for his own immediate consumption, but because of his status as a ward of the Dominion Government and because of conflict between wardship and provincial laws, no Indian had been able to secure an individual license for commercial fishing. However in 1923 the first step in removing such total disabilities for commercial operations was taken. It was possibly the beginning of the change in the economic status of Indians on the coast, for they could now become independent fishermen and entrepreneurs in that industry. This was, then, at least one concrete result coming from agitation and pressure. As important as it was, it could be looked upon only as a minor achievement for a major campaign.

In late 1923 the Allied Tribes had submitted a memorandum to the Department of Justice, asking questions of the Government of Canada. After some months of deliberation, the questions were answered in a reply stating that the Departments of Justice and Indian Affairs regarded Statute 51, of 1920, based on Bill 13, as intended "not for bringing about an actual adjustment of all matters . . . but for the purpose of bringing about a legislative adjustment of all such matters and

[60]*Ibid.*, p. 67.

thus effecting final settlement under the laws of Canada without the concurrence or consent of the Indian Tribes of British Columbia."[61] By this time the Allied Tribes considered itself the official spokesman for the Indian tribes of the province; since the Statute was enabling legislation for the passage of an Order in Council adopting the report of the 1912–1916 Royal Commission, the Allied Tribes dispatched a memorandum to the Government of Canada on February 29, 1924, opposing the passing of such an order. The Allied Tribes professed that the purposes of the Agreement and the Act had not been accomplished. When this action failed to stop the passage of such an order, the Executive Committee adopted the following resolution:

In view of the fact that the two Governments have passed Orders-in-Council confirming the Report of the Royal Commission on Indian Affairs, we the Executive Committee of the Allied Tribes of British Columbia are more than ever determined to take such action as may be necessary in order that the Indian Tribes of British Columbia may receive justice and are furthermore determined to establish the rights claimed by them by a judicial decision of His Majesty's Council.

Two months later a delegation of Indians met with the federal cabinet in Ottawa and presented a memorial on title claims. Yet no definite action towards getting their case before the Privy Council had been taken. In the House of Commons over a year later, the Hon. Mr. Stewart, still Minister of the Interior, indicated again that the Allied Tribes should try to secure a Privy Council decision and that the Government would give its sanction for doing so. He stated that the claim would have to be "something very concrete." Again Allied Tribes replied that their statement of December, 1919, was "something very concrete."

Apparently the Indians had neither the funds nor the knowledge to secure a decision from the Privy Council. A reading of the complete evidence and testimony as well as the documents which go back to 1909 indicates that Mr. O'Meara was seemingly not the best of general counsels and that his tactics in committee hearings were not esteemed by members of Parliament. For reasons we are unable to discover now, at this point a change in strategy was apparently in the making. On August 17, 1925, Mr. O'Meara dispatched at letter to the Minister of Justice in Ottawa, restating the history of the case and closing with the suggestion that a joint committee of Parliament be appointed for handling the issue.

In June, 1926, the change in strategy was clearly defined by a petition presented to Parliament. And a memorial was presented, interest-

[61]*Ibid.*, p. xxi.

ingly enough, to the Minister of Justice, claiming that "the Dominion of Canada is under obligation for providing all funds already expended and all funds requiring hereafter to be expended by the Allied Tribes in dealing with the Indian land controversy, in establishing the rights of the Allied Tribes, and in bringing about final adjustment of all matters relating to Indian Affairs in British Columbia."[62] To advise the Indians of this change of strategy, the Executive Committee issued a circular letter in December, 1926, stating the status of the case and the consequences of the political upheaval caused by the change of government. It also expressed hope for the appointment of a special committee. If this hope were achieved, then "The Special Committee will also consider the closely related matter of the first three prayers of the Petition asking for, (1) Safeguarding of the aboriginal rights of the Indian Tribes of British Columbia, (2) Defining of the issues between the Allied Tribes and the two Governments which require to be judicially decided and, (3) Helping forward the independent judicial proceedings of the Allied Tribes."[63]

In the 1926–27 session of Parliament, a Special Joint Committee was appointed to consider the Allied Tribes petition of June, 1926. On March 22, 1927, the Committee convened. The Premier of British Columbia, Mr. Oliver, advised the Hon. Mr. Stewart that no representative from British Columbia would be present. By April 14, 1927, the Report of the Special Joint Committee was concurred in. Extracts from the last two paragraphs are quoted:

It may be remarked with reference to the payment of annuities that the policy for the payment of annual sums to individual Indians was inaugurated in the early days, having in view the then conditions of the Indians, and that the annuity might be a source of revenue for their support, but conditions have changed so materially that the need and usefulness of such a per capita payment to Indians of British Columbia is negligible. In lieu of an annuity your committee would recommend that the sum of $100,000 should be expended annually for the purposes already recommended, that is, technical education, provision of hospitals and medical attendance, and in the promotion of agriculture, stock-raising and fruit culture, and in the development of irrigation projects. An annual expenditure of this amount for the purpose would seem to be far more applicable to the Indians in their present condition than in the payment of any per capita amount.

In concluding this Report your Committee would recommend that the decision arrived at should be made known as completely as possible to the Indians of British Columbia by direction of the Superintendent General of Indian Affairs in order that they may become aware of the finality of the findings and advised that no funds should be contributed by them to continue further presentation of a claim which has now been disallowed. . . ."

[62]*Ibid.*, p. xxii.
[63]*Ibid.*, p. 115.

A DEFEATED CAMPAIGN—1927

The land title question emerged during a period of unusually rapid and profound social change in the whole of the West. The gold rush of 1858, the developing exploitation of the forests and the sea, and the expansion of urban areas were the cause of numerous incidents between Indian and white as the settlement of the land progressed. A provincial government replaced colonial rule, and almost immediately Imperial policy was reversed with respect to land for natives. It is not hard to comprehend how the experiences of the natives gave rise to a resentment that developed into open hostility and hatred, and to feelings of inadequacy in coping with the problems of becoming a displaced population.

The most distinguishable and most inexplicable development was the change from mere feelings of resentment and hostility owing to specific incidents, to a persistent, sustained, and concerted effort which by 1917 had become a well-directed demand based upon a literature of injustice. Some of the Indians, prominent in the movement, demanded "justice" in the land title question, and in making this demand, they spoke for all Indians. Justice as an idea and as a term in both perspectives is still heard orally among them and found frequently in the *Native Voice*. If this transformation had not occurred, there would not have been a protest movement, for the feelings of resentment would have remained, we suspect, on an individual level of expression, and therefore unorganized and socially ineffective. It was the incorporation of hostility into a structure of ideas and conceptions of status which made the transformation of resentment of such central significance.

There were several not so obvious cultural changes during the period of agitation of the land title question which can be delineated from the materials presented previously. During the first stages of their protest the Indians were predominantly tribal in their orientation towards the world and in their social organization. But they were becoming increasingly literate and by the 1920's not only did many of the Indians who led their people have a fluent command of English but they had become steeped in the written history of the various issues in which they were now involved and of their relations with the whites. They had become better versed in the principles of Canadian law, and through the preparation of many petitions and their trips to Victoria and later to Ottawa, as well as to England, they had become better acquainted with Canadian political procedures. Thus, they were no longer completely dependent upon the missionary, the Indian agent, or the sympathetic white for the direction of their protest. Although these people continued to be present, they were there as functionaries retained for the Allied Tribes.

The importance of the growth in literacy among the natives as a result of the educational, religious, and commercial activities of the whites cannot be questioned. But, important as that was, a more significant fact was that it was the missionaries and other sympathetic white people who fostered the ideas and gave the early direction that converted resentment and hostility into a concerted and sustained protest. Thus their function was to define goals and formulate techniques and strategies which an organization needs for achievement. In so doing they gave meaning to even the lesser, vague feelings of a group undergoing rapid acculturation. These definitions clarified for the Indian the true source of his resentment and called forth sympathy from selected whites as well. The paramount problem, as they came to see it, was the injustice of the land title question. When Rev. Peter Kelly spoke to the writer about the federal and provincial governments he said simply: "They did not do what they said they would do."

The remarkable change in the Indians of the Northwest Coast culture area has been noted many times. It is an area where one can find the last totem pole carver, numerous examples of former Indian village life, an area where one finds the "most streamlined modern Indian," who has become an exploiter of his cultural heritage to earn a living—the same type as found in the professional Westerner, Southerner, or Cherokee. But even though the Indian was changing as a consequenc of the invasion of the Europeans and his close association with them, even though he was becoming more fully informed and skilled in the use of the political and legal means at hand to make life easier both in the new British Columbia and in Canada generally, it is just as true that Canadians and the Canadian system were changing. Thus we may point out an additional change during the historical period of the land title question: the change in their conceptions of Indians and the Indian's problems made by cabinet officials, members of Parliament, and other parties involved, and the changes of policy that resulted.

It has been said with pride that Canada inherited Imperial colonial policy; yet, while the Colonial Office stood on general principles, the colonies, at least British Columbia, attempted to reduce the Indian to a social and land-holding non-entity. But administrators and parliaments change and over the years of the protest movement, the federal parliament passed through the era of Sir John A. Macdonald, the wilful first prime minister of the Dominion, through the period of Sir Wilfrid Laurier, and into the days of Mackenzie King. During these important changes, one can see a shift in tactics and conceptions from the use of boundary commissions in the earlier days, to administrative investigations, and finally, in 1927, to a parliamentary hearing. For the Indians to have secured a hearing in Parliament was an achievement which one senses they considered as no less than revolutionary. The significance of these changes in tactics and in officials' conceptions lies in the difference between attention to boundaries merely from an economic point of view, which continues to be of major importance in reserve management, and attention to land titles as associated with legal rights and privileges. The social significance of each kind of attention is quite different. The latter is based upon symbols of status of the social system; it involves rights and privileges; it makes use of institutionalized means for redressing more general grievances even for wards; and it takes the issues to the national level of legislative concern and policy formation. For the Indians of 1927 a parliamentary hearing symbolized a far more acceptable recognition of their identity as a nation.

For the non-Indian, it is difficult to comprehend not only the means by which the resentment and open hostility of the Indian became transformed but also why, after transformation, the hostility persisted and seemed to preoccupy the Indians and become integrated into their self-conception. The persistence of this hostility was reinforced by the potlatch question, prompted by a resentment of the potlatch legislation and its intermittent local variation in enforcement. It will be recalled that the potlatch was an integral part of the cultural organization of each tribal group. Changes in the nature of the fishing industry, the relocation of the villages, the Christianization of large segments of some tribal groups such as the Tsimshian and the Haida, and the process of acculturation working informally through the assumption of European behaviour and formally through wardship and education caused the potlatch system to decline, to become transformed, or to disappear completely. Thus, although resentment was generated by the legislation, the potlatch was too limited an issue to be a unifying force. The conception of the potlatch had changed for many of the Indians. It had come to symbolize the old way of life, the traditional values which could never, in the new way of living, be restored. None the less thousands of Indians were sentimental about it; for them the legislation was just one more proof of the way in which the white man was attempting to do away with the Indian. The nature of potlatching was such that a movement to restore the potlatch could not inspire and catch the imagination or engage the loyalties of the Indians for any long, sustained, concerted group effort towards relating the Indian more acceptably and effectively to the social organization of British Columbia. Hence we may suspect that some of the hostility aroused by the potlatch went into the land title question movement where the Indian was attempting to uphold the same conception of justice and using the same procedures for securing it as were available to any other kind of Canadian. It was not until twenty-four years later, in 1951, that the Potlatch Law was rescinded.

The $100,000 settlement of 1927 continues to be interpreted as a defeat. It was a sudden letdown for the Indians who had been so long preoccupied with the issues. The Allied Tribes had been organized to try to develop some unity among the tribes, and now that the defeat was suffered, the organization simply collapsed. It had served its purpose, and upon reflection one can see that it undoubtedly served others, too. Its problem of the organization and formulation of policy quite naturally brought to the forefront the differences between the Indians of the coastal area and those of the interior. The differences were obvious in the economic foundations of Indian life, but the Allied Tribes showed clearly that these differences also existed in the social organization and heritage of the tribes. The function of the Allied Tribes was to develop a sense of accomplishment possible above the tribal unit. The coastal Indians, the ones whose ancestors had created the Northwest Coast culture area, had as a tribal heritage the fundamental conceptions of the old potlatching system based on a highly stratified, status-conscious, social system. They understood enterprise, not as the missionary wanted them to undertake it but in the way it was required for potlatching; they understood the manipulation of people, the use of wealth as a symbol of rank and generalized social status. They were, too, carriers of a tradition of great oratory, of great drama, of great feats—all skills required in tribal life in order to secure status. In fact, one can well entertain the hypothesis that it was these social skills—still manifested in Peter Kelly, Chief Scow, and the late Andrew Paull—that account for their turning the work of the missionaries, of Indian agents, and of other whites, such as the eminent anthropologists Franz Boas and Edwin Sapir, to advantage for the maintenance of group identity, an identity almost lost through the process of population displacement.

5. The Struggle For Identity: 1946-1951

THE DEFEAT of 1927 was followed closely by the great depression, and since minority groups are usually employed in the marginal occupations of an area, it is possible that the depression was felt sooner by the Indians. With their defeat in the land title debate and the acute depression shortly conjoining, one might have supposed that the collapse of the Allied Tribes would have, for some time, put an end to any further organizational efforts for an improved standard of living and acceptance in the community at large. Although these two goals had not been the explicit, direct purpose of the Allied Tribes, its methods did represent for many Indians the way to cure some of their troubles. And so, in spite of the disillusionment of 1927, only three years later a new organization came into existence—the Native Brotherhood of British Columbia—and it has continued to operate ever since.

The emergence of trade unions, particularly in the fishing industry in 1930, is of major importance as an indicator of the changes in regional social organization for both the Indians and the whites. This development has been described by Hawthorn, Belshaw, and Jamieson and by Drucker.[1] There we observe the long struggle for survival in its economic form. It is, however, the formation of the Native Brotherhood that reveals the determinative, collective efforts of the Indian to survive as a people; from then on these efforts provide a more clearly defined political orientation upon which to base strategy and tactics. The attempt to improve the position of the Indian in the regional social system has since been made within an institutional structure strictly Indian in origin.[2] The singular defeat in the land title question is in

[1]See *Indians of British Columbia* and *The Native Brotherhoods*. Drucker draws no conclusion about the future of the Indians in the industry. However, Hawthorn, Belshaw, and Jamieson are of the opinion that increasing competition and technological trends within the industry will make it increasingly difficult for the Indian to maintain a satisfactory place in it.

[2]Evidence regarding organization and direction of the Allied tribes suggests that it was highly dependent upon the missionaries, "Friends of the Indians," and particular people such as James Teit. The Native Brotherhood may retain non-Indian counsel now and then, but it is dependent entirely upon Indians for its leadership and officers.

perspective, thus, a turning rather than a terminal point in the Indians'
attempt to improve their status; fantasies of wealth prior to 1927 could
be sustained by the hope of a favourable decision, but when that hope
was killed, the problems of the Indians with or without such fantasies
continued, and they remained irritating, pervasive, and unsatisfactorily
managed—or even, perhaps, unmanageable. If the latter were the case,
then it remained to be demonstrated to the native Canadians as an
outcome of their own actions and conclusions rather than those of
agents or missionaries.

The Allied Tribes had been formed a decade earlier for the express
purpose of dealing with a single, basic question. To secure collective
action among people whose motives are dominated by loyalties to
clans and villages and who speak different languages is extraordinarily
difficult. In such conditions of divisiveness collective action is quite
likely possible only in extreme crises. Although all of the coastal
Indians were of the same culture area, their political organization was
bound to clan and village, and there were important barriers between
tribes based upon language differences. Since the initiation of language
classes by Mr. Duncan in 1857, missionaries and teachers have continued teaching English systematically. While there is no way of
establishing satisfactorily the extent to which English had become an
adequate language for inter-tribal communication by 1930, the very
fact of the organization of the N.B.B.C. and its continuance points to
the emergence of a generation of adult Indians in several tribes with
a sufficient command of English for political action. The work of the
first missionaries had included the task of learning the native tongues
for purposes of preaching and converting. The well-known Canadian
scientist, George Dawson, reported in his famous paper "Notes and
Observations on the Kwakiool People"[3] that the major problem of
Mr. A. J. Hall, who arrived at Alert Bay in 1878, was learning the
language. Mr. Hall set out to provide a dictionary of the Kwakiutl
language so that it could be learned more easily by succeeding generations of missionaries.[4] As one scans quickly the shelves of libraries of
divinity schools where mission work has been fostered, one can only
be deeply impressed by the amount of work which missionaries have
devoted to writing grammars and preparing dictionaries. As concerned
as Mr. Hall was about the Kwakiutl language for following generations

---

[3]*Transactions of the Royal Society of Canada*, V (1887), s. II, pp. 63–98.
[4]It will be recalled that the lay missionary Duncan spent five years learning
the language and customs of the Tsimshian before he started an intense programme of missionary work.

of mission workers, the trend in North America for the indigenous populations has always been towards the adoption of the European language—English, French, Spanish, or Portuguese—as a second language, and in some areas, the adopted language has become eventually the mother tongue. This trend has moved slowly and has not yet reached all sections. Increasingly the Indians of British Columbia are becoming aware of the necessity for a command of English as an important adaptation to contemporary living, although certainly the older ones still place a premium upon the use of their mother tongue. Indian tongues are important in local communities; for giving sermons in Kwakiutl at the Anglican Church in Alert Bay, interpreters were still in use in 1946—and are quite likely today. Where, however, the trend has brought about increased fluency in conversational and written English among enough Indians, then a new era in the life of the Indian has been initiated. The missionary or white man as a go-between is eliminated and an entirely new basis for the organization and direction of a protest movement is possible. The white man's techniques of propaganda, pressure, and political action are brought close to hand. And it is easier to use that major technique for handling minority group problems, namely, the judicial system. Moreover, the written history of Indian-white relations becomes accessible to the Indian in the formal documents of government, in the records of *Hansard*, and in the *Annual Report* of Indian Affairs. And of course, what are thought to be ancient customs and legends are gradually set down in writing. Thus, the emergence of the Native Brotherhood was one indication that a new era had formally arrived, and that the system of communication among the diverse language groups of the British Columbia Indians with their marked geographic isolation had changed.

THE NATIVE BROTHERHOOD AND ITS *Native Voice*

The development by the Indians of an organization to deal with their problems brought together several lines of Indian experience derived from their relations with British Columbians of both European and oriental descent. Gladstone and Jamieson have shown that in the fishing industry the Native Brotherhood is now the chief agent for collective bargaining. Here, there have been persistent problems owing to technological change as well as the conflicts among ethnic and racial groups within the industry. It was not only that the Indian, if he did not become a part of the organization of the industry, would receive lower prices for his fish, but that he would be given actually less opportunity to fish than other ethnic or racial groups.[5] In both the financial and management policies and in the actual fishing operations, the Indian has had and will continue to have an interest which is, one supposes from the evidence available, more important to him than to other groups. The paramount importance of fishing to the coastal Indians is based upon their historic relationship to the industry, their wide distribution of capital, the flexibility in their social organization, and a number of other factors, less clearly distinguished, such as occupational discrimination in urban areas, and the level of educational achievement. Fishing, lumbering, seasonal agricultural work, and casual labour, ranking roughly in that order, have so far been the major occupations of the coastal Indians.

As a foundation for a permanent protest organization, the potlatch question, in 1930, was clearly unsuitable. But the elimination of the potlatch had been an aspiration of the missionaries; a clause in the Indian Act had prohibited it, potlatchers had gone to jail, and Indians had been sued by lawyers for not paying professional fees—all these experiences, imposed upon the Indians by the white man and his government, had left an important, intense feeling as part of their attitude towards the white men. An analysis of the land title question indicates the same conclusions. It was these experiences coupled with an analysis of contemporary problems that gave birth to the Native Brotherhood and led it to develop into more than a mere trade union.

Until Philip Drucker studied the two native brotherhoods on the Northwest Coast, little research had been done on the origin and early days of the Native Brotherhood of British Columbia.[6] Some thirty years have passed since the defeat of 1927, and during that time the coastal Indians have changed very markedly as have the resident whites and therefore it is difficult to reconstruct the social conditions which gave rise to the N.B.B.C. The influence of the missionaries and

[5]Indians have so told the writer, and it appears from the *Minutes* of the Special Joint Committee that this discrimination continues. It would seem that the historical conflict and discrimination have led to the incorporation of a belief which the Indian now has about unfair charges, differential prices, differential wages, differential licensing of boats, and differential employment of Indian women in canneries. In contemporary relations, there are sufficient cases of discrimination for Indians to *know* that all they *claim* can be nothing less than generally true, even with respect to public policy.

[6]The first draft of the present manuscript was completed before Drucker's *Native Brotherhoods* was published. Note has been taken of Drucker's contributions; his work and the materials contained in this presentation supplement each other.

the role of the different denominations in the formation and development of the organization remain unrecorded; and yet, in doing field work one realizes enough of the depth of feeling, the play of politics, and the hopes of individuals to strike the profound, yet sufficiently general, motives for the development of an organization which will settle the "problems" of the Indians. Drucker reported the names of prominent Indians who initiated the organizational drive, and what actions they took in attempting to interest others among the Indian villages. On the same theme, Thomas Gosnell, at the meeting of the Special Joint Committee of Parliament on May 2, 1947, testified as follows:

I was one of the founders of the Native Brotherhood of British Columbia during the year 1930. I have been a councillor at the village of Port Simpson for about twenty years working under the advancement part of the Indian Act. I have been chief councillor about half of that period.

During the depression time of 1929 and 1930 things were very bad amongst the native people. The provincial government issued relief to citizens of British Columbia, and there was nothing available for the Indians in British Columbia. Depression times hit the country and everybody suffered. By reason of that council meetings have taken place to find an avenue to help the destitute Indians in the northern part of British Columbia. According to our meetings with the Indian agents there is no avenue open. An Indian either has to be sick or there had to be some actual starvation and destitution before he comes under relief, which calls for approximately $4.00 and some odd cents.

In answer to a question, Mr. Gosnell stated that it was $4.00 per month and not per week. He continued:

This was not available to the Indians during the depression time. The Indian Agent said, "You have to be sick." During our informal talks at the council meetings the question of helping the Indians came up. Before the birth of the Brotherhood started. The council does not sponsor it, but through discussion and talks with the senior members of the bands it was felt an Indian organization would be of benefit to the Indians. The problems concerning Indians cannot be dealt with by one individual village. . . . The birth of the Brotherhood took place in about six months following.[7]

As troublesome as the fishing industry has been for the Indians of the coastal area, their problems had broadened by 1930. The strategy of the Allied Tribes had proved to be a *rue fermée*. The Indians had wanted a general recognition of their problems, but these were converted by officials into a legalistic argument. The testimony of Thomas Gosnell is evidence that the great depression brought to the Indian

[7]*Minutes*, 1947, No. 17, May 2.

an entirely different conception of wardship. It was a period in which the glaring inequalities were demonstrated for all age groups and occupations among them. The Indian agent had told them that they were ineligible for any assistance. It became obvious not only that the old method of handling the problems of each village individually was inadequate—a fact apparently recognized as early as 1917 by the Tsimshian[8]—but also that all the Indians had common problems because of wardship and segregation. The Allied Tribes had, without much success, attempted to get all the Indians in British Columbia to support their actions in the land title question. The Native Brotherhood set out to organize the coastal Indians, all of whom had a stake in the fishing industry one way or another, and then go about the task of handling the problems relating to their general status and common welfare. What was done in the early days of the Brotherhood, outside of collective bargaining, is unknown. But one guesses that the annual conventions became increasingly important. Drucker noted that the problems of conscription and income tax led to important increases in membership in the Brotherhood. The more fully acculturated Indian was emerging, as was evident from the pages of the *Native Voice*, established in December, 1946, and from the testimony of witnesses and written briefs submitted to the Special Joint Committee, beginning about six months earlier.

Life along the British Columbia coast has been changed profoundly with the development of the internal combustion engine and the radio.

[8]Drucker's statement regarding the origins of the Native Brotherhood of British Columbia is of course the most comprehensive. He does not, however, make reference to the "Tsimpshean Agreement" which to some Indians is a part of the story of their struggle to gain unity.

The official organ of the Native Brotherhood, the *Native Voice*, February, 1948, makes reference to "the Tsimpshean Agreement." At the 1948 annual convention, Chief Arthur McDames attended and was said to be the only living survivor of the group who signed this agreement. Ten bands of "Tsimpshean" are listed; it is dated November 28, 1917, and drawn up as a legal document. Part of it reads:

". . . the above bands have agreed in the future in connection with all matters affecting the general rights and privileges of the Indians, and all matters not purely of a local nature, to cooperate and act together, and to form a Joint Special Council (general) for the purposes.

"NOW THEREFORE THIS AGREEMENT WITNESSETH that each of said Bands agree with the other bands as follows: . . . " There follows nine clauses regarding the organization of this Council.

It was the wish of Chief McDames that this agreement be published in the *Native Voice*. The purpose as stated was to let "it be known that the wishes of those Chiefs who died would still be carried on and that the Native Brotherhood now fully recognized as an organization can conduct its own affairs successfully."

The machines have impinged upon the Indian as they have the whites, though possibly in a different way. The scattered population and the slowness of communication due to physical conditions had always impeded efforts at collective organization. Some appreciation of these factors may be gained from the statistics given to the Special Joint Committee by Major D. M. McKay, then Commissioner for Indian Affairs in British Columbia, and now Director of the Indian Affairs Branch, Ottawa: a total Indian population in British Columbia of 25,515, of whom over 12,000 were under 17 years of age; a total of some 170 Indian villages, plus numerous communities with scattered habitations; 1,609 Indian reserves in British Columbia comprising in excess of 829,000 acres; and, for the purposes of administration, 19 agencies, 17 of them under the Commissioner of Indian Affairs.[9]

Although the developments of modern technology have lessened the significance of geographic features and eliminated some conspicuous parts of the traditional cultures, the social changes of the past century which have resulted in the modern Indian are also an outstanding achievement of the natives. Commissioner McKay in his testimony before the Joint Committee commented on this change as well as on the significance of community rejection.

. . . I recall that it was in 1850 that Sir James Douglas referred to the roving bands of savages being a menace to straggling white communities. In other words it is not much more than a long lifetime since the Indians of that province were regarded by the white people as in a state of savagery. I think when we endeavour to estimate the progress, or lack of it, that has been made through the years, we should bear that in mind. I doubt very much if any people in the world, with the obstacles that have confronted the Indians of that province, have made greater progress in the same period of time than the Indians in the province of British Columbia have made with all the obstacles to progress in Indian advancement. I would say that one of the obstacles has been that the better elements of white people have sought to ostracize the Indians. That has been a great handicap to begin with. . . . Another obstacle in the way is that all the governments, apart from the government of Canada, have washed their hands of the Indians pretty well. They do not consider that they have any responsibility whatever with respect to them. They simply say that they are wards of the Crown, the dominion, and it is their responsibility and not ours. I think that greater progress could have been made in the years if municipal and provincial governments had accepted some responsibilities, perhaps more responsibility than we have evidence of, in the matter of cooperation for Indian administration with the Dominion of Canada.

9*Minutes*, 1946, No. 4, June 11, p. 123.

The Indian's conception of his position in British Columbia and in the life of Canada as a whole was stated in part in the *Native Voice*.

It is conventional to expect the first issue of a paper to state its major purposes and editorial policies. But by its very nature, the first issue of the *Native Voice* was more than a ceremonial issue. It was expected to state not only the major issues which required a change of attitude on the part of the whites and their governments but also the sentiments which have developed around a broad series of Indian values. Although the more active Indian leaders had talked for some time about the founding of a newspaper by the Native Brotherhood, it was in the spring of 1946 that the publication of such a paper had clearly become an urgent need. Thousands of Indian veterans were now home from the war which had ended the preceding year. The fishing industry would no longer have the preferred place in the economy of the Dominion it had held during the war when its produce had been so urgently needed by the British Isles. And most important, in the spring of 1946 Parliament appointed a committee to investigate Indian problems in preparation for a thorough revision of all Indian legislation. It was obvious that 1946 was a year for important action by the Native Brotherhood.

The *Native Voice* thus provided a new means for continuing the old protest movements at a time when the Indian problem was once again under consideration in other quarters. As the official organ of the Native Brotherhood of British Columbia, it was directed by men who had been leaders in one of the two major parliamentary inquiries since the founding of the Dominion. It was while the government was in the process of establishing the Joint Committee and formalizing a point of view in regard to legislative and policy revisions that the *Native Voice* presented its initial statement. Through the newspaper, the N.B.B.C. announced that the time had arrived for an extension of its programme and activities.

The establishment of the *Native Voice* was an event of such singular importance that the front page of the first issue is reproduced here. One should note the conventional symbols of Indian culture and identification flanking the bold type of the paper's name: the thunderbird of the Northwest Coast on the left and the Plains Indian tepee on the right. The inside pages of this issue carried the conventional materials usually published in first or special editions—ads of congratulations, special letters, and special features—with one exceptional item: the picture and story of the Governor-General of Canada, Vis-

The Native Voice

OFFICIAL ORGAN OF THE NATIVE BROTHERHOOD OF BRITISH COLUMBIA, INC.

VOL. I.—No. 1.   VANCOUVER, B.C., DECEMBER, 1946   PRICE 10 CENTS

THE INDIANS ACT

[EDITORIAL]

In this initial presentation of "The Native Voice" to the people of British Columbia, we intend that the voice of the original Canadian will open a new era for our people who have striven to keep in step with all ranks in the march of time. An era in this atomic age where progress is measured for mankind the world over by scientific discoveries of learned people, who, by their individual and co-operative methods have the power to make this so-called Christian world a haven of content for every human being in existence.

"The Native Voice" will assert at the beginning the firm objectives at which we aim and hope to achieve in the not too distant future. An objective which will mean an honest guarantee of equality for the original inhabitants and owners of Canada. In Canada (A Canada) where under the Indian Act we suffer as a minority race and as wards, or minors without a voice in regard to our own welfare. We are prisoners of a controlling power in our own country—a country that has stood up under the chaos of two world wars, beneath the guise of democracy and freedom, yet keeping enslaved a Native people in their own home land.

Charity begins at home and it is up to those in control to sweep the steps of Parliament clean and bring into being a real democratic Canada, with freedom for all races—a Canada of which we can be proud. At this time, our Dominion is not in a position to point a finger of scorn at the treatment meted out by other countries toward their people, until she liberates her own original and subjected race.

We are in the position of the poor man mentioned in the Gospel who lived off the crumbs that fell from the rich man's table. This is particularly galling to us as the table and what is on it was at one time exclusively our own and we intend to and do demand our rightful positions on terms of equality with our fellow Canadians.

A square deal for the Native Canadians will mean a revolutionary change in so far as the Native peoples are concerned. We must be granted the status to which we are entitled by heredity—a status that should have been in existence for many years past and which will mean a free people in our own Dominion of Canada, susceptible to the influence of none.

The NATIVE VOICE will follow through with their aims and objectives with the co-operation of the Government, as they see fit. Those aims are stated clearly by the Native Brotherhood of British Columbia Inc. in their Constitution.

1. "To work for the betterment of conditions, socially, spiritually and economically for its people.
2. To encourage and bring about a communication and co-operation between the white people and Native Canadians.
3. To join with the Government and its officials and with all those who have at heart the welfare of the Natives of British Columbia and for the betterment of all conditions surrounding the lives and homes of the natives."

The NATIVE VOICE has definite aspirations within its pages. Our views are undenominational and non-political and all are welcome to use the freedom of the press within the pages of the NATIVE VOICE.

We do intend to have changed the attitude and governing methods employed at present in respect to the code at present in use. Methods that should have been voluntarily changed by one of the successive governments of the past on their own initiative, instead of waiting for the challenge of protest, that is heard now. The protest is not calculated to opening past discriminations, but a long awaited signal, that means, LET'S GO, LET'S BE CANADIANS and recognized as human beings.

The NATIVE VOICE, while invading the privileged sanctum of the press, heretofore not occupied by our people, does not find it necessary to apologize for its efforts which will be the long awaited stimulant leading toward a better way of life for all the Native people in Canada. News and views will be presented in our own way, catering always to the Native People, still, broad enough to realize that all people are human and are inclined to err, and with this thought in mind we should appreciate any comments from all races. We expect to give full co-operation with those who will meet us in a straightforward manner.

(Continued on Page 7)

Chief Wm. D. Scow, Alert Bay, B.C., President of the Native Brotherhood of British Columbia.

President's Message

As President of the Native Brotherhood of British Columbia, I most urgently appeal to all Native people to give their full suport to the NATIVE VOICE.

For many years we have discussed the ways and means of having a paper for ourselves but unfortunately never did progress beyond the discussion stage. Now we have started. We have established ourselves and will go forward. Through our NATIVE VOICE we will continue to be the best of our ability to bind closer together the many tribes whom we represent into that solid NATIVE VOICE, a voice that will work for the advancement of our own common native welfare.

The NATIVE VOICE will bring about a closer relationship between ourselves and our good white friends who we also appeal to at this time for their support in our struggle for advancement.

It is not my purpose at this writing to go into any details about the needs and problems that confront us native people as we in our own different villages and communities are conversant with the special problems that confront us locally. Through the NATIVE VOICE we will blend the whole of our problems into a common meeting ground for the discussion of whatever action that is necessary to benefit the well-being of all natives in B.C.

We will work together. The NATIVE VOICE will be the voice of the Native Brotherhood of B.C. in action which in turn is the voice for ALL the natives in B.C.

I appeal to all Branches of the Native Brotherhood and Sisterhood to see that news and material of interest is sent into your paper regularly. Regular correspondents must be appointed by each branch for the purpose of furnishing the news and views promptly. This is your job and mine, so please let us work for the 25,000 natives in B.C., but will finally form the basis of amalgamating the entire Native races of the Dominion into the powerful Brotherhood and Sisterhood that will finally talk with the solid expression of authority to all those whom we must confront on native problems. ALL POWER TO THE NATIVE VOICE.

THE "INDIAN ACT"

The year 1946 saw the start on a change to the Indian Act which has been in force in Canada since the year 1868. A special joint committee of the Senate and House of Commons to act on the long overdue "new deal" that is to come.

The resolution for the formulation of this joint committee was debated and passed early in May of this year.

The orders of the committee by way of resolution was:

Resolved—That a joint committee of the Senate and House of Commons be appointed to examine and consider the Indian Act, Chapter 98, R.S.C., 1927, and amendments thereto and to suggest such amendments as they may deem advisable, with authority to investigate and report upon Indian administration in general and, in particular,

1. Treaty rights and obligations.
2. Band membership.
3. Liability of Indians to pay taxes.
4. Enfranchisement of Indians both voluntary and involuntary.
5. Eligibility of Indians to vote at Dominion elections.
6. The encroachment of white persons on Indian Reserves.
7. The operation of Indian Day and Residential Schools.
8. And any other matter or thing pertaining to the social and economic status of Indians and their advancement, which, in the opinion of such a committee should be incorporated in the revised Act.

During the remainder of the session of the House, approximately two and a half months, the joint committee held 25 meetings, most of the witnesses appearing being Department of Indian Affairs officials or other government department heads or their officials.

An exception was made in their agenda when the chairman of the legislative committee of the Native Brotherhood of British Columbia Inc., Brother Peter R. Kelly, appeared in Ottawa to place a preliminary report, also to establish identity for the Native Brotherhood of B.C. in Canadian Indian affairs and the lead they take among the British Columbia Indians.

A digest of Brother Kelly's report will be found in another page of this paper.

The special committee foreseeing the difficulties in sight, had previously adopted a plan of procedure that would stretch out the hearing of witnesses giving evidence to cover the sessional year of 1946 to the hearing of Government department officials only. (Exceptions were made.)

The 1947 session would be devoted to the hearing of Indian, church and other organizations or individuals wishing to appear before them.

The 1948 session would be devoted to the—revision of THE INDIAN ACT.

During the sessions which covered many voluminous reports from department officials the special committee decided:

The hearing of department officials has disclosed the necessity for certain IMMEDIATE administrative improvements which can be effected without the revision of any existing legislation, and which, when put into effect, will remove some of the causes out of which have arisen grievances and complaints of many Indians.

In order not to break the continuity of the work envisaged by the Orders of Reference, your Committee hereunder makes certain recommendations to cover the period of the coming recess of Parliament.

(Continued on Page 7)

Canadian Indian Girls Train in New Zealand

Two Canadian Indian girls have recently made an important step in the annals of human welfare when they journeyed to far off New Zealand to take a special course in maternity nursing.

Miss Martha Soonias from Saskatchewan and Miss Doreen Gladstone from Alberta are now installed at St. Helen's Hospital, Wellington, N.Z., where they will undergo a special two years' course in their chosen field of nursing.

The girls have already had a year's training in their chosen profession at the Canadian Mothercraft Hospital at Toronto.

It is interesting to know that the curriculum used at the St. Helen's Hospital embraces the methods of the late Sir Truby King which he developed at Karatanee, methods so far advanced in their special field that they were the principal factor in putting New Zealand at the top of the list for better babies and low mortality for years.

PROGRESSIVE RACE

The two Canadian girls will be in direct contact with the most progressive Native race in the world. The Maori race of New Zealand has shown the world that they are able to hold their own in this world of progress. Those natives have their own members of parliament; they also have their own native members in many of the leading professions in that sister Dominion.

It is hoped that our two Indian girls will write to us relating to our readers their own impressions regarding their stay in a distant Dominion.

The most encouraging angle of the whole picture regarding our progressive-minded girls is their avowed determination to WORK AMONG THEIR OWN PEOPLE when they return to Canada.

It will be the duty of The Native Brotherhood of B.C. to keep in close touch with the girls and see to it that our Department of Indian Affairs at Ottawa has available in advance the proper positions that will enable our young Indian nurses to put into practical use for our Native people the valuable experience they have gained in their special line of human welfare work.

count Alexander of Tunis, being made a chief—the first white man, according to the article, to be so honoured.[10]

The materials of the first page deserve especial attention. First in importance is the editorial "The Indians Act". It is a long statement of purposes expressed in an interpretation of the Indian's position in the social system of the province. The first purpose is that of obtaining equality, "an objective which will mean an honest guarantee of equality for the original inhabitants and owners of Canada." There is no equality now:

. . . We suffer as a minority race and as wards, or minors without a voice in regard to our own welfare. We are prisoners of a controlling power in our own country—a country which has stood up under the chaos of two world wars, beneath the guise of democracy and freedom, yet keeping enslaved a Native people in their own home land.

. . . our Dominion is not in a position to point a finger of scorn at the treatment meted out by other countries toward their people, until she liberates her own original and subjected race.

. . . The NATIVE VOICE will follow through with their aims and objectives with the co-operation of the Government, as they see fit. Those aims are stated clearly by the Native Brotherhood of British Columbia, Inc. in their Constitution.

1. "To work for the betterment of conditions, socially, spiritually and economically for its people.

2. To encourage and bring about a communication and cooperation between the white people and Native Canadians.

3. To join with the Government and its officials and with all those who have at heart the welfare of the Natives of British Columbia and for the betterment of all conditions surrounding the lives and homes of the natives."

The paper would be "undenominational" and non-political, the editorial claimed, and continues:

We do intend to have changed the attitude and governing methods employed at present in respect to the code at present in use. Methods that should have been voluntarily changed by one of the successive governments of the past on their own initiative, instead of waiting for the challenge of protest, that is heard now. . . .

Furthermore,

The NATIVE VOICE, while invading the privileged sanctum of the press, heretofore not occupied by our people, does not find it necessary to apologize

---

[10]The initiation and the presentation of a totem pole, carved by Mungo Martin, were part of the Jubilee ceremonies celebrating the sixtieth year of the founding of Vancouver. The author was in Vancouver at the time and noted that some English-speaking Canadians resented the ceremony as "the representatives of the King bowed to the Indians."

for its efforts which will be the long awaited stimulant leading to a better way of life presented in our own way, catering always to the Native People. . . .

With respect to the Canadian citizens at large,

The new realm of endeavor in presenting the NATIVE VOICE will not review what the people of Canada through their elected Government did not do in the past, but will, however, explain our plight in so far as we see it and ask for the full support of the Canadian people.

With respect to residents of British Columbia the editorial claimed that:

The citizens of British Columbia have not shown a direct concern about our welfare in the past and the NATIVE VOICE is being printed for all people to lend a helping hand to bring about a change in the living conditions that held back an advanced mode of life for the original Canadian. The NATIVE VOICE will not be too concerned about the laxity of the British Columbia peoples in the past, but we will press forward our aims to release all prejudices against the Natives of British Columbia.

Finally,

. . . the NATIVE VOICE will be the means of uniting into one solid body the Natives of Canada by keeping them in touch with affairs relating to our people.

We have no equality with other Canadians except when the call to Arms or the Tax Collector comes.

It is to change that state of affairs that the NATIVE VOICE appears.

In no other issue of the *Native Voice* has the resentment towards the members of the majority group been expressed so directly, so extensively, and so vigorously. Important as that might be, the Indians also revealed in this first issue an awareness of some of the particular attributes of their relationship with the majority group. (1) To maintain its identity, a minority group cannot depend upon the majority, but must take and maintain the initiative and independence; (2) to secure increasing benefits from social change, the minority group must be well known nationally and provincially, and if possible, politically active either directly or indirectly; (3) the public reiteration of the basic ideals of the national state and its provincial organization is no guarantee of the equal distribution of justice, of security, or of prestige; (4) tribal tradition has to be recognized but subordinated to a new conception of a more general status, the status of Native Canadian, a status recognized and respected by some "good white friends."

The message from President Scow appealed for support, recognizing the need to bind closer the tribes "that we represent;" hoped to have better working relations with "good white friends;" and asked for contributions. President Scow left it to the editorial and feature writers to state the more basic issues of the conflict. Having defined their problems, the Indians prepared new strategies and tactics.

This first issue in providing a ceremonial occasion demonstrated at least the fourth of the points stated above: that of the subordination of tribalism. Chief Scow was a Kwakiutl from Alert Bay; the editor of the paper was Jack Beynon, a Tsimshian from Port Simpson, the area in which Mr. Duncan had started his missionary work in 1857; the chairman of the Legislative Committee of the N.B.B.C., Rev. P. R. Kelly, was a member of the Skidegate band of the Haida tribe, Queen Charlotte Islands; and Guy Williams, secretary of the N.B.B.C., was a Kitamat.

Greetings for success from a number of entrepreneurs were published, such greetings of course containing some of the polite prevarications of Western civilization. The major missionary and community church groups, the United Church of Canada, the Anglican Church, and the Roman Catholic Church also published their congratulations and wishes for success. As spokesman for the general public of the whites, one of the most vigorous columnists of British Columbia prepared what amounted to a feature article. Elmore Philpott wrote forthrightly on the fact that the "re-awakening" was due chiefly to agitation on the part of the Indians themselves; he took up the question of discrimination and reported that the Nanaimo School Board had rejected an Indian agent's request for the admission of Indian children into the Nanaimo school; the request was denied with the explanation "that it would retard the progress of the white children." Philpott closed by declaring that "the future of the Native [Indian] people will be decided by themselves. . . ."

For this first issue with its ceremonial function, the *Native Voice* had a solid underpinning of action to report. It could relate the actions of Ottawa and the activities of the chairman of the Legislative Committee of the N.B.B.C. A resolution by the House of Commons had started action on May 13, 1946; a Special Joint Committee was to be appointed. The order of reference specified eight major categories for inquiry: treaty rights and obligations; band membership; the liability of Indians to pay taxes; the enfranchisement of Indians both voluntary and involuntary; the eligiblity of Indians to vote at Dominion elections; the encroachment of white persons on Indian reserves; the operation of Indian day and residential schools; and any other matter or thing pertaining to the social and economic status of Indians and their advancement which, in the opinion of such committee, should be incorporated in the revised act. By an Order in Council, dated October 11, 1946, the work of the Committee was to be continued.[11]

This government action was fully discussed in the first issue of the *Native Voice*, after being introduced by a statement on the lack of revision of legislation since 1868. In addition, the major points of the "Third Report" of August 15, 1946, were restated in full, including the ten major recommendations.[12] Obviously the strategy of the editor and his advisers was to circulate information about what Ottawa was doing as widely as possible. The readers were informed also of what the N.B.B.C. was doing. As one considers the over-all actions of this organization, one realizes with what consummate skill the officers and the chairman of the Legislative Committee related themselves to the members of the Cabinet, to the officials of the Indian Affairs Branch, and to the members of the Special Joint Committee. Chief Scow, Rev. Peter Kelly, and Mr. Andrew Paull were by then old hands in Ottawa. This phrase was used informally by officials in Ottawa in the most complimentary manner, for it meant that they knew their subject, and they knew how to conduct themselves admirably according to Canadian standards of courtesy, an important matter in a public inquiry. Officials thus held in high respect the representatives of the N.B.B.C., who in addition to being old hands based their demands upon central issues.[13] It was, therefore, within a very meaningful context that Mr. Kelly made the "Ottawa Report" for the first issue of the *Native Voice*.

It is noteworthy that the bill to initiate the inquiry was passed on May 13 and that Mr. Kelly went to Ottawa almost immediately on June 23. Although the Committee had not planned to see representatives of groups during 1946, "an exception was made," and the Native

[11]*Minutes*, 1947, No. 1, March 5.

[12]These will be discussed more fully in the section following. The "Third Report" is found in *Minutes*, 1946, No. 21, August 13.

[13]It has, of course, been the experience of parliamentarians and administrative officials to have missionary, Indian, and other groups make small, even petty, demands with respect to Indian affairs. From the reserves close to Ottawa there are numerous individuals and many splintered groups going there to make representations. One would not wish to have the above interpreted as indicating that Ottawa did not have a respect for representatives from other groups. One need only to go through the reports to see that representatives from all parts of Canada were received cordially and given a respectful hearing. But also from the over-all reports, one receives an impression that the West Coast Indians, those from Alberta, and the Iroquois of Ontario seemed to be the most outstanding of all those who appeared or prepared submissions.

Brotherhood delegate was received. The Committee had decided that during the 1946 session it would hear departmental officials; in 1947 it would hear Indian, church, and other organizations; and in 1948 it would prepare the revision of the Indian Act. Mr. Kelly was advised by the responsible minister, Hon. J. A. Glen, that dates would be fixed, but Mr. Kelly did not wait; he called attention to the rhythm of life based on the fishing industry and the number of questions which needed to be clarified prior to the preparation of a brief. By taking the initiative in going to Ottawa, the chairman of the Legislative Committee was later able to report in his initial statement to the readers of the *Native Voice*:

. . . My purpose in appearing was not to give evidence at that time but rather to get a definite understanding from the joint committee regarding the appearance of the Native Brotherhood of B.C. representatives, also to discuss the possibilities of retaining counsel in the preparation of a brief.

On July 4th I attended another session of the joint committee when I was requested to give my views on behalf of the organization.

Due to the fact that the joint committee had established rules whereby only Government departments and officials would present submissions at that session, I believe that I may say that your chairman was treated with utmost dignity and respect to being granted the privilege of stating my case even to the extent of interrupting set Government committee proceedings.

Among other matters, your delegate had pointed out the importance of having Indian representatives working with the Committee in connection with the actual revision of the Indian Act in order that they may receive the benefit of the "Indian Point of View."

During my stay at the Capitol [*sic*], there were many interviews with high Government officials and Cabinet Ministers besides many members of Parliament, the outcome of which will be of much value to our committee when the time comes to finally present our case. Among my talks was a long period spent with the Hon. Mr. Glen, which I consider most important to our cause. However, at this time, it is not my intention to make a prolonged report, but I may add before concluding that after my experiences in Ottawa I consider that my trip was not only worthwhile but also necessary, as when the time arrives for our delegation to be heard they will find that a favorable ground has been paved and prepared so that the British Columbia Indians will be given a thorough hearing on their presentations.

Mr. Kelly closed by referring to the amount of time required for the preparation of a brief.

Available in the first issue, for any who would read, were the records of the sessions of the Committee. At the time and in larger perspective later, it was clear that the strategy and tactics of the N.B.B.C. were developed by men who could manipulate for advantage.

Although no Indian representatives were supposed to be heard, yet the British Columbians were first on the scene. Here is, in part,[14] the statement made to the Joint Committee by Mr. Kelly:

Mr. Chairman, honourable members of the Senate and the House of Commons: I appreciate this courtesy extended to me to speak to you during these brief minutes. I come before you not against your wishes; that is to say, I have received communications from the secretary of this committee informing our organization that it is not the desire of this committee to hear us at this time, but our committee took the ground that they would like to have certain matters clarified. Our people on the coast are largely engaged in the fishing industry. Fishing starts next Sunday evening. During that period of the next three months it will not be the best time for them to appear before your committee. Hence in our telegrams I said that what you kindly said to us, with the very best of intentions, was not altogether definite enough for our purpose and it was unsatisfactory because you could not give any stated time. That is one thing I would like to bring before you. . . . So I have been requested by them to come here and appear before you to suggest that some time after the end of September they be heard. That time would suit our people much better to appear before your committee. If that is not possible, then would you suggest an earlier date, so long as it is definite and we know when to appear before you. That is one thing they were very insistent upon, so that they will have in mind something very definite as the weeks and months slip by.

Members of the Committee agreeably arranged for the appearance of the Native Brotherhood at a time when they were not engaged in fishing. Then Mr. Kelly proceeded to state what was to the N.B.B.C. a very basic issue—that Indians in British Columbia were different from others; "I think we are peculiar in some ways." And after relating some economic facts, he proceeded to his main point:

. . . The reason I am bringing these facts out is this. It is no use repeating here. I do not bring it up as an argument, but just as a statement. The Indian is a minor in the eyes of the law; as far as being heard is concerned, he is in a stage of nonage. But for purposes of raising revenue he is taxed.

14For the full contents of this first appearance of Mr. Kelly before the Committee, see *Minutes*, June 27, 1946, No. 9. Attention should be called to the fact that Mr. Andrew Paull, a member of the Squamish band, North Vancouver, and president of the North American Indian Brotherhood, also appeared before the Committee on the same day. Mr. Paull was very active in the Allied Tribes and later in the Native Brotherhood of British Columbia. However, the latter organization seemed unable to develop the policies which he had in mind, and so he left it and organized the North American Indian Brotherhood which included some Indians resident in the United States. Members of this latter organization often appeared in Ottawa in traditional costumes, especially the feather head-dress as noted in *Minutes*, No. 9, p. 111. Such costumes excited press photographers who felt that this was good copy, and some editors apparently agreed.

He is taxable. When it comes to defense of his country his services, although he is looked upon as a minor, were accepted and were generously offered in this war as well as the war before. Yet he is denied any voice in the affairs of the land. Because of that, the Indians of British Columbia take the ground that they should not be subject to taxation. What I want to bring to your notice is this. We would request very respectfully that a counsel be appointed to represent the Native Brotherhood of British Columbia before this committee to argue out this matter of taxation. I know that it is a large request, and the man who has to do that would have to be a competent man, a constitutional lawyer. We are not in a position to present an argument in the manner in which we would like to do it. So we must submit to you that request should be granted to the Native Brotherhood of British Columbia. This matter of taxation is not peculiar only to British Columbia; it is a dominion-wide question. . . . it applies in greater measure to us. . . .

In this manner the Native Brotherhood of British Columbia established its identity with the Joint Committee, made a basic demand in a crucial issue, and initiated its significant role in the revision of the Indian Act.

Thus for a newspaper editor, it was indeed a happy time for opening shop. The war was over, and there had been 2,603 Indian enlistments.[15] The Japanese had been removed from the fishing industry of the Pacific coast, and the possibility of their return was only one of several problems. This period may be characterized by a long list of problems, but beneath it all was the fact that the great depression was over. The standard of living for the Indian appears, according to testimony in *Minutes of Proceedings and Evidence*, to have risen. A new generation had matured; thus there was a new platform from which to engage the opposition, if it could be located, in battle.[16] With respect to Indian legislation and the issue of community status, 1930 had been a year of

[15]*Annual Report* of Indian Affairs Branch, 1945. This report is published in full also in *Minutes*, 1946, No. 5, June 13, Appendix G.

For more detailed considerations of the Indian veteran, see the testimony and submissions of Col. George Patrick, an official of Indian Affairs, assigned to deal with the Veterans' Land Settlement Act, *Minutes*, 1947, No. 6, March 21, and in the same series No. 40, July 2. Quite naturally the testimony does not cover adequately the story of the Indian veteran.

[16]One should not underestimate the problem of a minority group in locating its opposition, of searching out the causes of their problems. At the end of the first year of publication, November, 1947, the *Native Voice* carried this significant paragraph in an editorial devoted to the fact that the Indians of Canada want opportunity:

"In fact we sometimes wonder who the Boogey Man is? Our dealings with the officials of the Indian Department have proved them to be courteous and willing to do more than their share. Our Doctors are doing a magnificent job and put in many weary afterhours. Our fight is more with the Unthinking, who in ignorance are prone to discriminate—and—with the present system of government which spoon feeds us. This spoon feeding cannot nourish respect or responsibility; it is up to us to discard the spoon."

organization and the several years following, years of preparation. It was not until 1946, with the appointment of the Joint Committee and the appearance of Mr. Andrew Paull and Mr. Kelly before it, that the offensive was launched and the campaign consolidated through the establishment of the *Native Voice*. The newspaper could consolidate the sentiments of Indians and non-Indians on the various issues, by its reports and editorials.

THE CANADIANIZED INDIAN

The significance of the *Native Voice* is embedded in a context greater than the fact that it is the official organ of the N.B.B.C., or that it is the second (the *Cherokee Phoenix* was the first) aboriginal newspaper of North America, or that it aspires to speak for all native Canadians as it has claimed since its conception and founding. The greater context is simple to state; some Indians have become very Canadian in their thinking and conduct. They now hold the modernized version of the Protestant Ethic. Though recognized by many Indians and other Canadians, this is still a fact difficult to secure data about, hard to analyze, and almost impossible to interpret. But the publication of the *Native Voice* is a product of this new Indian, and it is in the Canadianization of the Indian that one finds the significance of the paper for the national life of Canada and the changing, unvanishing Indian.

The first full expression in Canadian history of high quality Indian leadership is to be found in the record of the Joint Committee appointed by Parliament to consider revision of the Indian Act. The more statesmanlike members of the Indian Affairs staff, the better-informed members of the Senate and the House of Commons, many of the Indians themselves, a considerable number of clergymen, and many residents in local communities are aware of the extensive Canadianization among the Indians. In their total population this group is sufficient in number to be meaningful, and thus the *Native Voice* is far more than the name of a small newspaper published by some Indians in Vancouver. When the N.B.B.C. took up the question of enfranchisement in its brief to the Special Joint Committee, it asked for the "rights of citizenship to the Indians as such without the necessity of their enfranchisement." To discuss the subject, the writers of the brief divided the Indians into three main categories:

(a) There are Indians who boast of the fact that they are Indians and will die as Indians. They insist on being wards of the government in its fullest sense and do not want any part of progress. They are suspicious of any advancement from the past.

(b) There is a second group that want all the advantages of civilization and progress. They want education and all the medical care that the government has to offer, as well as other securities that come to them on the reserve life, but they do not want to even consider the responsibilities that these involve. They want to be carried along "on flowery beds of ease."

(c) There is a third group that see things just as they are. They appreciate all the advantages of civilization and realize all progress has its price, that the profits of civilization are fully appreciated only by those who have had to face some of the responsibilities for it. This group comprises the more virile type. They want to have all these advantages of civilization and profit by its spiritual and material values. They also have learned this means shouldering responsibility. They want the rights of citizenship but do not wish to surrender their hereditary rights all in one stroke.[17]

It was from among the latter group that the founders of the N.B.B.C. and the staff of the *Native Voice* came.

In the *Minutes* of the Special Joint Committee considerable space was devoted to statements by Indian witnesses and to briefs submitted by various Indian and white groups and government officials as well as experts on specially elected subjects. Furthermore, members of the Joint Committee who had visited reserves during the recess of Parliament also served as formal witnesses. In preparation for the revision of legislation, the work of Parliament in securing data, opinions, and points of view on small as well as large questions was handled by a Joint Committee of twelve Senators and twenty-two members of the House of Commons; the Committee held 128 meetings over a period of three years, during which 122 witnesses were heard and 411 written briefs received. The minutes and reporting of evidence filled 3,211 pages. Finally, there was, of course, considerable space in *Hansard*, devoted to the discussion of the bills to revise Indian legislation.[18] The first meetings of the Committee were held in the spring of 1946; its last meetings were held in 1948; the first public consideration of new legislation was in 1950; and a bill was finally enacted in 1951.[19]

When Mr. Kelly told the Committee during his first appearance that "they want to be heard and heard very thoroughly," he was actually speaking for people he did not represent, for not only Indians but

[17]*Minutes*, 1947, No. 16, May 1, pp. 766–7.

[18]The number of witnesses, etc., was tabulated by the *Native Voice*, June, 1950, p. 2.

[19]Apparently possible administrative changes were made as the work of the Committee revealed the need for them, for these are referred to in several places in the *Minutes*. Certainly the annual budget was increased significantly during the inquiry.

whites too felt more than indignant at the state of Indian affairs. They were morally shocked. They, too, wanted to be heard; they all felt that with revised legislation and a new era of administrative action the problems of the Indians could be solved, the sense of shame neutralized, and a new stage in national evolution achieved. Experts in the fields of medicine, education, and the social sciences, clergymen of several denominations, and administrative officials, along with the Committee and the witnesses, exhibited those acclaimed virtues of citizenship and public responsibility in the earnestness, sincerity and devotion with which they participated in the work of the Committee for the first two years. Canadians were shown some startling facts of the Indians' state, such as the high disease and mortality rates, utterly neglected school systems, and inadequate teaching personnel—in fact, so many extreme deviations from the ordinary sense of decency and of public responsibilty that some of the conditions revealed could be nothing less than shameful and shocking. If some of the revelations were shocking in their apparent simplicity, it is equally true that many were incomprehensible.[20] Interested Canadians, with the franchise, who had learned a great deal about themselves and their national life during World War II, were just as hard put for understanding as were the better-informed Indians. It is recognized, however, that through political behaviour and such political processes as parliamentary inquiries, not only individuals but groups of people learn something about themselves. The purpose of such an inquiry is exactly that—to find out what kind of "people we are." And it was in this process of discovery that the struggle for identity reached a peak; yet there was not a full revelation of that struggle as seen in the day-to-day moral crises in the lives of the Indians, or in the departmental and denominational bureaucrats. If more had been known of these, then

[20]One can point to the bureaucratic struggle reported in *Minutes*, 1948, No. 3, March 9, 11, 16, 17, 18, and 19; also continued in No. 4. Here are some data for studying cliques within bureaucratic structures, the struggle between the politician and the civil service, between the civil service and the bureaucrat, and the politician and the bureaucrat.

There are other examples difficult to comprehend such as the rules of the system of wardship, the political activities of denominations with a missionary interest in the Indians, and so on. As we shall discuss later, the common antipathy of the Indian towards the rules of wardship seem, just on a basis of common sense, to provide the foundation for unified action on the part of the Indians. It is therefore difficult to comprehend the political atomization of the Mohawk reserve at Caughnawagna near Montreal, or the absolute unwillingness of Indian Lorette to become a municipality, completely freed of the rules of wardship. In fact, the further one goes with examples the more incomprehensible the whole system becomes.

the public aspects of Indian affairs in Canada would have become clearer.

Early in the hearings of the Committee, testimony was presented by prominent West Coast Indians and by those who represented the Six Nations, a group better known and even more distinguished in the history of Indian and white relations. In addition, Brigadier Oliver M. Martin, a magistrate of York County, was called by the Committee not so much as a witness but as a prominent citizen who had made a survey of the problems, a person who could state problems as a former ward might feel them. Although he did not want to be considered an authority on the subject, Brigadier Martin explained, he was deeply interested in it:

> . . . during the past years . . . I have spoken frequently to service clubs, church groups and other organizations in behalf of a better deal for Canada's Indians. . . . I have taken every opportunity to assist the people of Canada towards a sympathetic understanding of the Indian, and have done what I could to show the Indian that his future welfare and well-being depend, in the initial instance, on himself. . . .
>
> I do know the Indian because I am one of them. . . . I have lived on the Six Nations reserve. My home was there until 25 years ago when I became enfranchised after the first great war. Just as you, whose ancestors came from Great Britain, fight to retain the union jack as part of our Canadian flag, and just as you, whose ancestors came from France, wish to retain some symbol of your ancestry in our national emblem, so I, a Canadian, am deeply thankful for this opportunity to say something . . . on behalf of my racial group which has played no small part in the development of our country. I am not, however, going to suggest to you that crossed tomahawks be placed on our flag. But what I hope is that the result of the work of this committee will be such that our distinctive new Canadian flag, which I understand is to come, will forever be a symbol to Canadians of Indian descent that their freedom was restored to them when that flag was born.

After speaking of the number of Indians with whom he had associated in the armed forces, and had lectured before and visited with in the provinces, Brigadier Martin then stated the first of his major conclusions.

> . . . I tell you this to let you know that my knowledge of Indians is not confined only to the Six Nations group. Indians vary, of course, to a mixed degree, across Canada, in appearance, manner of living, educational accomplishments, health standards and religious attachment; but they have one thing in common and that is antipathy towards the Indian Affairs Branch, more especially among the older people. It is most unfortunate that this is so, because the opposite should be the case. . . . In looking for the meaning of this feeling of distrust, and, in some cases, active antagonism which the Indian feels towards the Branch and its officials, if I tell you a few things

which took place between certain officials of Indian Affairs and my immediate family, and myself personally, you will perhaps see why Indians feel as they do, and I hope you will be more willing to show patience—which you are going to require—and sympathy towards these Indians and groups of Indians who may appear before you during the coming months.[21]

From his family experiences, Mr. Martin selected four to support his general conclusion regarding antipathy. One involved his own college and professional education; the second, his application to the federal civil service for appointment as an Indian agent; the third, his school teaching and farming experience; and the fourth, medical care for his sister.

In the early 1900's the Six Nations Council spent a great deal of money in legal fees paid to lawyers for services of one kind or another without getting any satisfaction with the result that after days of deliberation over a period of months they concluded that the only way they might hope to achieve anything would be to send one of their own people to take up the study of law. . . .

The people were willing to give up their interest money for that purpose and so expressed themselves. The boys were selected and the resolution forwarded to the Department of Indian Affairs at Ottawa for approval. The Department refused to sanction this expenditure and so far as I have been able to find out gave no reason for its refusal. I was one of the boys selected —the other was Jim Moses who was killed in action while flying over Germany as an officer in the Royal Air Force.

The civil service application for the Indian agency at Hazelton, B.C., was handled briefly: "I never got the job and never got an answer." Then while teaching school on the Six Nations Reserve, he was asked by the Indian agent to take over a repossessed farm which had been sold under the Soldiers' Settlement Act. In April the verbal agreement between him and the agent had been made; then in July he received a letter from the agent saying that because Martin had purchased a farm under the Soldiers' Settlement Act his "position as teacher was terminated forthwith." Finally, in 1935 the sister of Brigadier Martin was taken to the Toronto General Hospital for examination. She was diagnosed as a case of cancer requiring immediate operation.

. . . They kept her in the hospital that day to prepare her, but later on that evening she returned to our home saying that the hospital authorities, after finding out that her home was on an Indian reserve, would not do anything without her first obtaining authority from the Department of Indian Affairs. I immediately got in touch with the doctor on the reserve by telephone to get, as I thought, the required authority. . . . apparently he was helpless

---

[21]*Minutes*, 1946, No. 19, August 6, p. 746.

because he told me that due to the fact that there was a hospital on the reserve he couldn't authorize an operation in the Toronto General Hospital. She returned to the reserve where she was operated on some time later, and died—leaving two small children. I am not blaming the doctor—he is a good man who has done excellent work for many years on that reserve—but I do blame the system which apparently requires authorization from Ottawa before any action can be taken, even to meet an emergency of that kind. . . .

I note in your minutes that it is said the Six Nations Reserve is the most progressive one in Canada—if that is so—and since what I have told you represents some of the injustice suffered by one family during a quarter century and since the same sort of things must have been experienced, more or less, by every Indian family across Canada, all through the years since the Department of Indian Affairs was formed—you can see why Indians feel as they do towards departmental officials. . . .

Parliament had been grossly neglectful, admittedly so, in failing to give certain kinds of attention to Indian Affairs. Each year an *Annual Report* was published; each year the estimates for annual appropriations to support the activities of Indian Affairs went through the House of Commons, certainly without any searching questions, as one can now see from *Hansard*. Until World War II, enfranchised Canadians and their members of Parliament let Indian Affairs coast along. These are the high-level perspectives. Brigadier Martin took the Committee down to some of its consequences at a lower level, consequences of a kind of administration which had been tolerated over the years.

Phrased as it was in the form of a general conclusion supported by four examples of personal experiences, the intensity of antipathy of the Indian, his depth of feeling, was difficult to sense. Andrew Paull, in not following some of the finer rules of courtesy expected to be used in presentations before committees, helped support the conclusion of Brigadier Martin as well as portray a little more intensely the depth of feeling.

. . . I stand before you this morning not as a suppliant. I stand here before you representing somebody your equal. And now, let us get that understood before we go any further. . . . Now, gentlemen, we have spent a lot of time and through the assistance of honorable members of parliament in the House to bring this committee into being. . . . But this is not the kind of committee that we asked for. Now, while we are prepared to speak to you and present our grievances to you, I want this to go on the record; we asked for a Royal Commission to investigate "you" and "me."

When a member of the Committee indicated that these matters were not in the order of reference, Mr. Paull said that he wanted it on the record "that I want to speak my mind, and not for you to tell me what to say. . . ." And shortly thereafter he informed the Committee, "I might as well warn you that I am going to say a few disagreeable things, so you might as well be prepared."[22]

Wardship is a legal status, and in its administration it is a set of rules. Some discretion may be left to an individual agent, but the rules so infuriated Brigadier Martin that when he recognized how they would restrict his development, he got out from under them by becoming enfranchised and thus free of the system. Mr. Paull responded quite differently; he did not seek to be free of the rules; instead those rules provided him with an object of attack. In fact, he stated in the record that he had been studying the Indian problem since 1907.

I was chosen by my people to do this work when I was a youngster about 7 or 8 years old. They built a school and put me in there so that I might be their eye, ear and mouth. In the year 1907 I came out of school and from then on until the year 1911 I received my Indian education from the chiefs. Then I was brought before the Indian agent and sworn on the bible that I would always work for the interests of the Indians. Then I became secretary of an Indian organization in British Columbia. . . .
Later on I became recording secretary and later on secretary for the allied Indian tribes of British Columbia. The chairman of that organization was my friend, the Rev. P. R. Kelly. I have been interested in Indian work since that time.[23]

To study the problem, to engage in organizational activities related to the problem, to have the self-conception of having been chosen to do these very things, to have sworn by oath to work for the interests of the Indian—these aspects of a life-career in its development make for a "professional" Indian. Action in the case of Mr. Paull was directed towards building up a story from legal documents related to the history of land policy, from appraisals of conformance to treaty obligations, from the accumulation of cases displaying administrative ineptitude, intentional exploitation, and a disregard of Indian interests, and from attempts to organize the Indians, first in the Allied Tribes, then in the Native Brotherhood, and finally in the North American Indian Brother-

[22]See *Ibid.*, 1946, No. 9, June 27, p. 420.
[23]This statement is set down formally in *Ibid.*, 1947, No. 18, May 6, p. 867. Note that Brigadier Martin states that the Six Nations Council had selected two young men to send them to school. When the writer asked Chief Scow what his son was studying at the University of British Columbia, the Chief replied that his son had told him that he was preparing to go into law so that he could work on the problems of the Indians.
These two cases are an indicator of how the Indians define their problems and the manner in which they are handicapped in dealing with them. In numerous interviews with Americans and Canadians of Japanese descent, the writer never heard references to the need for educating minority group specialists as stated by the Brigadier and Mr. Paull.

hood. This work presents a life-career which was part of the struggle for identity, but conspicuously unlike that of Brigadier Martin who carried on the struggle through community work, and through careful analysis of his family and personal experiences in order to isolate crucial determinants and thus become as objective as possible. If one types the life-career of Mr. Paull as that of a "professional" Indian and thus one kind of Canadianization, then one would undoubtedly type Brigadier Martin as also Canadianized but on a more mature level. The former involves a career which has become centred around a continuing struggle with wardship whereas the latter has evolved into concern about the nature of the larger social system of the nation and the moral problems which characterize it.

The officials of the Canadian government did not, according to the public record, raise questions regarding the elimination of the system of wardship. That its disappearance was desirable was hinted at by members of the House of Commons, but there was no discussion of or planning for its elimination. The expressed ideal of the past century continues—assimilation. Although the conditions under which assimilation may be facilitated or even made possible have not been inquired into systematically, the work of Indian Affairs, the rationale for continued annual appropriations, and the concern about the levels of educational achievement all presume that that is the end in view.

It is assumed that for an indefinite period in the future there will be a fundamental segregation in the Canadian social system. Not only will there be the French and the English, but also the Indian peoples. The Canadianization of the Indian is not to be found, thus, in his wish to do away with this form of segregation, but rather lies in what he thinks can be done to change the system. Essentially two attacks have been made in an attempt to bring about a change. One, as we noted in the case of Mr. Paull, was the attack on the inadequacy of budgets and administrative policies and procedures, that is, on the conformance to treaty obligations. This attack was important. Brigadier Martin pointed it up very directly when he was talking about the operation of the rules in his own personal career prior to the time of his enfranchisement; but Brigadier Martin went a step further. Consistent with his higher level of social maturity he saw the significance of the Indian having no voice.

The other line of attack on wardship is found in discussions regarding political representation for the Indian, regarding citizenship, and in the forming of opinions about the franchise. In short, the first attack dealt with the reform of a system which by nature is bureaucratic and thus not easily adjusted to administrative discretion or to social changes in the wide range of types of community organization found in Canada. While this constitutes a set of issues which are problems in their own right, the second focus points up the consequences of Indians becoming more fully Canadian: a desire for a place in the political processes of the state. If such a place can be arranged while still managing improvements in the bureaucratic procedures, then the Indian will have his freedom restored, to express it in the manner of Brigadier Martin.

During the latter part of World War II, a quickening sense of Canadian national identity led Parliament to give considerable attention to the establishment of Canadian citizenship, the new act being proclaimed on July 1, 1946. Although a revision of Indian legislation was just getting under way at the end of this debate and the new plan for Canadian citizenship agreed upon, the Indian was not given citizenship status, as an editorial in the January, 1947, issue of the *Native Voice* noted.

January 1st, 1947, saw the dawning of a new stage in the lives of Canadian people. With the birth of the New Year all peoples residing in Canada regardless of their birthplace, foreign or British, are entitled by law to call themselves Canadians. Much publicity has already been given through the press and radio on the forward step taken by the Dominion Government which makes a further comment from THE NATIVE VOICE unnecessary at this time excepting to mention that under Canadian laws INDIANS ARE NOT PEOPLE.

In the February issue, considerable space was given to the church choir from Metlakatla, Alaska. These were the descendants of the Tsimshian who had left Canada with Mr. Duncan at the time of the great conflict with the Church of England. The settlement in Alaska has become renowned as an ideal Indian village, supported by cooperative enterprises. The use of such historical facts are part of the propaganda and tactical techniques used by the Canadian Indians; that is, they select favourable aspects of Indian policy in the United States, or in New Zealand, in an effort to shame the Canadian people, parliamentarians, and bureaucrats into changing. After several paragraphs about the choir, the editorial writer remarked:

The sharp contrast is that all members of the Metlakatla Choir are "people." They are free, voting responsible citizens of the United States of America. In Alaska they are running their own Native candidate for the House of Representatives.

After a short statement on the origins of Metlakatla, the editorial writer concluded by recommending that the Special Joint Committee "will be well advised to make a thorough study of the advanced methods the United States Government employs in advancing the way of life of their original people. Canadian Indians are 'wards' or 'minors.' United States Indians are 'citizens' or 'people.'"

It would be an inaccurate representation and analysis to indicate the use of such comparisons as limited to a tactic of shaming and goading the government into a change of policy and administration. The problem is more basic. The Canadianized Indian is searching for hard facts to demonstrate the achievement of other Indians in economic development and political activity. When the brief of the Native Brotherhood of British Columbia was under discussion, Mr. Williams, a former officer of that organization, returned to statements regarding Metlakatla.

In connection with the development of our Indian people, we want to substantiate or we want to back up our position in the brief with some of these statements. It has been pointed out by Mr. Gosnell this morning that in Alaska—Metlakatla, Alaska—there is quite an industrial development. This has been stressed a great deal, but that is not the only place where the Indians have developed industries, the salmon fishing industry. For example, a little further north there has been a development around Hydaburg and places such as that.

. . . They have their canneries, they have good sized stores and they maintain businesses just as other white brothers are doing in that part of the country.

I should just like to make this statement. In Alaska the Indians have outdistanced their cousins to the south of them by leaps and bounds, beyond the expectation of the American government. They were put on their own and they responded to treatment. In their village life and also living in towns like Ketchikan, they are taking their place with the citizens of that territory in the industrial life as well as the educational life. They are marching everywhere shoulder to shoulder with the other citizens. They realize the value of personal dignity as they never thought it possible to do before.

I should like to refer to what happens in Prince Rupert, for instance. There, in a theatre, where the price of admission is the same for all, Indian, white, or any other race, every Indian who comes into the theatre is given one corner or one section. He is segregated. The effect, psychologically, I think, is damaging. . . . An Alaskan Indian came into that theatre with his wife. They were very well dressed. He came in and was going to sit down in the body of the theatre. The usher came to him and said, "No, you cannot sit here: Indians do not sit here." He wanted to know why. He was told why. He said, "I appeal to the manager; I am a citizen of Alaska. I have never been treated this way before and I have a right to sit where I please. I have paid the same admission fee as anyone else." The manager was brought. The manager apologized to him and told him to pick his seat.[24]

---

[24]In the testimony of Guy Williams, *Minutes*, 1947, pp. 829–30. In the summer of 1946 the author was told of this incident by Mr. Kelly. There are sections of northern British Columbia where Indians are segregated, where they are not

One can think of at least two groups of reasons why the same Indians are searching for evidence of the achievement of other Indian peoples. On the one hand, are all of the reasons based upon wardship, for example the problem of securing credit for small, personal businesses or even larger band enterprises.[25] The Indian has a very profound security in the reserve system; his land, his house, and his chattels are fully protected. He cannot be sued with respect to them. But for that security system, he has, if we wish to use the term, paid the price of withdrawal from normal economic expansion. He has not been an integral part of the competitive system.

On the other hand, they are concerned with demonstrated achievement owing to their profound conceptions of Indian abilities and traits of character. Official policy has taken little account of the trends of thought regarding race relations as they are now investigated and taught in the schools and universities of Canada and the United States: that is, the fundamental points of view of social psychology with respect to the development of character traits, with respect to the significance of one's self-conception in regulating conduct, or with the role of varying cultural backgrounds in the formation of personality. Since 1881, European scholars have studied the development of the child and the personality of the adult, and new ideas based on careful research are contrary to a system of government which assumes significant racial differences in educability. Thus Mr. Williams, Dr. Andrew Moore, the Manitoba educator, and Dr. Diamond Jenness, the former Dominion anthropologist, discussed with the Joint Committee the factor of racial discrimination and the feelings

permitted to walk even with or ahead of a white man, and where one's reputation is likely to suffer seriously if one maintains friendly relations with an Indian. The hostility toward mixed bloods is also very marked. This claim was supported in personal conversations with Dr. Diamond Jenness. On March 25, 1947, Dr. Diamond Jenness testified before the Committee and stated that "In the little town of Hazelton, . . . I was gravely reprimanded for walking by the side of a fine old Indian gentleman 20 years my senior. In that district Indians walked behind a white man like a dog."

"Again I asked the keeper of the pound on the Sarcee Indian reserve near Calgary why he did not try to increase his miserable income by working as a harvester for some of the white farmers round about. 'I used to,' he answered, 'but because I am an Indian the white farmers pay me only $2.50 a day instead of the $4.00 they pay their white labourers, although I work just as hard as the white labourer.'"

[25]While the writer was visiting with an Indian agent in the Okanagan area, an Indian of about 30 called to say that an agent of an oil company had been discussing with him the installation of a service station and asked the agent to "say a good word for me." The agent explained rather quickly that the deal would not go through as the Indian had no security, no experience, and in any case it was doubtful if there would be much business attracted to the proposed site.

of inferiority it has engendered. It is noteworthy that Mr. Williams, Chief Scow, and Mr. Kelly were the ones who pointed the evidence towards the system which prevents sources of credit from developing for Indians, which prevents the Indian from participation in the political work of the state, and which degrades the Indians through active segregation. In pointing to the life of the Alaskan Indian, the argument of the Canadian Indian was simply that people of a similar race have achieved economic goals equal to whites; they share in the political life of the community; and they consequently have feelings of dignity and have achieved an identity as a group. Metlakatla is a very specific demonstration, Mr. Gosnell stated:

If you visit the school in Metlakatla, Alaska, you will find seven or eight teachers who are native girls. If we go out and look over their health establishment you find two or three nurses there—all people who were educated in Alaska. They are certified nurses and certified teachers. This, we think, is possible in B.C. If it is possible in Alaska it is also possible in British Columbia. At one time the Indians in British Columbia were far ahead of the Indians in Alaska, yet today the Indians in Alaska are far ahead of the Indians in British Columbia, and we give credit to the United States government.[26]

Thus Canadianized Indians are searching for an argument whose basis is more than an appeal to general notions of humanity or justice. The history of racial discrimination as well as its contemporary liveliness forces them to search for these demonstrated abilities of other native peoples.

It is especially true in the case of the coastal Indians of British Columbia that an analysis of the factors responsible for their economic status was urgent and should be undertaken and understood. Among the generation of Mr. Kelly, Chief Scow, Mr. Gosnell, and Mr. Paull, there is a developed sense of what the process of displacement has done to the Indian groups; they know, for example, about the effects of smallpox and other consequences of civilization. But more important, they know what the coming of Scandinavian immigrants did in creating competition in the fishing industry; they know of the threatened extinction of the salmon itself. They have made bitter denunciations of the Japanese, and when the opportunity came to take a stand about the removal of the Japanese during World War II, the Indian was one of the main supporters of evacuation. It is in the fishing industry that experiences over some decades have provided a demonstration at home, in Canada, that racial differences are superficial as far as the

[26]*Minutes*, 1947, No. 17, May 2, p. 787.

industrial business worlds are concerned. During the war, the Indian took the place of the Japanese, and as Mr. Gosnell pointed out, "looking over the records four years prior to the war and the four years during the war, the canned salmon production is equal if not better during the war than it was before the war."[27] But there are other demonstrations too, chiefly in the professions, in the names and occupations of Indians with whom Brigadier Martin was acquainted. Here the more prominent acquaintances and relatives were mentioned—physicians, surgeons, teachers, and military men—and the number practising outside of Canada was a significant percentage. The Indians have accumulated sufficient evidence to know that racial heritage is unimportant as such but that racial discrimination is crucial. Hence, the government's policy is far more significant than it might be in other aspects of national management since it impinges so directly upon the entire life of individuals and families.[28]

In making comparisons in order to point up crucial factors, the Indians have presented evidence for the necessity of political representation. The rules of wardship have until recently isolated all Indians from political participation in the life of the community and state. On May 2, 1947, when the representatives from British Columbia had their last meeting with the Committee, Mr. Reid, M.P., asked Mr. Kelly if he had "given any thought of the future. . . ." In reply the witness made a rather lengthy statement which was an excellent summary of one group's over-all point of view. It showed, further, a broad comprehension of social trends.

Well, one must of necessity give a great deal of thought to that. I think the Indian reserves and villages at one time served a very fine purpose; they acted as a protection for the people. I believe the time has come when the Indian of today has just marched a little past that. The reason we are stressing so much the necessity of Indians attending the public schools of the land is so that the growing generation will meet with the other children and will compete with them . . . and play with them; and will develop with them and will think as they do and see as they do. . . . Some organizations, the organization which is to appear before you very shortly, have referred to the Native Brotherhood of British Columbia as championing enfranchisement, and have proclaimed a sort of war-cry against our organization because of that. . . . As our brief points out, we would like the Indian to hold on to his aboriginal rights, and not to take all that away from him at one stroke but extend to him the right of citizenship. Only by so doing do we think that gradually if men will go to them—from what I have seen all men who conduct election campaigns, they go to every place; if the Indian

---

27[Ibid.]
28See *Ibid.*, 1946, No. 19, Aug. 6, p. 750.

has the vote they will go to him; and not only go to him, but they will see that he is properly treated. Now, he cannot engage in a public work of any kind unless there is no one else to do the job. If there were 1,000 Indians and a half a dozen white people the white people would get the job, but if he has any voice he will be treated with equality, and by so doing we believe his better self will come to the fore and be encouraged until he reaches the full measure of manhood. . . .[29]

The Native Brotherhood had incorporated in its submission, under "4. Enfranchisement of Indians," a statement regarding the Maoris of New Zealand. Because enfranchisement as provided for in Canadian legislation involves the surrender of hereditary rights, few Indians have availed themselves of the opportunity to become Canadian citizens. In fact the mention of enfranchisement to almost any Canadian Indian would result in a highly emotional rejection of it. It is a response which indicates clearly a very strong anxiety. But the N.B.B.C. boldly set down more than a mere reference to the Maoris:

. . . A system of native representation such as the Maoris enjoy in New Zealand could be the pattern followed in Canada. There the Maoris retain their aboriginal rights, but at the same time have full representation in parliament. See *New Zealand Year Book* (1944). Why cannot this be done in Canada?
The incentive to advance is noticeable where the rights of citizenship are enjoyed by the native people as they are in Alaska.[30]

Then the British Columbia Indians stated their conception of the three major types of contemporary Indians, quoted above: the chaps "who want no part of progress"; the ones who want the advantages of civilization but wish to avoid responsibility and "be carried along on 'flowery beds of ease' "; and those who want the advantages of civilization and are willing to share the responsibility and pay the price. These generalized definitions worked out specifically in the revision of legislation when such basic issues as taxation and voting privileges were considered. As an example, according to the *Minutes* of the Special Joint Committee for April 30, 1951, when members of the Committee and the Hon. Mr. Walter Harris, the responsible minister, were preparing final changes in a bill for presentation to the House of Commons, Mr. Harris said:

. . . we have three groups of Indians. We have a group who refuse to have anything to do with a vote, on any terms whatever; they were opposed to voting, they were opposed to other Indians demanding the vote. In the alternative you had the Indian who demanded the vote. In between you

---

[29]*Ibid.*, 1947, No. 17, May 2, p. 833.
[30]*Ibid.*, 1947, No. 16, May 1, p. 766.

had the other group, which I think represented by far the larger number of Indians whose attitude was one of difference; who said, in effect, we would like to take part perhaps, perhaps we would not, but the paramount thing is to retain our privileges as we now have them. Well, I think the solution here is the only solution in the light of their position, we must take the Indian at face value. The one who does not want to vote . . . because it is a matter of principle with him not to take part in national proceeding, is still protected. The one who wants to vote has that right on the basis of equality with non-Indians. (pp. 269–70)

Mr. Harris's statement followed five years of intensive work by the committee in securing evidence, hearing testimony, and private discussions as well as in the preparation of legislation. By 1950, members of the House were becoming curious about the fact that no bill had been presented, and the Indians were becoming restless. On May 5 Mr. Diefenbaker, then a prominent member of the Opposition, asked Prime Minister St. Laurent when a bill could be expected; according to *Hansard*, he went on to say:

I make this suggestion in the spirit of trying to remove all resentment, unjustified no doubt as it is, in particular arising from the hunger strike of Jules Sioui. Apparently his action has aroused the representatives of Indian reservations throughout Canada. If the Prime Minister can see his way clear to arrange it before the legislation is introduced, I think a meeting with the Indian chiefs would go a long way toward removing this feeling of resentment.

The Prime Minister replied that he was unable to set a date for the introduction of legislation, but a month later, on June 7, Bill 267 was given its first reading. By June 21, when this Bill received its second reading, its inadequacies had been thoroughly expressed by the resentful Indians and the disappointed Canadians. So on June 22, the Minister of Citizenship and Immigration indicated briefly that this bill would have "to stand for further consideration." As one analyzes the debate of the day before, it is quite clear that the major newspapers of the Dominion, the Members of Parliament who had large Indian reserves in their constituencies, and the opposition under the leadership of Mr. Diefenbaker were all disappointed in Bill 267. Mr. Harris and the Special Joint Committee went to work to prepare a new bill. While they were working in that late spring and summer of 1950, representatives of the Native Brotherhood of British Columbia again went to Ottawa. Although they did not appear before the Special Joint Committee, conferences were held by the Department of Citizenship and Immigration to which delegates of Indian organizations or reserves were invited. Among those attending the conferences were

William Scow, President of the N.B.B.C., Dr. Peter Kelly, still chairman of the Legislative Committee of the N.B.B.C., and Mr. Andrew Paull of Vancouver, President of the North American Indian Brotherhood. When the Special Joint Committee met on April 12, 1951, to consider the new legislation, Bill 79, the minister explained the procedures used and the Indian organizations asked to confer with him and his staff so as to eliminate the objections found in Bill 267.

No longer did the Indians of British Columbia, or from any other part of Canada, think of going to England to seek an audience with the King or Queen; no longer did they think in terms of pagan and Christian Indians, those in opposition to or those in support of the potlatch law. While Indian languages and cultures might have sentimental value and certain utility, the campaign of the British Columbians was used to define a different type of future—one characterized by justice, development of reservations, occupational opportunities, educational achievement, and feelings of dignity and self-worth.

It is difficult to evaluate the influence of the British Columbian group of Indian leaders with respect to the revision of the Indian Act. But apparently their appearances and the representatives of the province in the House of Commons at that time made a very deep impression and helped establish the fact that conditions in British Columbia were different from those in other parts of Canada, that those Indians had become civilized quickly, and that possibly there should be a special section of new legislation or even an independent Indian Act for British Columbia. The Chinese and the Japanese problems had earlier helped to define British Columbia as a special province in the national affairs of Canada; now the Indian had contributed an additional twist to the place of that province in the legislative processes of Parliament. In fact, as a consequence, the Dominion Government requested and financed a special, administrative study, reported in *The Indians of British Columbia*, directed by Dr. Hawthorn of the University of British Columbia. Thus in 1946 when Mr. Kelly reported in the first issue of the *Native Voice* that he felt more hopeful than ever before, he was unaware that such eloquent pleading by him and moral resentment by many Canadians would be expressed and delivered through parliamentary proceedings. Thus, in this one way at least, the native Canadian has become more intimately associated with national affairs.

6. Again the Northwest Coast

In the history of the Dominion, each province has had its own arresting features of settlement and economic development with their accompanying provincial and national issues. Of the ten provinces Quebec and British Columbia seem to have generated and sustained the most dramatic of these. Conquest, colonization,[1] and extreme acculturation are often picturesque as well as tragic, but especially so when associated with rapid economic expansion and population decline and growth as shown by the accompanying chart. For almost a century, Indian-white relations in British Columbia have been notable for dramatic transactions in acculturation, in the sense of Georg Simmel, between Indian and non-Indian, between band councils and Ottawa, and between the federal and provincial governments. Now and then as part of the historic interchange, smaller public spectacles have been staged, such as the Indian village arranged as part of the Diamond Jubilee celebration of the founding of Vancouver, with Chief Mathias Joe telling visitors about the taking of the land; or the Indian dancers on the parade float with newspapers reporting the next day the allegations of discrimination in hotel accommodations and food allowances; or, again, the cultural revival expressed through Mungo Martin, the last of the totem pole carvers, who has been working for the Provincial Museum of Natural History and Anthropology in Thunderbird Park, at Victoria, where a number of Haida and Kwakiutl poles have been carved.[2]

The province of British Columbia has appeared again and again in the widely varied facets of Canadian history—the heroics of the early discoveries, and the problems of international diplomacy, as well as domestic political issues involving the Pacific railroad or oriental immigration. Now we find our most modern drama manifested in large corporations exploiting resources in the mountain areas adjacent to

---

[1]The conquest of Mexico by Cortes is a great story of conquest, colonization, and acculturation. At the present writing one thinks also of Africa; possibly for purposes of rather enlightening comparisons, one thinks specifically of Kenya with the recent Kikuyu uprising. See Jomo Kenyatta, *Facing Mount Kenya: The Tribal Life of the Gikuyu*; D. H. Rawcliffe, *The Struggle for Kenya*.

[2]The *Annual Report*, 1956, of the Museum, a branch of the Department of Education.

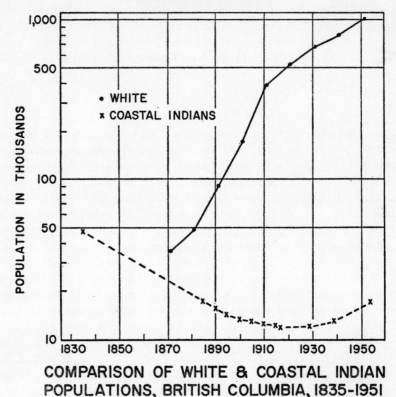

COMPARISON OF WHITE & COASTAL INDIAN POPULATIONS, BRITISH COLUMBIA, 1835-1951

FIGURE 1: Selected from statistics prepared by Wilson Duff, published in Hawthorn, Belshaw, and Jamieson, *The Indians of British Columbia*.

coastal waters. Thus the dramatic features of life in the Northwest continue to be expressed in the new technology and engineering feats; a site near an Indian reserve, Kitamat, has become a centre of aluminum production, along with Arvida, Quebec, in the Maria Chapdelaine country.

The struggle for an identity in coastal British Columbia was, in its first phase, a struggle of the colonists to remain true to the British conception of what the dominant population type should be in the area of new settlement. As far as the relations of the British with the native Indians were concerned, the problem of consistency in social organization was easily solved through the isolation of the Indians physically and socially and the establishment of the system of wardship already used in eastern Canada. Since the prevailing assumption was that the Indians would eventually disappear, the consequences of acculturation were of no concern for some time. But the consistency of policy which characterized the controlling group in 1871, when the province joined the Dominion, later broke down. The philosophy of colonialism which held sway in British Columbia at that period, and which was based in part upon the Protestant Ethic, particularly its secular form, could not continue even though an empire was built upon it. The breakdown of these old premises of action seems to have been slow. Seventy-eight years elapsed between the year of union, 1871, and the provincial enfranchisement of the Indians in 1949. During that time the Indians have evolved culturally from the traditional type of potlatchers and ceremonial cannibals, to operators of radios and diesel engines, preachers of the Gospel, and members of the Legislative Assembly; at the same time the whites have changed also.

The degree of success so far achieved by the Indians in their struggle for identity is the result of various trends that tend to establish a more secure identity for all British Columbians. Although we cannot argue a direct causal relationship between the kinds of people in the province and this more secure identity for British Columbians, yet some gross statistical evidence helps build a circumstantial case for such an argument. Tom Kent has claimed that as a country of diverse races and creeds, Canada is conspicuous for its tolerance, and this, he claims, is the basis for its unity.[3] For British Columbia this has not always been true; our claim is that tolerance in that province is mainly the result of two factors: first, through legislation the threat of extensive migration from the Orient was controlled; and secondly, in each decade an increasingly greater proportion of migrants to the province have been Canadian-born. As social trends based upon economic and political development changed, the struggle to remain British shifted to the problems of being Canadian. Both the legislation against the orientals and the segregation of the Indians and their changed status today are to be interpreted as part of that shift, as part of the emergence of a national Canadian identity which has been a continuing struggle since 1867.[4]

Reference to the suspected function of population changes in this struggle was made above. In 1911 only 43.14 per cent of people resident in the province were Canadian-born; by 1951 the number had increased to 70.88 per cent.[5] And of the Canadians in the province,

[3]See his *Liberal Economics and Canadian Federalism.*

[4]For separate studies and statements on this specific problem, see Mason Wade, *The French Canadian Outlook*; *Report of the Royal Commission on National Development in the Arts, Letters and Sciences*; Tom Kent, *The American Boom in Canada*, particularly the section on "The Way to Stay Canadian"; William H. Hessler, "Canada's Case of the American Jitters," *The Reporter*, February, 1959.

[5]Data taken from *Racial Origins and Nativity of Canadian People*, census monograph No. 4, Ottawa, 1937, p. 250, and *Census of Canada*, 1941, p. 330.

figures for 1951 show that 56.5 were born in British Columbia, while Ontario contributed 8.45 per cent, Manitoba 7.60 per cent, Saskatchewan 13.02 per cent, and Alberta 9.47 per cent. Immigrants from the British Isles, it will be recalled, have been important in the settlement and governing of the province; but the percentage of such immigrants in British Columbia has declined from 21.38 in 1941 to 16.07 in 1951. The contemporary ethnic origins of government officials have not been examined, but world affairs and dominant interests in the province would have made British-born provincial officials far less influential, we suspect, than they were in the mid-1800's and early 1900's.

Other factors beside population change have entered into making these trends. World affairs, although certainly desperate and unstable in 1958, do not present the same kind of a threat to British Columbia that they did between 1914 and 1945. The struggle over Asiatic immigration ended decades ago; the Japanese have been fairly well removed from the province, and those now resident have been enfranchised. Japan, again a national state in competition with the British Commonwealth, provides in the foreseeable future no prospect of grave danger. Thus in the larger context of world affairs, British Columbians and the entrepreneurs can continue to develop the economy in relative regional security, under conditions of expansion. A dominant population type has thus been established, and its political control appears stable in spite of the loss of offices suffered by the older Liberal and Progressive Conservative parties. In 1949 when the coalition of the two oldest parties enfranchised the Indians, there was no prediction that within six years the coalition would be dead and the Social Credit party would have gained enough political power to capture the provincial government.

As with other groups, the history of the Indian's struggle for survival and identity has not been and cannot be written adequately. Although government officers, missionaries, and other white people were involved, the evidence points to the struggle for identity becoming increasingly political in character as the Indians became more learned about and skilled in pressure group functions. Increasingly, the Indians became capable of making their own decisions about what they could and would do to change their status. And those things they wanted to do, they did, independent of the majority about them or the functionaries who served them.

The political institutions of the native culture at the beginning of settlement were not highly developed. Organization of political life extended no further than each village. Furthermore, in each village there was provided only a limited foundation for handling the problems which emerged after the settlers of European origins attempted to take over the land, the forests, and the sea. Discussion, manipulation, and compromise are the three essential components of the political life developed by the Europeans. Particularly for the British, these components have been institutionalized within highly developed legislative assemblies and political parties. The first two—discussion and manipulation—are found in potlatch behaviour, but compromise seems to have been absent. In many respects the culture of the Northwest Coast was a "business culture," a set of rules for gaining credits and paying debts, for manœuvering to the advantage of self, family, and village. By the time the extensive revision of Indian legislation came under consideration, the additional component, that of compromise, for entrance into the political life of the Dominion and province had been acquired by enough leaders and followers so that the values of a new identity were emergent. The native "business culture" of the Northwest Coast provided a psychological foundation for manipulation and oratory; so organized by experience were Chief Scow, Rev. Peter Kelly, and Mr. Andrew Paull that they were well versed in the new rules of the game at an important juncture in the history of Indian legislation and Indian aspiration.

There is no denying that the Indians of the province felt that the $100,000 increase in the annual budget for British Columbian Indians was a defeat in the land title issue. This interpretation has been made too explicit to be doubted. None the less, protest continued, the N.B.B.C. emerged, and the *Native Voice* was established. Shortly afterwards an opportunity to play a very important role in national life occurred, and Mr. Paull and Mr. Kelly hurried to Ottawa to make certain that the opportunity was fully realized. The senators and members of the House were deeply impressed, and so must be any one else who reads their testimony and brief. But our thesis that many of the Indians by 1946 had become quite Canadian and politically astute also means that they cannot stop in their political action. It is this political compulsion that enables us to draw the tentative conclusion that one type of struggle for identity is recognizable political action and such actions constitute one of its major attributes.

For reasons not readily available but surely a part of a campaign, the officers of the N.B.B.C. in 1947 submitted a brief to Mr. Hart, Premier of British Columbia. The *Native Voice* stated that: "Owing to the misunderstanding on the question of citizenship privileges for our Native Indians and our educational facilities, executives of the Native

Brotherhood of British Columbia Chiefs and active members went to
Victoria and presented a brief to Premier Hart and the cabinet members."[6] In January, Chief Scow, president of the N.B.B.C., had dispatched a telegram to Mr. Hart. In reply Mr. Hart acknowledged the
telegram with respect to "granting the franchise to aborigines of this
Province. You may be sure that your representation will be given every
consideration."[7] With the February issue of the *Native Voice* all readers
learned that their representatives were attempting to do something
about the provincial vote. The brief which the N.B.B.C. submitted
to the Joint Committee in Ottawa asked for enfranchisement and for
eligibility to vote in Dominion elections. When Mr. Williams appeared
as a witness before the Joint Committee on May 2, he stated:

. . . There seems to be a theory of a master race over an inferior race
which has to be followed. I have heard it said that the Indians cannot think
for themselves. Therefore, somebody has got to do their thinking for them.
I am sorry to say in practice in a great many instances that is borne out. . . .[8]

But the representatives of the N.B.B.C. would not accept the theory
of a master race, and for them political action was required as a central
part of their campaign for change in status and practice.

It will be recalled that during 1946, 1947, and 1948 the Joint Committee of Parliament went about the business of gathering evidence
and working towards the writing of proposed legislation. Before the
new legislation could be presented, unexpectedly, in March, 1949, the
Native Voice announced the granting of the vote to Indians in British
Columbia.[9] In a message dated March 14, 1949, the Attorney-General
of the province, Mr. Gordon Wismer, sent a message to the *Native
Voice*:

I feel that in granting them the franchise, this Government has recognized
a principle which should have been invoked long ago. These new voters are
the only true Canadians; the rest of us came to this country from other
lands and it is only fit that they should have a voice in the affairs of their
own country.
I might point out that the amendment to the "Elections Act" does not
grant to the Indians any more than the franchise itself, but this is a price-
less possession to free men in a free country and thus for the first time the
Indians of British Columbia will have an opportunity of voicing their claim
to all of the other privileges which are accorded Canadian citizens. It also

---

[6]March, 1947, p. 1.
[7]February, 1947, p. 1.
[8]*Minutes*, No. 17, May 2, 1947, p. 831.
[9]In contrast, affairs in Ottawa regarding Indians voting in federal elections
appeared to be quite confused during the 1949–1950 session of Parliament.

PRESERVES ANY RIGHT HE HAD IN THE PAST, but it gives him only the additional right to vote in the elections OR BE A CANDIDATE IN THE ELECTION. . . .

It seems to me that this step of the Province of British Columbia will have a profound effect upon their very reasonable request that they be given the vote at Federal elections. . . .

Quite naturally the announcement by the *Native Voice* was, for its purposes, the most important announcement it had ever had the opportunity of making. Among all the individuals quoted about their interpretation of such news, most pertinent to our interest was the statement of Mr. Kelly.

This has opened the door to the way that leads to everything. I have visited the Attorney-General and the Premier. They gave the Indians of B.C. the first real chance they ever had. Mr. Attorney-General assures me he wishes to help and explained that the vote in no way jeopardized Indian rights.

I sometimes have felt very discouraged since my last trip to Ottawa, but now I am full of hope.

And so party politics for Indians started. In the May issue "Citizens Welcome 'Boss' Johnson" described a meeting of some Indian chiefs with Premier Byron Johnson. In the same issue, the C.C.F. party advertised an Indian candidate, Mr. Frank Calder, who later won the election and became the first Indian representative in the provincial Assembly. In early 1950 Chief Scow, accompanied by Frank Assu, as president of the N.B.B.C. went to Victoria and thanked the Assembly for the right to vote. Certainly this mode of behaviour is outside the traditional or even the modified forms of potlatch conduct; but it is the type of deference to high authority that has characterized the Northwest Indians since the days of Queen Victoria.

The March issue of the *Native Voice* was notable, as suggested above, for the Indian was now in politics. In this issue not only was "Boss Johnson" campaigning, but there was an advertisement for his government which was running for re-election. Along with the Premier, the Minister of Finance was included in the photograph, and the message referred to hospitalization, roads, social services, trade and industry, education, public power, flood control, and municipal financial aid—all these items were points of significant gains, it was claimed, in legislation and action since the fusion government had taken office. As one looks over these items and compares them with the legislation of Ottawa and the experiences of the Indians under wardship, one wonders just how long the Indians will be content to stay under the jurisdiction of the federal government. If this is what other British Columbians get, then why not us? And in the same issue, the C.C.F. candidate, Frank Calder, was claiming that:

The CCF is the best friend we have

The CCF has fought and will fight to bring us full rights as Canadians

The CCF preaches equality and proves it by more than empty promises. That is why I shall be elected to carry our just fight for better conditions to Victoria. I have the support of Fishermen, Miners, and Workers to help our people win a spokesman in a new and honest government.

Wherever you are, vote for your local CCF candidate. He will put his promises into action and help us get education, good homes, good health and equal standards of pay income and opportunity.

VOTE CCF[10]

Further news about Calder indicated that he had been a student of theology at the Anglican College of the University of British Columbia, that he was active in the fishing organizations, and that he was also secretary of the N.B.B.C.

Finally, the *Native Voice*, of May, 1949, could point out that the Indians were to vote in two elections, the provincial one on June 15 and the federal one on June 27. For the latter, they now needed only to sign a tax exemption waiver. And thus, with good reason, the front cover of this issue said:

TWO HISTORIC ELECTIONS

On June 15 next and again on June 27, Native Indians will, for the first time in Canadian history, have the opportunity to take part in the democratic process. . . .

We hope that EVERY eligible Native Indian voter will go to the polls on June 15 and again on June 27 and vote for the candidates of their own, free choice. The Native Voice does not presume to tell its readers, free Canadian citizens, whom to vote for.

Remember, the ballot is secret! Under the system in which Provincial and Dominion elections are conducted in Canada no other person may know how the individual voter marks his or her ballot paper. This secrecy is guaranteed by law.

Vote for whomever you choose but Get Out and Vote!

A consequence of provincial enfranchisement can be observed in the actions of the first session of the 22nd Parliament of British Columbia, February, 1950, when the Government passed an act authorizing an inquiry into the status of rights of Indians in the province. In contrast it will be recalled that during the whole of the many conferences and with respect to numerous petitions dealing with the

[10]This ad was published by the CCF Campaign Committee, Vancouver.

land title question, the provincial government had refused to participate. How the Indians will change as a result of their new political status and the new basic attitudes expressed by provincial officers and legislators remains to be seen. The Government which amended the provincial Elections Act in 1949 lost control in the election of 1952. Premier Johnson and Attorney-General Wismer went out with their party when the coalition changed from 39 seats to 10 in a 47-seat Assembly. But historically it is the first time that the Indian had been a voter when an investigation of his status and rights was intended and authorized.

When the officers of the N.B.B.C. included in their brief a classification of Indians with respect to progress and community status, it was clear that they themselves were interested in paying the price of progress. They sought enfranchisement but felt justified in asking for the retention of Indian rights. Although this retention makes a legally recognized Indian peculiar to the general social system, there are major issues in the struggle for identity, in addition to the question of political participation, which suggest that the struggle for identity will continue into the indefinite future.

Political enfranchisement cannot solve the problem of occupational immobility based on racial discrimination; it may increase some opportunities, but discrimination still keeps the Indian in logging, fishing, and seasonal agriculture, if he remains in British Columbia. The continuing struggle will be marked by the hopes of younger people for new jobs, for places in the professions, or for better conditions in logging and in the catching and packing of fish. Questions of schools, scholarships, and undeveloped abilities are peppered through the records of the Joint Committee and in the columns of the *Native Voice*. This struggle for identity involves a conception of educational opportunities and satisfying occupational choices.[11]

[11]For the investigator an unusual turn in this problem is that many Indians have migrated out of the Northwest, some into eastern Canada, some into the United States, and some, apparently, to Europe, this latter being uncertain. Apparently the group in British Columbia is a "residual" group, for the author met people who lived in Seattle and Long Beach, California, and heard of others who were working in New Jersey, and one who was a deck officer on a Cunard liner. If one notes the addresses given by Brigadier Martin in his testimony before the Joint Committee, one is impressed with the number of professionally trained Indians who are practising in the United States. Then, too, in Vancouver and in eastern Canadian cities some of the mixed bloods have disappeared into non-Indian groups. Hence, any study of the occupational discrimination as found on the Northwest Coast should, it seems, consider the factor of out-migration for employment purposes. We do not include here the seasonal migration of Indians into the state of Washington for the picking of berries and small fruits.

Contemporary preoccupations of Indians about jobs and education represent a different period than the one in which the missionaries and Indian agents were the ones concerned with the precepts of the Protestant Ethic in its secular form—concern about the indifference of Indians to the European notions of the way work should be done, routinized, and carried on day after day without regard to the seasonal character of salmon runs; concern about the perseverance needed to amass wealth and eliminate idleness, casualness, and inefficiency; concern about time schedules and punctuality; concern about neutralizing vanity, egotism, and personal rewards. These earlier concerns of the agents of European civilization have been reduced or transformed. It is the Indians themselves, in their own way, who have stated the issues and the proposed solutions.

The effort to gain control of one's fate is crucial in the life of any member of a minority group. In the struggle for identity, two major components apparently enter into the conception of what this control actually is. First, it is doing something about defining the past. All three types of Indians referred to in the N.B.B.C. brief did do something about the past as represented in a definition of the traditional Indian culture, symbolized in part by the potlatch. Identification with one of the types indicates clearly what a tribal group or an individual believes to be required for the control of its or his fate. But regardless of type, all three have this in common: they wish the dominant community to be tolerant and understanding of the traditional culture. Some Indians may not want to participate in efforts for cultural revivals or in the building of museums, but all wish for tolerance.

In the effort to control one's fate, the second basic factor is the desire for political equality and participation. It may be claimed that for years the Canadian Indian had informal political representation through the members of Parliament who paid attention to the conditions of the reserves in their respective ridings. But this is not equality; the Indian without a vote can appeal only to decency and morality. As important as they are, decency and morality are insufficient to symbolize equality. In a social system such as Canada's, political participation is the symbol for equality. As one American Iroquois told the writer, "I can vote but they can't make me." To him it was important to have the opportunity; but he still carried the resentment so well expressed and elaborated upon by the distinguished Iroquois orator Red Jacket.[12]

[12]See William L. Stone, *The Life and Times of Red-Jacket or SA-GO-YE-WAT-HA.*

If the struggle involves acquiring a more suitable "vocabulary of history" as Richard Wright would phrase it, and if it involves a demand for political participation, it is also a struggle not to get left behind, as Peter Kelly interpreted it, in economic development. By not getting left behind, Indians will have access to occupational careers which will provide satisfactory choices and opportunities; today there is a wider range expected by them than was available when Mr. Duncan set up his new economic order. They have demanded recognition of their modern training, aspirations, and rights based upon natural law.

The demand formulated is a contemporary conception of the secular form of the Protestant Ethic, a conception which has been formulated through years of engagement in the struggle for survival.[13] This extended engagement created a new institution and modified old ones so that the Indians can survive in a technologically based, urban social system without demanding a Northwest coast type of revenge for their defeat in 1927, or without denying their cultural past.

[13]The emphasis in this study has been on the processes of institutional origin. It is well known that in areas where significant cultural change is under way, there is considerable personal disorganization which can also contribute to institutional organization and development. For a study of the less creative aspect of cultural disintegration see the significant study of Edwin M. Lemert, *Alcohol and the Northwest Coast Indians.* Particularly will the well-informed reader want to pay attention to Lemert's discussions in his footnotes. For an approach to the acculturation process as it develops personality orientations and configurations, see George D. Spindler, *Sociocultural and Psychological Processes in Menomini Acculturation,* especially p. 17ff.

BIBLIOGRAPHY

Bibliography

ARTICLES AND CHAPTERS OF BOOKS

BARNETT, H. G. "The Nature of the Potlatch," *American Anthropologist*, n.s. 40, 1938.

CARELESS, J. M. S. "Frontierism, Metropolitanism, and Canadian History," *Canadian Historical Review*, XXXV, 1946.

DAWSON, GEORGE. "Notes and Observations on the Kwakiool," *Transactions of the Royal Society of Canada*, V, 1887.

DRUCKER, PHILIP. "Rank, Wealth and Kinship in Northwest Coast Society," *American Anthropologist*, n.s. 41, 1939.

EISELYN, W. H. "Christianity and Religious Life of the Bantu," in I. Schapera, ed., *Western Civilization and the Natives of South Africa*, 1934.

GLADSTONE, PERCY. "Native Indians and the Fishing Industry," *Canadian Journal of Economics and Political Science*, XIX, 1953.

HARDING, JOHN F. "Libel and Right of Privacy Problems Involved in the Publication of National Magazines," *Conference Series No. 10*, The Law School, University of Chicago, 1952.

HARPER, ALLAN G. "Canada's Indian Administration: The Treaty System," *America Indigena*, V, VI, VII, 1947.

HESSLER, WILLIAM H. "Canada's Case of the American Jitters," *The Reporter*, February, 1959.

HOWAY, F. W. "Indian Attacks Upon Maritime Traders of the Northwest," *Canadian Historical Review*, VI, 1925.

—— "Discovery of the Northwest Coast," Canadian Historical Association, *Report*, 1926.

IRELAND, WILLARD E. "Pre-Confederation Defence Problems of the Pacific Colonies," Canadian Historical Association, *Report*, 1921.

JAMIESON, STUART, and GLADSTONE, PERCY. "Unionism in the Fishing Industry of British Columbia, *Canadian Journal of Economics and Political Science*, XVI, 1950.

KENNEDY, RAYMOND, "Colonial Crisis and the Future," in Ralph Linton, ed., *Science of Man and the World Crisis*, New York, 1945.

KNAPLUND, PAUL. "Gladstone's View on British Colonial Policy," *Canadian Historical Review*, IV, 1923.

—— "Arthur Mill's Experiment in Colonization," *Canadian Historical Review*, XXXIV, 1953.

MacINNES, T. R. L. "The History and Policies of Indian Administration in Canada," in C. T. Loram and T. F. McIlwraith, eds., *The North American Indian Today*, Toronto, 1943.

—— "History of Indian Administration in Canada," *Canadian Journal of Economics and Political Science*, XII, 1946.

MARTIN, CHESTER. "The Colonial Policy of the Dominion," *Transactions of the Royal Society of Canada*, Series III, XVI (1922).

McILWRAITH, T. F. "Anthropology in Canada," *Canadian Historical Review*, XI, 1930.

—— "Ethnology, Anthropology, and Archaeology," *Canadian Historical Review*, XXXIII, 1952.

MEMORIAN, BROTHER. "Roman Catholic Missions in Canada," in C. T. Loram and T. F. McIlwraith, eds., *The North American Indian Today*, Toronto, 1943.

MILLS, LENNOX. "The Real Significance of the Nootka Sound Incident," *Canadian Historical Review*, VI, 1925.

MUNGER, EDWIN S. "Economics and African Nationalism," *Current History*, July, 1953.

ORMSBY, MARGARET A. "Canada and the New British Columbia," Canadian Historical Association, *Report*, 1948.

RAY, VERNE. "The Historical Position of the Lower Chinook in the Native Culture of the Northwest," *Pacific Northwest Quarterly*, XXVIII, 1937.

RIDDELL, R. G. "A Cycle of the Development of the Canadian West," *Canadian Historical Review*, XXI, 1940.

RUSSELL, NELSON VANCE. "The Indian Policy of Henry Hamilton: A Reevaluation," *Canadian Historical Review*, XI, 1930.

SAGE, WALTER N. "The Gold Colony of British Columbia," *Canadian Historical Review*, II, 1921.

—— "Sir James Douglas, Fur-Trader and Governor," Canadian Historical Association, *Report*, 1925.

WESTGATE, REV. T. B. R. "The History, Policy, and Problems of Protestant Missions of the Indians in Canada," in C. T. Loram and T. F. McIlwraith, eds., *The North American Indian Today*, 1943.

BOOKS

ARCTANDER, JOHN M. *The Apostle of Alaska: The Story of William Duncan of Metlakahtla*, New York, 1909.

BAKER, ARCHIBALD G. *Christian Missions and a New World Culture*, New York, 1934.

BARBEAU, MARIUS. *Totem Poles: A By-product of the Fur Trade*, Washington, 1942.

BASS, ALTHEA. *Cherokee Messenger*, Norman, 1936.

BEGG, ALEXANDER. *History of British Columbia*, Toronto, 1894.

BENEDICT, RUTH. *Patterns of Culture*, New York, 1946.

BOAS, FRANZ. *Ethnology of the Kwakiutl*, Washington, 1921.

BROWN, ARTHUR J. *The Foreign Missionary*, revised edition, New York, 1950.

BURKE, KENNETH. *Permanence and Change*, New York, 1935.

CODERE, HELEN. *Fighting with Property: A Study of Kwakiutl Potlatching and Warfare, 1792–1930*, New York, 1950.

COLLIER, JOHN. *The Indians of the Americas*, New York, 1947.

COLLISON, W. H. *In the Wake of the War Canoe*, New York, 1915.

COREY, STEPHEN J. *Ten Lessons in World Conquest*, Cincinnati, 1911.

CREIGHTON, DONALD. *John A. Macdonald: The Young Politician*, Toronto, 1952.

CROSBY, THOMAS. *Among the An-ko-me-nums or Flathead Tribes of the Pacific Coast*, Toronto, 1907.

DEBO, ANGIE. *The Road to Disappearance*, Norman, 1941.

DENNY, C. E. *The Law Marches West*, Toronto, 1939.

DRUCKER, PHILIP. *Indians of the Northwest Coast*, New York, 1955.

—— *The Native Brotherhoods: Modern Intertribal Organization on the Northwest Coast*, Washington, 1958.

FARRIS, JOHN. *The Cherokee Story*, Asheville, 1950.

FORD, CLELLAND S. *Smoke from Their Fires*, New Haven, 1941.

FOREMAN, GRANT. *The Last Trek of the Indians*, Chicago, 1945.

—— *Sequoyah*, Norman, 1937.

FOSTER, GEORGE E. *Se-quo-yah, The American Cadmus and Modern Moses*, Philadelphia, 1885.

FURNIVALL, J. S. *Colonial Policy and Practice*, Cambridge, 1948.

GIRAUD, MARCEL. *Le Métis canadien, son rôle dans l'histoire des provinces de l'ouest*, Paris, 1945.

GOSNELL, R. E. *The Yearbook of British Columbia and Manual of Provincial Information, 1911*, Victoria, 1911.

HALLIDAY, WILLIAM. *Potlatch and Totem*, Toronto, 1935.

HAWTHORN, H. B., BELSHAW, C. S., and JAMIESON, S. M. *The Indians of British Columbia*, Berkeley, 1958.

HOWARD, JOHN KINSEY. *Strange Empire*, New York, 1952.

KENYATTA, JOMO. *Facing Mount Kenya: The Tribal Life of the Gikuyu*, London, 1953.

KNAPLUND, PAUL. *The British Empire, 1815–1939*, New York, 1941.

KNORR, KLAUS E. *British Colonial Theories, 1570–1850*, Toronto, 1944.

KRAUSE, AUREL. *The Tlingit Indians*, Seattle, 1956. Translated by Gunther, Erna, from Krause, *Die Tlingit Indianer*, Jena, 1885.

LAVIOLETTE, FORREST E. *Canadian Japanese and World War II*, Toronto, 1948.

LEMERT, EDWIN M. *Alcohol and the Northwest Coast Indians*, Berkeley, 1954.

LLEWELLYN, K. N., and HOEBEL, E. ADAMSON. *The Cheyenne Way*, Norman, 1941.

LINTON, RALPH, ed. *Most of the World: The Peoples of Africa, Latin America, and the East Today*, New York, 1949.

LORAM, C. T., and McILWRAITH, T. F., eds. *The North American Indian Today*, Toronto, 1943.

McLEAN, JOHN. *The Indians of Canada*, Toronto, 1889.

MACMILLAN, W. M. *Africa Emergent*, Pelican Edition, 1949.

MAYNE, R. C. *Four Years in British Columbia and Vancouver Island, 1862*, London, 1862.

MEARES, JOHN. *Voyage from China to the Northwest Coast of America*, London, 1791.

MOERAN, J. W. W. *McCullagh of Aiyansh*, Edinburgh, 1923.

MORICE, A. G. *History of the Northern Interior of British Columbia,* Toronto, 1905.

PRICE, A. GRENFELL. *White Settlers and Native People: An Historical Study of Racial Contacts between English-Speaking Whites and Aboriginal Peoples in the United States, Australia, and New Zealand,* Melbourne, 1949.

RAWCLIFFE, D. H. *The Struggle for Kenya,* London, 1954.

REISSMAN, LEONARD. *Class in American Society,* Glencoe, Ill., 1959.

SPINDLER, GEORGE D. *Sociocultural and Psychological Processes in Menomini Acculturation,* Berkeley and Los Angeles, 1955.

STEELE, C. B. *Forty Years in Canada,* Toronto, 1915.

STONE, WILLIAM L. *The Life and Times of Red-Jacket or SA-GO-YE-WAT-HA,* New York and London, 1841.

WADE, MASON. *The French Canadian Outlook,* Toronto, 1946.

WELLCOME, HENRY S. *The Story of Metlakahtla,* London, 1887.

WIESCHOFF, H. A. *Colonial Policies in Africa,* Philadelphia, 1944.

WISE, JENNINGS C. *The Red Man in the New World Drama: A Politico-Legal Study with a Pageantry of American Indian History,* Washington, 1931.

WOODSWORTH, CHARLES J. *Canada and the Orient,* Toronto, 1941.

GOVERNMENT PUBLICATIONS

Annual Report, Indian Affairs Branch, 1871–1950, Ottawa.

Anthropology in British Columbia, British Columbia Provincial Museum, Victoria, 1950, 1951, 1952, 1953–4.

Annual Report, Provincial Museum of Natural History and Anthropology, Victoria, 1955, 1956, 1957, 1958.

British Columbia: Atlas of Resources, Victoria, 1956.

British Columbia Papers connected with the Indian Land Question, 1850–1875, Victoria, 1875.

Claims of the Allied Indian Tribes of British Columbia, As Set forth in Their Petition Submitted to Parliament in June, 1926: Report and Evidence, Ottawa, 1927.

Eighth Census of Canada, Dominion Bureau of Statistics, Ottawa, 1941.

House of Commons, *Debates,* 1867–1951, Ottawa.

Minutes of Proceedings and Evidence, Special Joint Committee of the Senate and the House of Commons, 1946, nos. 1–20; 1947, nos. 1–41; 1948, nos. 1–5.

Series G 1. Public Archives of Canada, Ottawa.

Racial Origins and Nativity of Canadian People, census monograph No. 4, Ottawa, 1937.

Report of the Royal Commission on Indian Affairs for the Province of British Columbia, 4 volumes, Victoria, 1916.

Report: Royal Commission on National Development in the Arts, Letters and Sciences, Ottawa, 1951.

Statutes of Canada, "The Indian Act," 1880, I and II, ch. 28; 1884, 47 Vic., ch. 27, sec. 3; 1895, 58–59 Vic., ch. 35, sec. 6; 1951, ch. 29.

UNPUBLISHED MATERIALS

POTLATCH FILE, Department of Citizenship and Immigration, Ottawa.

ANNAKIN, VIRGIL. "The Missionary, An Agent of Cultural Diffusion." Unpublished doctoral dissertation, Ohio State University, 1940.

BARBEAU, MARIUS. "The Totemic System of the Northwestern Indian Tribes of North America." Unpublished thesis presented at Oxford University for Degree of B.Sc., 1910.

BLANCHET, GASTON. "Etude de la communauté de Lorette." Thèse de License en Sciences Sociales, Laval University, 1946.

FALARDEAU, JEAN-CHARLES. "Préhistoire et description contemporains de Hurons canadiens." Unpublished manuscript for B.A., Laval University, 1939.

MacINNES, T. R. E. "Report on the Indian Title in Canada with Special Reference to British Columbia." House of Commons, Sessional paper no. 47, Ottawa, 1914.

SHANKEL, GEORGE EDGAR. "The Development of Indian Policy in British Columbia." Unpublished doctoral dissertation, University of Washington, 1945.

NEWSPAPERS, PAMPHLETS, AND MISCELLANEOUS

Administrators of Indian Affairs: Historic Sketch, Department of Indian Affairs, Ottawa, n.d.

Summary of Main Provisions of Canadian Indian Treaties, Indian Affairs Branch, Ottawa, n.d.

Atlantic Monthly, December, 1956.

Clippings from The Potlatch File, Ottawa:

   Daily Columbian

   Gazette

   Toronto *Empire*

   Vancouver *Daily Province*

   Victoria Daily Colonist

   Victoria Daily Times

   Victoria Weekly Colonist

Kent, Tom. *Liberal Economics and Canadian Federalism*, Winnipeg, 1956.

—— *The American Boom in Canada*, Winnipeg, 1957.

Log of the Columbia, Vancouver, Oct. 1931; Nov. 1931; Feb. 1932.

Native Voice, Vancouver, 1946–1951.

Saturday Night, Toronto, Feb. 2, 1952.

Time Magazine, New York, Sept. 5, 1955.

Times-Picayune Daily, New Orleans, Aug. 10, 1954.